affectionately —
Joy

Five Frames for
the *Decameron*

Five Frames for the *Decameron*

Communication and Social Systems in the *Cornice*

~ Joy Hambuechen Potter ~

PRINCETON UNIVERSITY PRESS
PRINCETON, NEW JERSEY

Published by Princeton University Press, 41 William Street,
Princeton, New Jersey
In the United Kingdom: Princeton University Press,
Guildford, Surrey

Library of Congress Cataloging in Publication Data will be
found on the last printed page of this book

Publication of this book has been aided by a grant
from the National Endowment for the Humanities

This book has been composed in Linotron Palatino

Clothbound editions of Princeton University Press books
are printed on acid-free paper, and binding materials are
chosen for strength and durability

Printed in the United States of America by Princeton
University Press, Princeton, New Jersey

To Glauco and Marlis Cambon
maestri e amici

~ CONTENTS ~

~ ACKNOWLEDGMENTS ~

MOST OF THE RESEARCH and a considerable part of the writing of this book were done during a year's Fellowship for Independent Research from the National Endowment for the Humanities, to which I would like to express my gratitude. I would also like to thank the University of Texas Research Institute for a typing and xeroxing grant.

My grateful thanks go to the many people who have contributed in various ways to such good qualities as this book may have. Foremost of these is A. D. Sellstrom, without whose encouragement as friend and chairman this study might not have been written and whose sensitive and intelligent editing greatly improved the quality of my prose.

Others who read parts or all of the manuscript have improved it through their valuable suggestions. They include Glauco and Marlis Cambon, Gian Paolo Biasin (to whom I owe my title), Terese de Lauretis, Richard Koffler, the two readers who commented on the manuscript for Princeton Press and Gail Filion of the Press. Professors Ruggero Stefanini, Franco Fido, Ciriaco Moròn-Arroyo, Cesare Segre, and Umberto Eco have all been generous with their time and friendship and with suggestions to which my work owes a great deal. My colleague Millicent Marcus, herself author of a book on the *Decameron*, generously shared bibliographical information. Warm thanks also go to Roger Abrahams, to Barbara Babcock, and to Victor Turner. All are the kind of people who give true meaning to expressions such as "the community of scholars."

Mrs. Kay Stephenson not only typed my often messy manuscript beautifully but proved to be a kind and warmhearted friend.

Last I would like to thank my daughter Karen Antonia for cheerfully living with "the book," and George, whose support has meant so much to me.

Five Frames for
the *Decameron*

~ INTRODUCTION ~

A RECENT STUDY of Boccaccio's other works referred to the *Decameron* as "possibly the most enigmatic text in continental medieval fiction, richly difficult to fathom."[1] It has been called escapist and realistic, nostalgic and historical, utterly amoral, godless and profoundly moral, deeply Christian. It has been read as a book permeated by medieval naturalism and as one that warns against the dangers of concupiscence, as a purely aesthetic text and as a paean to worldly intelligence, as pure entertainment and as national epic, the "*chanson de geste* of the paladins of a mercantile world." Lately interest has focused on the metaliterary aspects of the book, and it has been approached as an illustration of the transforming powers of the word, "a fictitious universe . . . which shines with the unabated radiance of lying"; as a study of the deceptive powers of language, a work whose "mode of being is one of marginality in relationship to existing literary traditions, cultural myths and social structures, to that which, in one word, we call history," possibly implying the marginality of literature itself, and as a warning to the reader against gullibility.[2]

The extreme divergence of critical opinions and interpretations in the case of this particular work is not due only to the differing historical times and to the diverse ideas and temperaments of the critics.[3] There is after all no debate as to whether the *Divine Comedy* should be regarded as "escapist," "realist," or "moralist" writing, while there is a very definite continuing debate as to Boccaccio's aims.[4] The discussion on the *Decameron* is provoked by the fascinating ambiguities inherent in the book itself. Some of these are caused by our distance from the period: after all, as Paul Zumthor has pointed out, "the text is the product of an encoding operation, carried out on the basis of the structural and cultural integrity of a state of language [*langue*, not *langage*]. An intentional element has been introduced, whose function is to orient the decoding; but nothing is less resistant to time than this effect."[5] We know a little more about Boccaccio's universe than we do about that explored by Zumthor, partly because of its later date and the rich documentation that has been and is still being explored by both literary critics and historians, but it would be foolish to pretend that we have mastered it. The more we learn, in fact, the more complex it proves to be.

The ambiguities also stem from complex historical reasons and from intricate structural and stylistic systems built into the *Decameron* by its author. The latter reflect both the normal "encoding operation" based on the standard cultural codes of the period to which Zumthor refers and special systems deliberately created by Boccaccio the artist as part of his aesthetic idiolect. This book proposes to explore some of these.

The *Decameron* is clearly a product of the historical and social crises of fourteenth-century Italy, a society in transition. Vittore Branca and Giorgio Padoan have shown the ways in which the work reflects both the old aristocratic, feudal world and the emergent humanistic and mercantile society of Florence.[6] I propose to show some of the ways in which it reflects Boccaccio's *awareness* that his world is in crisis and his society in transition. While it may not always be conscious, this awareness is traceable in the structure of the work as a whole, in the author's attitude toward the Church, and in certain of his stylistic and organizing devices. In almost all cases, the evidence is in the *cornice* or frame tale and most of this study is devoted to it.[7] Individual stories are discussed only insofar as they have a dialectical relationship with or may be said to function as part of the *cornice*. The partial exception is Chapter II, in which certain stories are discussed as evidence of the way in which Boccaccio used his medium (discourse) to make his point about religion.

The problems raised by the *cornice* are interesting in

themselves as well as being the key to Boccaccio's purpose in writing the *Decameron*.[8] The *cornice* is not only a far more elaborate frame tale than its predecessors in literature, but it is itself also, as it were, "framed," not by another tale, as in a Chinese box structure, but by a double lie. Boccaccio opens his work by telling his readers that he is writing for a select and a restricted audience—lovesick ladies—and that he is moved to do so by the memory of his own hopeless and consuming passion, which has fortunately passed. We now know that his love for "Fiammetta" was as mythical as the lady herself, and even a superficial reading of the *Decameron* shows that the book was not intended merely for the restricted audience described. On one level the problem could be dismissed as resulting simply from Boccaccio's use of a schema typical of medieval literature and rhetoric, one that he had already used in other works. On another, it takes on added meaning, for lying, as the recent tremendous upsurge of interest in the subject by anthropologists, sociologists, and semioticians of all sorts shows, is a very special subject. Umberto Eco remarked that "the possibility of lying is the *proprium* of semiosis just as (for the Schoolmen) the possibility of laughing was the *proprium* of Man as *animal rationale*."[9] Although Eco was not in this passage remotely concerned with the *Decameron*, the quotation strikes me as particularly well-suited to a book so filled with both lies and laughter. "Every time there is a lie there is signification. Every time there is signification there is the possibility of using it to lie" (*Semiotics*, p. 59).

The question, of course, is *why* the lies? *Why* the laughter? What was Boccaccio trying to communicate and for what purposes? Unlike Petrarch, Boccaccio did not see himself as a seeker of sylvan solitudes, and I can think of no greater contrast in literature than Petrarch's "Solo e pensoso i piú deserti campi" (thought filled and alone [I seek] the most deserted fields) and the *Decameron*, whose pages are filled with every variety of human interaction and reaction. It is very clearly a book whose focus is on what Aristotle so aptly labeled the *zoon politikon*, whose distinguishing char-

acteristic is sociability, which is in turn based on the ability
to communicate effectively. Indeed, without communication, no society of any kind can survive, and the more
complex the society is, the more complex its communication systems will be. (There is a great difference between
the letters of *Les Liaisons dangereuses* and the changes of
color of an amorous fish, though they ultimately communicate much the same thing.) It seems to me logical, therefore, that a study of a work such as the *Decameron* should
be approached not only from what literary scholars might
consider to be its own ground (philology in its broadest
sense) but from disciplines that can be said to deal explicitly
with communication: semiotics, sociology, and cultural anthropology.[10]

From this perspective again, understanding the *cornice*
seems the single most important factor in understanding
the book, for it describes a small society constituted at a
time of severe crisis, whose behavior is so stylized as easily
to be read as ritual and which spends the better part of
two weeks recounting stories. Here too Boccaccio's statement about his reasons for writing the book shows itself
to be a lie: if he were merely telling tales for lovesick ladies,
why would he need a *cornice*? And above all, why would
he wish to set those tales against the background of the
Black Death? But, if I may wrench Eco's concept severely
out of context, "every time there is a lie there is signification." Perhaps these particular lies signify just that, and
their meaning is to be found by reading them as lies and
taking the *Decameron* as a work so serious that it needs a
claim of frivolity to protect both itself and its author.

The contrast between the horrifying description of the
plague and the serene life of the *Decameron*'s ten protagonists is one of the unsolved mysteries of the book. There
is no apparent structural reason for the chilling pages that
open the *Decameron* proper, or for the apology with which
Boccaccio introduces them. He could easily have reduced
both to a sentence: "At the height of the terrible plague of
1348 seven young women and three young men . . . ."[11]

Why begin a supposedly "happy" book with such a carefully elegant, rhetorically subtle description of a shattering crisis? It seems paradoxical and is hard to justify on grounds such as "contrast" or "aesthetic unity." Perhaps, however, that crisis is indeed the *raison d'être* of the work, which then can be seen to be a profoundly social one. I am convinced that this is so, and that an approach which borrows from the theories of certain cultural anthropologists can provide valid insights into this and other problematic areas. One of these areas is the very existence and prominence of the *cornice* and of its ten stylized protagonists. If, as I argue, they are meant to be ten representatives of a society in which Boccaccio wholeheartedly believed,[12] ritually secluded during a time of extreme crisis so that they may examine their social universe and learn its values, then the pages on the plague are justified as an integral part of the work's meaning, and the constant reminders of the protagonists' presence at the end of each day and at the opening not only of each day but of each story acquire a worthwhile semantic content. The existence of the stories themselves also acquires a new semantic content: they exist not merely to entertain but to teach, and to teach far more than the social *saper vivere* posited by Getto (p. 11). This in turn proposes a partial explanation of another puzzling feature of Boccaccio's book: the mixture of very traditional values and of quasi-revolutionary concepts that can be found in the hundred tales. The society was in a period of transition and while many old values still obtained, new mercantile values were emerging. Branca has conclusively demonstrated their presence and importance in the world of the *Decameron*.

If the *Decameron* was deliberately written in order to preserve those older values that Boccaccio found to be valid, to attack some values and social structures that he believed to be harmful, and to reaffirm some of the newer customs and ethical codes that better reflected and influenced the prevailing society of the time, there should be textual evidence to support that theory. It is ample and of two kinds:

structural and symbolic. A careful study of the *cornice* shows that it is actually a fivefold concentric structure, with the hundred stories at the center—the most precious and protected place, as we learn from medieval architecture and from works such as the *Roman de la Rose* or the *Divine Comedy*. At the same time, a carefully engineered system of framebreaks[13] ensures "contact" between Boccaccio's audience (the readers of the book) and his message (contained in the stories). The fivefold system not only emphasizes the value of the story content but acts as a protection for the author, as the message is in some cases too controversial to present openly. Chapter V contains a detailed explication of this system, whose theoretical bases are derived from the work of Gregory Bateson and Erving Goffman.

The symbolic evidence that Boccaccio wanted his work to transmit a definite set of values and a body of knowledge about his society is more subtle. A reading of the *cornice* in terms of plot pure and simple shows ten young people, all of noble and prominent families (hence logical future leaders), leaving Florence during a time of extreme crisis and withdrawing to a series of secluded country retreats, where they tell each other stories for two weeks. They then return to their plague-stricken city. The plot itself and many details of the protagonists' carefully described behavior symbolically reflect actions and behavior universally shown during liminal rituals as studied by Victor Turner. The first chapter examines the similarities and looks at the use of storytelling and drama as instruments of learning.

The second chapter explores the *Decameron*'s attitude toward religion and the Church. There is no denying the virulence of Boccaccio's attacks on the latter, both in the stories and in the comments in the *cornice*, but there are grounds for discussion both about the reasons for his virulence and about his attitude toward Christianity. The behavior of the ten initiands, who refrain from telling stories on Fridays and Saturdays out of respect for the Passion, does not always seem to fit in with their comments and their jokes, or with the statements made in the stories.

Boccaccio was most certainly a Christian, but I believe his religion to have been socially oriented and I have examined his attitudes in the light of a theory of the anthropologist Roy Rappaport, which seems best to explain the apparent anomalies.

Boccaccio makes it clear that he takes his book seriously, both by indirect statements and by the quality of the codes,[14] texts, and authors to which he alludes in the course of his *cornice*. The codes were universally acknowledged to be authoritative and weighty ones; the authors were men of dignity; and the texts all belong to the *genus grave*. This is not in the least typical of medieval comedy, and should be regarded as a message in itself, as I will show in Chapter III.

The *Decameron* is a work of art *par excellence*, one of the most "aesthetic" of the world's great literary texts. According to Umberto Eco, the aesthetic text is one in which "many messages, on different levels and planes of the discourse, are *ambiguously* organized" (pp. 270-271). The organization of these messages is not in the least random, but follows a precise design, so that all levels exert pressure on all other levels. Several different systems of messages (what Eco would call s-codes, as each is "a set of signals ruled by internal combinatory laws," p. 37) are studied in Chapter IV, since "the aesthetic text has a self-focusing quality, so that its structural arrangement becomes one of the contents that it conveys" (*Semiotics*, p. 272). The theoretical basis for this chapter is the work of Juri Lotman and of Boris Uspensky, as well as that of Eco.

Dante's presence will seem ubiquitous in this book and calls for some explanation. I have used the *Divine Comedy* for example and for contrast because Boccaccio himself very probably had it in mind when he wrote, as is shown not only by the ten-by-ten structure he used for the *Decameron* but by the many references and allusions that the critics have traced.[15] There is another reason, however: the *Commedia*, for all its frequent focus on the throng of human beings who so richly populate its pages, was written as a reflection of a universe conceived to be itself a reflection of the mind of God. It is essentially a religious work and the offspring of an essentially religious world. The *Decameron* is no less serious and in its way no less Christian a work, but it is the offspring of a later period, one in which people were beginning to leave the divine sphere to God and to concentrate on humanity-in-the-world as opposed to God-as-reflected-in-the-world. The contrast may help in understanding both works and the different world views that engendered them.

~ CHAPTER I ~

Society and Ritual
in the *Cornice*

THE FOURTEENTH CENTURY in Italy was a period of social, philosophical and economic crisis. New classes, new institutions, new socio-political values and new ideas on the universe were emerging everywhere in the aftermath of phenomenal changes in Europe, such as the growth of the towns, the emergence of national monarchies in some countries and the overthrow of Boniface VIII. William of Occam's work was calling new attention to Nominalism, and Marsilius of Padova's treatise *Defensor Pacis* (1324) was spreading the revolutionary idea that the previous relationship between Church and state should perhaps be reversed. Tensions between old and new forms of life and ideas were pronounced, and in the case of Florence they were exacerbated by class struggles and economic crises as well as by demographic pressure and later by the plague.[1]

Florence in the first half of the fourteenth century was at the crisis of a major transition. The end of the thirteenth century and the early years of the fourteenth were a period of unprecedented growth and prosperity for the city: in 1338 only Venice, Milan, Naples, and Paris had greater populations; both ecclesiastical and private construction were booming and Florentine bankers and merchants were spreading the city's influence throughout the known world. The closed, suspicious temper of Dante's times, clearly shown by the inward-turned, huddled towers compressed by the city walls in contemporary frescoes, was beginning to give way to a somewhat more open urban style, less designed to protect the government from internal as well as external enemies. Most of the Duomo was built between 1296 and 1396; Giotto's tower was begun in 1334 and completed in 1359. The contrast between these buildings and the grim fortress that is the Palazzo del Podestà or Bargello (completed in 1255) graphically illustrates the difference in outlook of the two societies.[2]

Private construction was to some extent replacing the emphasis on communal construction of the previous century, and housing, factories, and warehouses (especially for the flourishing wool trade, which produced seventy to eighty thousand rolls of wool a year) were springing up everywhere. According to the chronicler Giovanni Villani, a contemporary of Boccaccio's, Florence at the beginning of the fourteenth century had 100,000 inhabitants, a hundred and ten churches, forty banks, and two hundred workshops. The level of education was also exceptionally high. Again according to Villani, all the eight to ten thousand children in the city could read and write.[3]

Clearly this was no feudal, agrarian society, but a flourishing and mobile one that had for some time been divided into several classes, as Dante testifies in his remarks about "new people and sudden wealth" ("la nuova gente e i subiti guadagni" of *Inferno* XVI, 73-75). In Boccaccio's time there were at least five easily identifiable social classes: the older aristocracy, the upper middle class who belonged to the more important guilds, a middle and a lower middle class (the medium and minor guilds), and a proletariat, most of whom were immigrants from the surrounding countryside and many of whom were wool workers, *i Ciompi*, whose uprising in 1378 was on a par with the great city revolts of Flanders or England (Procacci, pp. 56-57).

The Florentine republic was governed by a balance between aristocratic and egalitarian principles: the greater and medium guilds participated in government after the reforms of 1293 (Giano della Bella's *ordinamenti di giustizia*), and all offices were rotated on a regular basis. On the whole, the upper levels of the society were rather open and flexible. The more prosperous of the merchant class were also landowners, and they were rapidly developing an aristocratic mentality, as Procacci shows:

> the difficult times of the fourteenth and fifteenth centuries reawakened and revived in Italian merchants and burgesses that *rentier* spirit that had always existed in them . . . it seemed clearer to them that property investment . . . was the only way to protect from the blows of circumstance the wealth they had accumulated by trade and speculation. So the first noble palaces rose in the towns, and the first villas in the country. . . . This trend towards property did not always or necessarily go with a corresponding drift away from trade and production. Indeed the reverse was often the case: at this point—the point where wealth became opulence—the merchants of various Italian cities became an aristocracy: that is, they became aware of their privileged position and their rank. This was the moment when they naturally began to transform their wealth into power, and to use that power as the natural right of their wealth (p. 47).

The class mentality described in this passage can easily be recognized in the *Decameron*.

There was also, however, a firmly entrenched social tradition according to which prominent families identified themselves with certain neighborhoods of the city, from which they mustered support among friends, dependents, and family. Classes in such districts were mixed, and in spite of the pressures created by the expanding lower classes' desire to share in government, neighborhoods were still the bulwarks of family political power, which was extended and reinforced by carefully planned matrimonial structures. The latter were extremely significant for determining social status, the important criteria being wealth, ancestry, and the possession of high office. Economic decline on the part of a family was often the prelude to a drop in the social hierarchy because it led to the loss of political influence and thence to the inability to contract good marriages.[4]

The web of power-oriented marriages among influential families was a conservative factor in city life, as was the Church, venerably and deeply rooted in the city's traditions and history. Religious and secular public ceremonies further contributed to the conservative forces, as both were not only "bread and circuses" but also extremely structured events designed to stimulate community feeling and pride. The forces of insularity and parochialism were equally strong. In spite of the many cosmopolitan features of Florentine life introduced by the city's far-reaching banking and merchant activities, Florentines were fearful of the outside world, suspicious of all foreigners and highly reluctant to follow the European custom of inviting distinguished visitors to their city. Princes and prelates seeking invitations were usually rebuffed, and no pope or emperor visited Florence between 1273 and 1419 (Brucker, *Renaissance Florence*, p. 238).

We thus have a picture of a closed but prosperous and expanding society dominated by aristocrats and merchants, suddenly undergoing internal pressures from an at first rather well-contained but clearly delineated class struggle. There were also external pressures because of Florence's attempts at territorial expansion. The city was in serious rivalry with neighboring Pisa, and was financially fully extended by adventures such as the purchase of Lucca in 1341 for 150,000 golden florins. Territorial expansion and protection were expensive: the Florentines had become a people of craftsmen and merchants, and the city was one of the first to rely on mercenaries for both offense and defense.

The prosperity of Florence was founded on its banking and commercial operations, and so the failure of several Florentine banking houses who had ignored early warning signals and continued to lend vast sums of money to the King of Naples and the King of England proved catastrophic as the latter suspended all payments in 1339, pro-

voking widespread bankruptcies. The citizens put themselves under the protection of an adventurer, electing Walter
of Brienne, called the Duke of Athens, as *seigneur* for a year
in 1341, but the experiment failed amid general discontent.
The minor guilds insisted on participation in government,
and their victory in 1343 led to a series of challenges and
power plays on the part of the members of the major guilds
(known as *il popolo grasso* or the "fat cats"). Minor outbreaks
of plague in 1340 and 1342 had not helped matters, and
the terrible outbreak of 1348, which killed about one-third
of the population of Italy, France, and England, and by
most accounts reduced the population of Florence by one-
half to three-fifths, led to unprecedented civic chaos and
economic depression.[5]

The crises—not only the Black Death but the previous
economic and social problems of the mid-century years in
Florence and the severe political and economic problems
concomitant with the sudden reduction in population—
were in themselves enough to provoke serious reassess-
ments. They also came about in part as the result of previous profound changes in the society. The increasing power
of the merchant class and its growing pretensions to gen-
tility were changing both dominance structures and social
values.[6] Boccaccio himself belonged to the middle echelons
of this emerging bourgeoisie, but he was also—due to his
stay at the court of Naples and his study of letters—imbued
with many of the values of the older aristocracy. He had
returned to Florence in 1341 and become increasingly involved in civic affairs in the seven years before he witnessed the social and moral chaos engendered by the plague.
It is entirely logical that the *Decameron* should reflect his
ideals for a better society, and that these in turn should be
aristocratic and at the same time grounded in practical experience and filtered through the down-to-earth spirit and
sense of humor that were not only personal but "Tuscan"
characteristics reflected in the contemporary and later literature of the same region.[7] The *Decameron*, as so many
critics have pointed out, is in many ways a middle-class

book, and part of its ambiguity—torn between bourgeois desires and aristocratic ideals—is due to this factor and arises very directly from its times.

When compared to several contemporary accounts, Boccaccio's description of the total collapse of law, custom, and all civic and civilized institutions from communal norms to personal family ties during the plague is no exaggeration but sober and balanced reportage in spite of the literary traits of its style and structure.[8] The picture that emerges from the *cornice* of the *Decameron*, when its formal expression and the pages on the plague are properly taken into account, is not one of ten young aristocrats (specifically described as being "of noble blood" in I, Intro., 49) fleeing their responsibilities but one of ten young members of the ruling class who temporarily leave the chaos of their world in order to undergo a retreat (in the third meaning given by Webster's dictionary, "a period of group withdrawal for prayer, meditation, study, and instruction"), during which they both learn and reassess the values of their society.

The whole process has certain analogies with the liminal phase of rites of passage and could be described as what Victor Turner calls a "liminal" (as opposed to "liminoid") phenomenon.[9] The key differences are that whereas liminal phenomena essentially reinforce the social structure and are almost always collective events, liminoid phenomena tend to be more critical of society; in this sense they are revolutionary and are generated by specific individuals or groups. The former tend to flourish in tribal and early agrarian societies, the latter in post-industrial-revolution times, although Turner points out that liminoid phenomena also sometimes appeared in city-states that were in the process of changing to empires (of the Graeco-Roman type) and in feudal societies, as well as in societies similar to the Florentine one described above (Turner, "Liminal," pp. 84ff.).

According to Turner's view, satire is defined as "a conservative genre because it is pseudo-liminal [rather than liminoid]. Satire exposes, attacks, or derides what it con-

16

siders to be vices, follies, stupidities, or abuses, but its criteria of judgment are usually the normative structural frame of values" ("Liminal," pp. 47-48). This is important in view of the *Decameron's* satiric attitude toward clerical behavior, which is one of the factors that could, on the surface, cause the work to appear *liminoid*.

Another crucially important insight presented in Victor Turner's article is that liminal phenomena "tend to be collective, concerned with calendrical, biological, social-structural rhythms *or with crises in social processes whether these result from internal adjustments or external adaptations or remedial measures* [conditions that clearly fit the *Decameron*]. They are thus enforced by sociocultural 'necessity,' but they contain *in nuce* 'freedom' and the potentiality for the formation of new ideas, symbols, models, beliefs" ("Liminal," pp. 79-80, italics mine). The apparent tug-of-war between tradition and innovation in the *Decameron*, one of its most marked characteristics, is thus not entirely a product of its polysemous nature. In fact the overall impact of the hundred stories follows Turner's statement: "But to my mind it is the analysis of culture into factors and their free or 'ludic' recombination in any and every possible pattern, however weird, that is of the essence of liminality, liminality *par excellence*" ("Liminal," pp. 60-61). The ten protagonists study their cultural cosmos through the hundred stories told during their ten-day (or two-week) sequestration, and the storytelling is definitely not "play" as opposed to "work" or "escape" as opposed to real life. It is a careful education for the protagonists' role in society. Although these stories include many feudal or "medieval" ideals and values along with the current ones of the merchants and aristocrats in Boccaccio's world, as Branca, Getto, Baratto, and Padoan have shown, the author's strictly secular approach bears the seeds of the subversion of the medieval world as Dante portrayed it. The fact that Boccaccio's theories, especially on naturalism, were not in themselves new (one of the valuable contributions to be

17

derived from Scaglione's erudite book) does not in any way lessen the "revolutionary" *impact* of his work.

It is, of course, tricky to apply anthropological theory to literature, and in studying the liminal attributes of the *Decameron* I am well aware that I am not dealing with an actual liminal period in a real rite of passage. Some of the key characteristics of liminality are *not* present in the *Decameron*, notably the "reversals, inversions, disguises, negations, antitheses of quotidian, 'positive' or 'profane' collective representations" ("Liminal," p. 85), which do not appear in any way in the frame tale. Perhaps a case could be made for the presence of some of these in the stories themselves, but it would be tenuous and asystematic. Nor are there any instances of the grotesque in the frame tale; in fact the few monsters in disguise in the *Decameron* as a whole are on the same level as the not very large black horned beast on which Bruno and Buffalmaco induce Mastro Simone to ride to his dip in the cesspool (VIII, 9).

Nevertheless, there are many similarities between the conditions that generally lead to liminal rites and the actual social crisis that was the matrix of the *Decameron*. There are also enough correspondences between liminal rituals and the structure and details of the frame tale to justify the eliciting of the parallels and to allow the cross-disciplinary approach that Turner advocates in his "essay in comparative symbology." As Clifford Geertz pointed out, "anthropological writings are themselves interpretations" and *Madame Bovary* and an informant's account are equally fictions—"makings."[10] Both may reflect universal patterns, and Turner's frequent and brilliant analogies in all of his work show how many of the customs, rites, and ceremonies he has studied can be compared to those of both past and modern urban civilizations.

The group structure and action the young people of the *Decameron* set up for themselves reflect both the ritual quality of the retreat and the closeness of its ties with reality.[11] The latter is indicated by the fact that Boccaccio goes out of his way to tell us that the ten were actual, living citizens of Florence, whose names he has withheld so that their reputations will not be blemished for telling and listening to stories that might be considered too risqué in the somewhat more puritan climate that followed the plague (I, Intro., 50). As so often in the *Decameron*, this can be read on several levels. It could be a purely literary device or an indication of a serious and realistic social meaning. Inasmuch as the women are to be among the leaders of the post-plague society, their reputations must be spotless. There is a further possible ritual meaning that will be examined later.

The social structure of the group also closely reflects the Florentine life of the times, which was more oligarchic than democratic. It would have been easy for Boccaccio to create a purely idyllic and unreal "space" around the young people by simply omitting all humdrum details of daily organization. Instead, he took care to equip the company with servants whose Greek comedy names are for the most part belied by their function in the work. There is one exception: the much discussed "realistic" irruption of Licisca and Tindaro's quarrel in the Introduction to Day VI as to whether Sycophant's bride went to him as a virgin, an episode that bears out the servants' Greek comedy origins and firmly classifies them as belonging to the lower orders (hence fit subjects for comedy). Otherwise the servants are mentioned in the Introduction, and the literary flavor of their comic names is immediately counteracted by the listing of their functions: Parmeno is made seneschal, Sirisco steward, Tindaro is to take care of the men's quarters, Chimera and Strattilia of the women's, and Misia and Licisca are to cook (Intro., 98-101). Except for Licisca and Tindaro, the servants are not mentioned by name again. The seneschal, however, is insistently shown carrying out his duties, usually expressed by a phrase such as "having arranged the following day's dispositions with the discrete seneschal" or "the seneschal left early and set everything up." Such phrases appear at the beginning and again at the end of almost every one of the ten days, and serve as

19

constant reminders of the division of the classes.[12] The fight between Licisca and Tindaro, firmly put down by the queen in a manner that is a dead give-away of Boccaccio's class position, may also reflect the constant egalitarian pressure of the minor guilds and the proletariat within the Florentine social system.[13]

A further mirroring of the actualities of Florentine life is furnished by the rotating rulership. Although the title "queen" or "king" reflects both the literary code of courtly love and the social customs of the groups that cruised the city streets in fun-seeking bands, there is also a more serious side of this aspect of the *cornice*, as expressed by Pampinea:

> However, nothing will last for very long unless it possesses a definite form. And since it was I who led the discussions from which this fair company has come into being, I have given some thought to the continuance of our happiness and consider it necessary for us to choose a leader, drawn from our own ranks, whom we would honor and obey as our superior, and whose sole concern will be that of devising the means whereby we may pass our time agreeably. But so that none of us will complain that he or she has had no opportunity to experience the burden of responsibility and the pleasure of command associated with sovereign power, I propose that the burden and the honor should be assigned to each of us in turn for a single day (p. 65).[14]

The Florentine insistence on the regular rotation of high offices clearly comes into play here.

The symbolic ritual aspects of the *cornice* are even more interesting. Several details fit the pattern closely. In the course of his remarks on the rituals pertaining to doors and gateways, Van Gennep broadens his field of speculation: "This evolution from the magic portal to the monument seems also to have occurred in the case of the Roman arch of triumph. The victor was first required to separate himself from the enemy world through a series of rites, in order to be able to return to the Roman world by passing through the arch" (p. 21). Van Gennep also speaks of "the portal which separates the sacred world from the profane world" (p. 23) and concludes that, "in order to understand rites pertaining to the threshold, one should always remember that the threshold is only a part of the door and that most of these rites should be understood as direct and physical rites of entrance, of waiting, and of departure—that is, as rites of passage" (p. 25).

In the case of the *Decameron* the portal is the Church of Santa Maria Novella, one of the most famous in Florence. Its quality as a ritual gateway is underlined. The protagonists meet there originally (I, Intro., 49) and return to the world through it after their two-week absence: "and with their wise king leading the way they returned to Florence. Having taken their leave of the seven young ladies in Santa Maria Novella, *whence they had all set out together*, the three young men went off in search of other diversions, and in due course the ladies returned to their homes" (pp. 826-827, italics mine).[15]

The sacredness of the space in which the ten live and learn during their two-week liminal sojourn is borne out by their privileged position with respect to the plague that is raging in the countryside all around them (they are only two or three miles from the city) and which is hardly ever mentioned during the ten days. It is further borne out by the repetitious stylization and unreality of their lives and by a comment by the author at the beginning of the ninth day: "They all wore wreaths of oak, and carried fragrant herbs and flowers; anyone who had encountered them could not but have said: 'Either these people will not be vanquished by death or it will overcome them in a state of happiness.' "[16] The oak was sacred to Jupiter and stood for strength and long life, a fact that takes on additional meaning in view of the plague.

The special names assigned to the ten young aristocrats may also be interpreted in a liminally ritual way. According to Van Gennep, when a child is named he/she is both individualized and incorporated into society (p. 62). Victor Turner has shown that liminal personae are structurally invisible: they simply cease to exist as members of society for the duration of the ritual, "they are at once no longer classified and not yet classified" (*Forest*, p. 96). Turner also lists absence of names as a sign of liminality (*Ritual*, pp. 102ff.; "Liminal," p. 59). When Boccaccio endows his invented creations with literary names and underlines the fact that these are not their "real" names, his device functions to show their temporary absence from or non-existence in their normal state in society for the duration of the liminal period. (This, however, in no way precludes his also having had other possible reasons for doing so, as will be seen.)

Another aspect of the liminal state is that it takes place in sacred space and sacred time, which are both demarcated from secular space and time.[17] The analogy in the life of the *cornice* is carried by several factors. Sacred space is implied not only by the absence of the plague but by the series of gardens in which the tales are told, with their increasing formality of shape (the shape of the first is not described; the second is rectangular or square with a fountain at the center: "the garden was surrounded and crisscrossed by paths of unusual width, *all as straight as arrows*" [p. 232, italics mine];[18] the third is perfectly round). The second garden is described as a Paradise on earth (III, Intro., 11), and both it and a thicket near the third are filled with wild animals that act tame, as if they were in a Gothic-current fresco rather than in any form of reality. The stylized and repetitious life together with the almost total absence of the plague also creates a sacred space around the ten protagonists. The quality of time is changed and made "sacred," no longer belonging to the everyday world, by Boccaccio's device of counting only the ten days on which stories are told (*Decameron*) even though we know that two weeks of "real time" elapse. The device functions rather

better for the reader than for the protagonists, of course—
a reminder that we are dealing with a work of fiction.

The *Decameron* analogy to the "phase of separation" characteristic of liminal rites is the formal departure of the group
of young women and men from the Church of Santa Maria
Novella, which takes place after their discussion of the
legitimacy of letting convention go by the board because
of the exceptional nature of the times (I, Intro., 81-85).

One of the more striking characteristics of liminality is
the "leveling" of the initiands. Often all signs of pre-liminal
status are destroyed, and the initiands are regarded as absolutely equal among themselves, although this does not
apply to the relationship between them and their instructors. The latter have total authority, and the behavior de-
manded of the former is complete submission. There are
no figures analogous to the instructors in the *Decameron*,
and it would be farfetched Pirandellism to try to assert
authority over the storytellers by the characters in their
tales, but there is an equivalent to the equality factor. Males
and females are completely equal in the life of the *cornice*
and take their turns at authority as if there were no social
difference between the sexes. This was most certainly not
the case in "secular" life. Boccaccio himself tells us so in
his prefatory reasons for writing a book to help socially
captive women while away the pangs of love, and in the
Introduction both Filomena and Elissa argue the superiority of men:

> "You must remember that we are all women, and every
> one of us is sufficiently adult to acknowledge that
> women, when left to themselves, are not the most
> rational of creatures, and that without the supervision
> of some man or other their capacity for getting things
> done is somewhat restricted. We are fickle, quarrel-
> some, suspicious, cowardly, and easily frightened; and
> hence I greatly fear that if we have none but ourselves
> to guide us, our little band will break up much more
> swiftly, and with far less credit to ourselves, than would

23

otherwise be the case. We would be well advised to resolve this problem before our departure."

Then Elissa said: "It is certainly true that man is the head of woman, and that without a man to guide us it rarely happens that any enterprise of ours is brought to a worthy conclusion" (p. 62).[19]

These passages come *before* the group's discussion of the proprieties of going with the young men and *before* their formal departure, while they are still outside the liminal moment of the *Decameron*. Once inside, the male superiority practically disappears, in spite of one or two later comments by some of the women, and the first ruler is Pampinea.[20] The equality among the sexes is limited to their experiences in the liminal state, however, and is not part of the values they are to learn. This is clearly shown by Emilia's prefatory remarks to IX, 9:

"Lovable ladies, if the order of things is impartially considered, it will quickly be apparent that the vast majority of women are through Nature and custom, as well as in law, subservient to men, by whose opinions their conduct and actions are bound to be governed. It therefore behooves any woman who seeks a calm, contented and untroubled life with her menfolk, to be humble, patient, and obedient, besides being virtuous, a quality that every judicious woman considers her especial and most valued possession.

"Even if this lesson were not taught to us by the law, which in all things is directed to the common good, and by usage (or custom as we have called it), Nature proves it to us very plainly, for she has made us soft and fragile of body, timid and fearful of heart, compassionate and benign of disposition, and has furnished us with meagre physical strength, pleasing voices, and gently moving limbs. All of which shows that we need to be governed by others; and it stands to reason that those who need to be aided and governed must be submissive, obedient, and deferential

24

to their benefactors and governors. But who are the governors and benefactors of us women, if they are not our menfolk? Hence we should always submit to men's will, and do them all possible honour, and any woman who behaves differently is worthy, in my opinion, not only of severe censure, but of harsh punishment" (pp. 721-722).[21]

There is an ironic contrast here to the frequently decided and noble female (indeed, sometimes feminist!) characters within the stories themselves. This is a problem that has not been studied and that certainly merits attention.

Another interesting possibility is inherent in the basically oligarchic structure of the *cornice*. Where there are elders in liminal rites, their authority is absolute, but it is not based on legal sanctions; it is in a sense the personification of the self-evident authority of tradition. The authority of the elders is thus absolute because it represents the absolute, the axiomatic values of society in which are expressed the "common good" and the common interest (*Forest*, pp. 99-100). The lack of "elders" or any authority except their own may thus also connote denial of any axiomatic values or truths in this universe, where the ten future leaders of society are indeed, as stated earlier, learning some of the traditional values in their world, but are perhaps also being taught not to take anything in the human realm for granted or to accept it just because authority (the Church or the Philosopher) says it is so. This is, of course, a very "renaissance" aspect of the book and in no way surprising. Boccaccio and Petrarch, after all, stand at the beginning of the age that was to turn *credo ut intelligam* into *intelligo ut credam*.

Other factors underline the ritual aspects in the life of the protagonists of the *cornice* in ways that can be described as more and less "formal" in terms of symbology. The dance and *canzone* that invariably end each of the ten days of storytelling are a less formal way of ritually affirming the group's own aristocratic and elitist values. The separate bathing, first of the seven women and then of the three men, in the clear pool at the center of the round and theater-like valley of the ladies, is far more formal in terms of symbolic meaning.[22] The idea of ritual purification that underlies it is very clear, and it is related to one of the most widespread of taboo categories, that connected with women, who are regarded as dangerous in a great number of cultures. The Catholic culture that is the *Decameron*'s matrix is certainly no exception, and despite Boccaccio's naturalism[23] and the lack of such prejudice in the stories, he seems to be taking some precautions, crossing his fingers as it were, by means of this unemphasized and understated but very definitely ritual purification, which introduces the topic of female artifice.[24] The episode is presented in a completely serious way, and there can be no question here of satire or joking as there frequently is in the stories. The bathing takes place at a very crucial moment, just after the announcement of the following day's theme, set by Dioneo: "the tricks which, either in the cause of love or for motives of self-preservation, women have played upon their husbands, irrespective of whether or not they were found out" (p. 515).[25] This is touchy material in any society, and even more so in the Catholic Florence of the period, which was by no means free of misogyny.

The subject of marriage is a basic one in the *Decameron*, probably because of its importance to the social structure that is frequently reaffirmed in different ways throughout the book.[26] A consideration of the social function of marriage in the Florence of the time may therefore provide the key to a somewhat puzzling anomaly in the *cornice*, the repeated emphasis on the chastity of the ten protagonists. Critics have often ascribed this to their aristocracy, taking the line that they are above behaving like the characters in the stories they tell, but such an interpretation conflicts with the obvious high-mindedness of personages such as Ghismonda, the daughter of Prince Tancredi (IV, 1), whose greatness of soul cannot be denied, and of many other protagonists whose nobility does not entail chastity and whose lack of that quality in no way diminishes their great-ness.[27]

A partial explanation lies in the fact that sexual prohibition is frequently a part of most kinds of ceremonies among peoples for whom coitus implies impurity or magico-religious danger. Both connotations are clearly present in the sexual attitudes of the Catholic culture of fourteenth-century Florence, and it is by no means unlikely that a similar prohibition is functioning within the *cornice* to underline the special nature of the retreat. This is obviously not to say that Boccaccio deliberately set out to create an anthropologically based example of ritual-in-fiction. He did, however, more or less deliberately draw on certain frequent if not universal structures and formats that consciously or unconsciously act to confer ritual importance and solemnity on the group retreat.

A more sociological approach yields another and even more functional reason for the group's chastity, connected with contemporary marriage customs. As representatives of the ruling class, the ten protagonists gather in ritual formality and seclusion to undergo a learning experience that will better fit them to lead the society that is to be regenerated after the death and dissolution of the great plague of 1348; as such, they have certain duties to that society. Given that marriage was a known and accepted means of preserving, extending, or acquiring power and influence at the time, group exogamy in the *Decameron* is entirely logical and fitting. Lévi-Strauss has argued that the reason for the prohibition of incest is that marrying out leads to the founding of interdependent networks and gives rise to new families. The exigencies of cultural life thus produced exogamy. Leslie White has argued along similar lines that exogamous rules resulted from the need to gain compulsory and extensive cooperation and make life more secure. It is apparently debatable whether such reasons may be said to account for the origin of incest taboos, but when the much later society of the *Decameron cornice* is seen against its historical and sociological background, similar reasons for exogamy within the group make very good sense.[28]

Internal evidence also upholds this theory. Various critics have argued that the frame characters represent certain virtues, echoes of Boccaccio's literary past, and the aristocratic classes.[29] They may well do so, but they also, despite their stereotypic nature, represent a varied cross-section of sound qualities for living: one has only to think of Pampinea's calm good sense, Filomena's prudent wisdom, the modesty and piety of Neifile, or the gaiety and beauty of Fiammetta. The men also represent a good variation of character: Filostrato's inclination to melancholy, Panfilo's essential practical goodness, and Dioneo's more complex nature (there are moments when he reminds one of Shakespearian fools, and others that recall some—but by no means all—aspects of trickster figures) all contribute toward making the group of ten a representative social one that is well fitted to extend itself and reconstruct society.

The relationships within the group are nuclear and represent many of the possible permutations of love and family. The three young men are in love with three of the women and are related to several of the others (I, Intro., 79). This nuclear concentration of affections may in part symbolize the rather beleaguered state in which the aristocracy felt itself to be. The pressures from the other classes in Florence and the peculiar combination of Florentine insularity with the cosmopolitanism introduced by the citizens' widespread trade and banking activities could not but cause some measure of "identity crisis." Mary Douglas's concept of "grid and group" (classification and personal pressure), although it is not fully worked out and therefore somewhat unclear and difficult to work with, does afford some further insight into the symbolic and artificial life of the *Decameron* group.[30] Speaking of the Manichaean cosmology as a "typical sectarian," strong grid, strong group concept, Douglas writes: "Their small, tightly organized group maintained its identity by elaborate rituals, ruthless rejection of the bad outside and affirmation by symbolic means of the purity of the group and of their inner selves." The grid and group situation of the *cornice* fulfills these qualifications to some degree. The group is small, tightly organized by ties of family and affection, and changes locus twice to avoid "contamination" by outsiders: "Furthermore, since we shall have stayed here for four days, if we wish to avoid new people coming upon us to join us here, I think it advisable to leave here and go elsewhere."[31] The fact that people will have heard of the group and will attempt to join it is also one of the reasons given by Panfilo for breaking it up after the tenth day of storytelling. The ritually repetitive life style has already been pointed out, and the purity of the group is symbolically affirmed not only by the bathing episode but by its continual emphasis on its own chastity.

The love relationships among the protagonists are also considered to be dangerous, however, as Neifile points out:

> Then Neifile, whose face had turned all scarlet with confusion since she was the object of one of the youth's affections, said:
> "For goodness' sake, do take care, Pampinea, of what you are saying! To my certain knowledge, nothing but good can be said of any of them. . . . But since it is perfectly obvious that they are in love with certain of the ladies here present, I am apprehensive lest, by taking them with us, through no fault either of theirs or of our own, we should bring disgrace and censure on ourselves."
> "That is quite beside the point," said Filomena. "If I live honestly and my conscience is clear, then people may say whatever they like; God and Truth will take up arms in my defense" (p. 63).[32]

This does not necessarily constitute an argument against Boccaccio's exogamous intent, however. The love ties among the group, which are frequently alluded to and which represent a fairly complete gamut of possible types of love, belong to the realm of *amour courtois*, which was by definition quite separate from the practical realm of marriage.[33] The *De arte honeste amandi* specifically excludes the possibility of love between marriage partners. Furthermore, it is almost always in the *canzoni,* themselves an artificial formula for the closing of each ritual day, that the love permutations are presented.

Discretion and secrecy were cardinal rules of *fins amours,* and neither would have been possible under the circumstances in which the *brigata* spend their fifteen days. The young people's restraint thus bears out Thomas Greene's theory of the essentially social nature of the *Decameron*: the deceptions practiced by the lovers in the stories affirm the importance of social sanctions on sexual matters, and where such deceptions and secrecy are not possible, passion must be controlled.[34] The ten future leaders of a regenerated society must learn to understand the passions that form part of everyday living and to give both reality and the ideal their due. As the incredibly rich gamut of the stories shows, they must also learn to control their desires when it is necessary for the greater good of society. It is an often repeated lesson among the humanists, to whom Petrarch and Boccaccio stand as fathers. The emphasis on the absence of "endogamous" affairs thus has both ritual and social significance, if, *pace* Durkheim, one may momentarily separate the two for the sake of emphasis.

The very existence of the *cornice* and the high degree of stylization in the life of its protagonists has its own significance. In her book *Purity and Danger,* Mary Douglas argues that social relations are impossible without symbolic acts and that ritual provides a frame and alerts a special kind of expectancy (p. 63).[35] Again: the *cornice* of the *Decameron* is not, properly speaking, a ritual, but it does possess ritual qualities, and the constant emphasis on its presence, the repetitive living patterns of the narrators that open and close each day of storytelling, alert a special expectancy in the reader. Other statements in Douglas's work also open up interesting possibilities of meaning for the book as a whole, notably the theory that there is danger in transitional states because they are undefinable, leading to the extreme importance of ritual as a protective factor during a state of transition (p. 96).[36] The aristocracy of the protagonists and the strong class hierarchy evident in their relations with their servants, reaffirmed because of the pressures toward social change of the 1340s in Florence, come to mind. Douglas affirms that the weaker and less elaborate the social organization, the fancier and more complex the rituals become (p. 92), and this too is paralleled by the very existence of the orderly and stylized life of the *cornice* during the time of disorder consequent on the plague.[37] The effect of religious rites is to create and control experience: "The object of the ritual is to reformulate past experience" (pp. 65-67). The overt aim is stability: "rituals enact the form of social relations and . . . enable people to know their own society" (p. 128). The ten days of storytelling, set within this secluded and artificial frame, certainly enable the ten protagonists to know the society of their time. The stylistic elaboration and Boccaccio's emphasis on his own literary style (to be shown in Chapter III of this study) also function to underline the ritual aspect of the whole experience.

There is further evidence, beyond their sheer bulk, that the stories are an intrinsic (and the most important) part of the ritual experience. In spite of his totally irreverent and indeed markedly antagonistic attitude toward the official Church of his time, there is no doubt that Boccaccio was profoundly Christian in his beliefs.[38] Invocations to the Deity in his work should therefore be taken seriously and looked at carefully.

An examination of the invocations of God in the Preface, the Introduction, the Introduction to the Fourth Day, and the Author's Epilogue, in contrast to that in the first story, shows how deeply serious and ritually significant the storytelling itself is. The invocations in the framing sections of the book are more or less formulaic, in spite of their gradation from greater to lesser levity. A comparison shows an increase of seriousness not only from beginning to end

31

but also from "outer to inner layer." It corresponds to the shift in action from the author's alleged reason for writing the book (to amuse lovesick ladies) through his description of the circumstances in which the tales were told, his defense of his art (Introduction to Day IV and Epilogue) to the inner core of the *Decameron*, the stories themselves.

> However, the One who is infinite decreed by immutable law that all earthly things should come to an end. And it pleased Him that this love of mine . . . should in the course of time diminish of its own accord (Preface, p. 45).

> If this [that the ladies derive pleasure and useful advice from the stories] should happen (and may God grant that it should), let them give thanks to Love, which in freeing me from its bonds . . . (Preface, p. 47).

> I say, then, that the sum of thirteen hundred and forty eight years had elapsed since the fruitful Incarnation of the Son of God, when the noble city of Florence . . . (Introduction, p. 50).

> Being confident that God and you yourselves [the ladies] will assist me, I shall proceed patiently on my way . . . (Introduction to Day IV, pp. 330-331).

> And so, after giving thanks, firstly to God and then to yourselves [the ladies], the time has come for me to rest my pen and weary hand (Author's Epilogue, p. 829).

> . . . for the time has come for me to bring all words to an end, and offer my humble thanks to Him who assisted me in my protracted labor and conveyed me to the goal I desired. May His grace and peace, sweet ladies, remain with you always (Author's Epilogue, p. 833).[39]

This final quotation is from the next to the last and the last

sentences of the *Decameron* and is clearly serious enough
to suggest that Boccaccio had not planned a mere "human
comedy" in the modern sense of the word (the contrast to
Dante's *Divine Comedy* in the medieval sense has been all
too repeatedly underlined since De Sanctis's times). It is
notable, however, that in every one of the passages cited,
except for the last, God and the ladies Boccaccio addresses
are mentioned together, frequently as if they were on the
same plane. In the vocative at the beginning of the first
story, on the other hand, the ladies are clearly placed in a
different category. Boccaccio is no longer allowing himself
any levity and the opening invocation within the first story
is very solemn:

> It is proper, dearest ladies, that everything done by
> man should begin with the sacred and admirable name
> of Him that was maker of all things (p. 68).[40]

In the Italian, the play is on the words *"fa"* (whatever
man *does*) and *"facitore"* (God as "doer" or Creator of all
things). The critic's temptations when faced with such a
sentence are many: one could argue that Boccaccio's love
for etymological play is evidence for a "forerunner of the
High Renaissance" theory, according to which he could
have been setting up the well-known later image of "man
as creator in rivalry with God" (but this is unlikely, given
the religious attitudes both of Boccaccio and of his times).
One could equally well or perhaps better argue that the
sentence reflects the more docile and Dantesque attitude
(with respect to man's relation to God, the combination is
not oxymoronic) that it is humanity's duty on earth to imitate God and His works to the best of its poor ability. The
undeniable solemnity of the sentence remains regardless,
and its possibly ambiguous continuation (the much discussed story of Ser Cepparello is proposed as an example
of "one of His marvelous works") does not detract from
this solemnity. The continuation is in fact part of a complex
framing system and belongs to a different discourse, pertaining to the implicit moral of the story itself.

Historico-social matrix, ritual aspects, and Boccaccio's choice and handling of his signifiers thus all point to the telling of the hundred tales as something more than amusement, more than escape, more than the portrayal of a civilization that is disappearing or than an affirmation of life in the face of death. Nor is it only, as several critics have said, a portrayal of the world written by a lay moralist and reflected through "the art-play of storytelling."[41] It is designed, as Boccaccio himself wrote, to give some "useful advice" and to show "what should be avoided and likewise what should be pursued" (p. 45).[42] This advice is addressed to his audience on the first plane, the ladies whom he claims to be addressing, but it is also repeated in his Epilogue, addressed directly to his readers, where he says of the stories that, like everything else in the world, they may be harmful or useful, depending on how they are taken. A few lines later he writes:

> Everything is in itself good for something, and if badly used it can cause great damage, and so I say about my stories. If anyone wants to get evil advice or derive wicked plots from them, they will not forbid it if they have such things in them or if they be twisted and distorted so as to have such things in them; and to him who wishes to derive usefulness and fruitful advice from them, they will not deny these things, *nor will they ever be called or held to be other than useful and honest if they are read in those terms and by those persons for which they were told.*[43]

The theme of the stories' usefulness is also repeated frequently by the young people (or initiands into the leadership of their society) themselves. Fifty-five of the hundred stories are introduced as having some sort of moral aim by their narrators, and the adjective "useful" is used again and again.[44] At times one could almost believe one were reading a work by Alberti, whose favorite adjective was *utile.*

It is clear that Boccaccio has taken care to reaffirm the

importance and civic usefulness of his stories on all three of his narrative levels, so that they will be valid for all three of his "audiences." These are constituted by "real people," his own narrators (who are, as was recently pointed out, the projection of (1) the ideal reader, (2) the figure of the audience, (3) the figure of the author himself—as they too are narrators),[45] and the fictitious narrative audience, made up of the ladies to whom both Boccaccio *qua* author and his narrators constantly address themselves. The essential functionality of the storytelling is also pointed up by two examples of stories within stories that are overtly teaching devices, both in the very first day: the tale of how Melchisedech the Jew averts a trap set for him by Saladin with a story of three rings (I, 3) and the story of how Bergamino cures Can Grande della Scala of a fit of parsimony by telling him about the Abbot of Cluny (I, 7). The whole implicit theme of the stories as vehicles of knowledge and custodians of civilized ideals is further underlined by the narrators' not infrequent habit of breaking into their own narration to open a discussion on the life of their times.[46]

The physical situation of the *Decameron* experience may also be read in the light of ritual although it, too, is capable of bearing multiple interpretations. Various critics have noted that the gardens in which the stories are told correspond closely to the classic *locus amoenus*, and this has been used to argue that the whole experience is an idyllic escape, taking place in the "green world."[47] The *cornice* landscape has also been seen as the "good natural world" in contrast to the "negative urban world" and its closeness to the city as a sign that the *brigata* will return and help shape a better urban society.[48] But the locus, though not urban, is more suburban than rural, and considerable emphasis is placed on the elegance of the man-made villas in which the party sojourns. The gardens in which the stories are told are likewise places where nature and culture meet, as opposed to the realm of pure nature. This is true even of the "natural" Valley of the Ladies, which is described as being "perfectly" circular, with a "regular" series of terraces that are arranged like the seats in an amphitheater.

The idea of telling the stories in a place where nature and culture are reconciled in harmony, such as a garden, is perfectly in keeping with Thomas Greene's thesis that the true message of the book is the reconciliation of nature (human nature) and society. The locations (within two or three miles of Florence) furthermore are not only in keeping with this theory but could also reflect the liminal character of the whole work. Liminal rites are usually situated in specially prepared locations that are outside the limits of, but in a sense still part of, the tribal villages or clusters of villages they serve. Dioneo's often quoted statement:

> I know not what you intend to do with your troubles; my own I left inside the city gates when I departed thence a short while ago in your company. Hence you may either prepare to join with me in as much laughter, song and merriment as your sense of decorum will allow, or else you may give me leave to go back for my troubles and live in the afflicted city (p. 64).[49]

could also be in part interpreted as an affirmation of entry into a separate, liminal world, where the old identity is left behind together with its problems and preoccupations.

A basic question remains, and that is whether Boccaccio and his contemporaries could have seen the idea of storytelling as either a "rite of modernization" or as a "rite of conservation." In *Rites of Modernization*, a study of *ludruk*, the proletarian theater in Java, the anthropologist James Peacock has shown how *ludruk* "helps . . . apprehend modernization movements in terms of vivid and meaningful symbolic classifications, seduces . . . into empathy with modes of social action . . . involves the participants in aesthetic forms that structure their most general thoughts and feelings in ways stimulating to the modernization process."[50] Peacock's year-long intensive observation of *ludruk* and its audience's reactions led him to conclude that in the evolution of this type of drama the original opposition between what is refined and what is crude became useless because it served to "read" the past, traditional society. It was gradually replaced by an opposition between progressive and conservative elements, with plays geared toward the former point of view achieving a definite lead in popularity and frequency of performance. Vittore Branca's fundamental conception of the *Decameron* as the epic of the merchant classes in some ways leads to similar conclusions. The book's enormous popularity was ascribed to the fact that it reflected the values of the rising merchant class. A parallel point of view may be found in the essay of Antonio Staüble, who sees the *brigata* as a sort of audience for whose benefit the scenes narrated in the stories take place.[51] It is a somewhat fanciful concept, but becomes very useful for Staüble's subsequent classification of their "audience reactions," which are usually *group* reactions and "reveal quite similar and rather generic intellectual, moral and spiritual attitudes." The generic reactions, however, are in keeping with the liminal aspect of the whole experience and well suited to the *brigata*'s role as future leaders and models.

Boccaccio set out to teach his ten protagonists a good set of values that would enable them to preserve the old virtues and also to function effectively as leaders in their world. This world had been and was still changing, as Boccaccio certainly realized, and it is perhaps after all not so strange that the *Decameron* tales praise the traditional values its author wanted to protect and at the same time mirror a new society in which a doctor's daughter such as Giletta can be more noble-minded than a count's son (III, 9) and bakers such as Cisti can remind influential and powerful Florentine leaders of their manners (VI, 2). Boccaccio believed that the best of the old traditions should and could be kept by the society that found itself in a state of transition. This accounts for the curious mix of the *courtois*, feudal, and romance ideals with the "naturalism" and "modern" or humanist values to be found in the book.

The idea of using stories to transmit a message was certainly not new. The comedies of Terence and Plautus served as literary models with a moral, as Boccaccio himself pointed out in the *De Genealogiis* (XIV, 9). A similar use of stories was to be found all around him in the *exempla* that rang from every pulpit, most notably that of Santa Maria Novella itself, where the famous Jacopo Passavanti, author of the well-known collection of *exempla, Specchio di vera penitenza,* preached his sermons.

Boccaccio's use of *exempla* is an interesting topic, one which critics have not failed to discuss.[52] Enrico De' Negri has shown the similarities between Boccaccio's rhetorical strategies and those of the typical medieval *exemplum* and argued that Boccaccio pokes fun at the *exemplum* as a literary genre by his gross exaggeration in the first story of the *Decameron*, that of Ser Cepparello. Salvatore Battaglia argues that the *Decameron* transformed the genre by freeing it from the necessity of expressing only preset Christian verities and rendering it more flexible and better able to express the problems of the world. Millicent Marcus writes that Boccaccio believed "the author must disabuse his public of the tendency to interpret stories in exemplary terms by making the *exemplum* discredit itself . . . thereby exposing the obsolescence of the genre" (*An Allegory of Form,* p. 12). All these comments focus mainly on the literary or metanarrative aspect. Some of Boccaccio's stories do indeed seem exaggerations of the *exemplum* (notably both the first story in the book and the last, that of the exasperatingly patient Griselda), and others seem ironic perversions of the genre (notably the story of Nastagio degli Onesti [V, 8], who stumbles across a supernatural vision that is clearly borrowed from one of the many "hell hunts" in the *compendia* and uses it to liberalize the mores of the ladies of Ravenna). But the exaggeration and the irony could be aimed at the specific content of these tales as well as at the genre in general. Boccaccio himself uses an *exemplum* in the Introduction to Day IV, speaking directly to his readers in his quality as author, and though he uses it ironically, it cannot be argued that in this case he does so to attack a literary genre.

Though its "moral" is very different, Boccaccio's story of Filippo Balducci and the geese is otherwise a faithful reproduction of one of the most popular of all known *exempla*.[53] It tells of how Fillippo Balducci, suddenly finding himself a widower, resolves to remove himself and his two-year-old son from the temptations of the world. He takes the child to live as a hermit in a cave on the slopes of "Mount Asinaio," where he carefully segregates him from all worldly things and limits his life to the contemplation of the glories of God and His angels. When the boy is eighteen, his father takes him to Florence, as the old man is growing too frail to undertake the occasionally necessary trip there himself, and wishes to teach his son to do it for him. The boy is fascinated by all that he sees and is eagerly questioning his father about it when they run across a group of young women. The father tells him to avert his eyes from these evil beings and, in order to protect him further, does not tell him their real name, calling them geese and repeating his injunction to avoid them. It is unavailing, however, for the son replies that they are more beautiful than the pictures of the angels and begs to take a goose home to feed. Boccaccio ends the tale on a pun ("you don't know where/wherewith they feed")[54] and on the father's realization that human wits cannot overcome the urges of nature. There is nothing exaggerated about this story by medieval standards, and even the deft switch in morals (the standard version ended by pointing out the horrifying and dangerous power that women have) is—if I may be allowed the pun—a natural one. If Boccaccio was attempting to do away with the *exemplum* as a genre, why would he so openly use it to present an important message during a serious defense of his work? The not-so-hidden meaning may be that his stories do transmit important messages and that his literary audience would do well to participate indirectly in the frame tale initiands' experience. The exaggeration in some other *exempla*, like that of Ser

Cepparello, which De' Negri rightly calls a caricature, is almost always aimed at the contemporary hagiographic "credibility gap" and the exaggerated expectations about which the clergy preached while their own behavior so frequently and clearly exemplified the unnaturalness of the mores they prescribed for others. Boccaccio's message in the story of Filippo Balducci is thus a double one: not only does it teach us that stories teach, but it teaches us that to model oneself on the *exempla* to be found in church sermons is absurd.

~ CHAPTER II ~

God, Church, and Society
in the *Decameron*

THE MUCH DISCUSSED problem of whether the *Decameron* is religious, areligious, or anti-religious can also be approached from an anthropological point of view.[1] There can be no doubt that many ecclesiastic customs come off very badly at Boccaccio's hands, but it could be argued that they come off no better at Dante's, whose faith has never for a moment been questioned. The difference lies in the fact that where the *Divine Comedy* boils over with honest indignation at corrupt clerical practices while belief in Church dogmas and sacraments is openly stated, and the Church itself as an institution is fully accepted, the *Decameron* makes fun of the corruption and points out the lies and deceit of the clergy without making any statements about the religious institution itself. It also makes hardly any about God. Yet Boccaccio was by no means irreligious or heretical. It therefore behooves us to examine closely the workings of the religious "frames" in the *Decameron*.

God and Church are carefully separated in the text, and while the former is treated with great reverence, His place within the *Decameron* is clearly limited. In the tale Boccaccio tells us about his book in the Proem, the presence of God is not at all marked, and, with the exception of the almost flippant hope that He will grant lovesick ladies a cure, it is formulaic. This is not true of the innermost of the circles that make up the *Decameron*. The most notable and serious invocation of God is found in the opening sentence of the

41

first story: "It is a fitting thing, dearest ladies, that everything done by man should be begun by the admirable and Holy name of Him who was the maker of all things."[2] Even here, however, religion is seen in a human framework. In the Italian, the construction is not passive; it reads "everything that man does," and the name of man is mentioned before that of the deity. The latter's presence is portentously underlined, however, and presides over the central learning content that is the crux of the liminal experience.

God's presence is also serious and strongly marked in the description of the plague, where He is mentioned twice, both times in the guise of angry and awe-inspiring Old Testament Lord. The deadly plague is said to have raged "either because of the influence of the heavenly bodies or sent by God's righteous wrath to rebuke us mortal men for our iniquitous way of life"; and some people fled Florence "almost as if God's wrath would not send that plague to punish men's wickedness wherever they were, but would only visit it upon those who happened to be within their city walls."[3] The description of the plague forms the third world of a fivefold concentric system, and it is the outermost in the series that depicts the protagonists of the ritual. The "skeleton plot" of the *Decameron* could in fact be described as the story of a visitation by God that precipitates a ritual in which the élite of society are taught the enduring values of their world. The Church as an institution is not treated as valuable, however, and religion is not emphasized in the pages on the plague. The bulk of the description (an impressive bulk) underlines not God's visitation but the ensuing breakdown of society. Boccaccio's interest is social and oriented toward humanity-in-the-world. This is amply demonstrated by his only apparently offhand remark about the enormous loss of life in Florence (over a hundred thousand deaths): "such was the cruelty of Heaven and perhaps in some measure that of man."[4] The paratactic syntax and the fact that the second phrase is a hendecasyllable in Italian, whereas the first is a less "noble" heptameter, work to counterbalance the "perhaps" and to assign equal responsibility to mankind.

The Church is conspicuous by its absence in the *cornice*. *Qua* institution it is not mentioned at all and there are very few references to formal religion or even to the clergy. In the pages dedicated to the otherwise detailed description of society during the plague, we find only the following mentions:

[1] Nor were the countless petitions humbly directed to God by the pious, whether by means of formal processions or in any other guise, any less ineffectual (p. 50).

[2] In the face of so much affliction and misery, all respect for the laws of God and man had virtually broken down and been extinguished in the city. For like everybody else, those ministers and executors of the laws who were not either dead or ill were left with so few subordinates that they were unable to discharge any of their duties (p. 53).

[3] . . . and there would be a contingent of priests, whose numbers varied according to the quality of the deceased; his body would be taken thence to the church in which he had wanted to be buried. . . . But as the ferocity of the plague began to mount, this practice all but disappeared entirely . . . (p. 55).

[4] . . . taking up the coffin and hauling it swiftly away, not to the Church specified by the dead man in his will, but usually to the nearest at hand. They would be preceded by a group of four to six clerics, who between them carried one or two candles at most, and sometimes none at all. Nor did the priests go to the trouble of pronouncing solemn and lengthy funeral rites, but, with the aid of these so-called sextons, they hastily lowered the body into the nearest empty grave they could find (p. 55).

[5] And times without number it happened that two priests would be on their way to bury someone, holding a cross before them, only to find that bearers carrying three or four additional biers would fall in behind them; so that whereas the priests had thought they had only one burial to attend to, they in fact had six or seven, and sometimes more (p. 56).

[6] Such was the multitude of corpses (of which further consignments were arriving every day and almost by the hour at each of the churches), that there was not sufficient consecrated ground for them to be buried in, especially if each was to have its own plot in accordance with long established custom. So when all the graves were full, huge trenches were excavated in the churchyards, into which new arrivals were placed in their hundreds, stowed tier upon tier like ships' cargo . . . (pp. 56-57).[5]

Of the six passages that allude to the role of religion, the Church, or the clergy, one (1) describes religion's impotence in the face of God's wrath; one (2) alludes to religion's social failure; three (3, 4, 5) depict the perfunctory haste and impersonality with which the clergy perform their office of burial, which is tantamount to depicting their failure at ritual office, and one (6) uses the telling mercantile simile of the ships' holds to further desacralize Church and churchyards.

The actual *function* of the Church within the plot structure is a rather interesting one. It plays no active role but merely serves as a gateway, first into the liminal experience, and subsequently back into the chaotic world of the plague. The protagonists of the *cornice* meet in the church of Santa Maria Novella and return to it as their dispersal point. This implies a very basic change in role: from that of valid institution, in whose rules and customs one can dwell, to that of threshold, a place of transition through which one passes to a valid experience. The contrast can best be seen by comparing the institution's symbolic role in Dante's *Purgatorio*, where it is presented as an integral part of life, which also serves to open the gates of Purgatory and thus of eventual salvation for the sinner.

The end result of Boccaccio's handling of the themes of God and Church is to maintain the religious attitude toward God while at the same time desacralizing the official institution. There is a clear statement of this theme in Neifile's introductory comment to her story of Abraham the Jew, whose conversion to Christianity was brought about by his witnessing of the depravity of the papal court: "Panfilo has shown us in his tale that God's loving kindness is unaffected by our errors, when they proceed from some cause which it is impossible for us to detect; and I in mine propose to demonstrate to you how this same loving kindness, by patiently enduring the shortcomings of those who in word and deed ought to be its living witness and yet behave in precisely contrary fashion, gives us the proof of its unerring rightness; my purpose being that of strengthening our conviction in what we believe" (p. 82).[6]

The treatment of clergy and of Church customs in the stories as well as in other comments made by the protagonists of the fourth world of the *cornice* (that in which they exchange their tales) is consistent and reflects contemporary public opinion. There are clever and highly derogatory puns on the names of Church-certified saints or angels, such as the *"ragnolo* Braghiello," a contamination of *agnolo* (angel) by *ragno* (spider) and of Gabriel by pantaloons (*braghe*).[7] There are examples of joking prayers used in extremely profane contexts, such as St. Julian's *pater noster*, and equally profane references to saints and religious customs that have become contaminated by avarice, such as the allusion to the anointing of the hands of a holy inquisitor with a "goodly amount of St. John Golden-Mouth's ointment (a highly effective remedy against the disease of galloping greed, common among the clergy . . .)" (p. 97).[8] Finally, there are indignant denunciations of the clergy by the protagonists of the *cornice*, like the one by Pampinea in IV, 2:

> There is a popular proverb which runs as follows: "He who is wicked and held to be good, can cheat because no one imagines he would." This saying offers me ample scope to tell you a story on the topic that has been prescribed, and it also enables me to illustrate the extraordinary and perverse hypocrisy of the members of religious orders. They go about in those long, flowing robes of theirs, and when they are asking for alms, they deliberately put on a forlorn expression and are all humility and sweetness; but when they are reproaching you with their own vices, or showing how the laity achieve salvation by almsgiving and the clerics by almsgrabbing, they positively deafen you with their loud and arrogant voices. To hear them talk, one would think they were excused, unlike the rest of us, from working their way to Heaven on their merits, for they behave as though they actually own and govern the place, assigning to every man who dies a position of greater or lesser magnificence there according to the quantity of money he has bequeathed to them in his will. Hence they are pulling a massive confidence trick, of which they themselves, if they really believe what they say, are the earliest victims; but the chief sufferers are the people who take these claims of theirs at their face value.
>
> If only I were allowed to go into the necessary details, I would soon open many a simpleton's eyes to the sort of thing these fellows conceal beneath the ample folds of their habits. However, for the time being we must hope that God will punish their lies (p. 343).[9]

The most excoriating comments are to be found in the innermost frame, within the story of Abraham the Jew, and are thus made part of the learning experience that is at the core of the ritual. Again, Boccaccio takes care to separate God and Church. At the papal court Abraham settled down, without telling anybody why he had come, and cautiously began to observe the behaviour of the Pope, the cardinals, the other Church dignitaries, and all the courtiers. Being a very perceptive person, he discovered, by adding the evidence of his own eyes to information given him by others, that practically all of them from the highest to the lowest were flagrantly given to the sin of lust, not only of the natural variety, but also of the sodomitic, without the slightest display of shame or remorse, to the extent that the power of prostitutes and young men to obtain the most enormous favours was virtually unlimited. In addition to this, he clearly saw that they were all gluttons, wine-bibbers, and drunkards without exception, and that next to their lust they would rather attend to their bellies than to anything else, as though they were a pack of animals.

Moreover, on closer inspection he saw that they were such a collection of rapacious money-grubbers that they were as ready to buy and sell human, that is to say, Christian blood as they were to trade for profit in any kind of divine object, whether in the way of sacraments or of church livings. In this activity, they had a bigger turnover and more brokers than you could find on any of the Paris markets including that of the textile trade. They had applied the name of "procuration" to their unconcealed simony, and that of "sustentation" to their gluttony, as if (to say nothing of the meaning of the words) God were ignorant of the intentions of their wicked minds and would allow Himself to be deceived, as men are, by the mere names of things (pp. 84-85).[10]

None of this is new, and all of it can be found in other examples of the literature of the time. But there is a difference: the tone of the *Decameron*'s commentary on organized religion is bitter rather than funny; the jokes are extremely subversive and the attacks demonstrably virulent.[11]

The reason for such bitterness in an otherwise good-humored book has a profoundly social basis. It lies in the failure of the contemporary organized religion to preserve the sacred, and its consequent inability to perform its social function, as demonstrated by the role assigned to it in the description of the plague (one of impotence and absence).

The social importance of the concept of the sacred in human life is by now beyond discussion, and the work done on various aspects of the problem by anthropologists continues to show its crucial position and Protean manifestations in the life of all societies. It comes as no surprise, then, to find it occupying an important place in the *Decameron*, where its prominence reflects its role in contemporary civic life. "It is by re-inserting the work into historic evolution as a whole and by relating it to social life as a whole that the researcher can show the *objective* meaning of which even its creator is often not very much aware."[12] There is a sense in which the *Decameron* does, in the middle of the fourteenth century, what Martin Luther was to do in the first quarter of the sixteenth (though it does so in a very different way). Boccaccio's work, both in the *cornice* and in the stories, reflects the fact that the blatant corruption in the Church was costing it a great deal of moral power. This reflection is obvious and does not need discussion. What is interesting is exactly *how* the *Decameron*, as a book, contributes to the desacralization of the Church, as an institution. A very specific theory, rather than a more general "anthropological approach," leads to some insights into the problem.

Roy A. Rappaport has emphasized the importance of the concept of sanctification in preserving the reliability of human communication.[13] The sacred plays a crucial role by its certification of the trustworthiness of certain messages, and thus, although it is a notion that belongs essentially to the realm of discourse, it exerts strong influence in the realm of social life. Rappaport argues that, since human communication relies mainly on symbols, lying is far more possible in human than in animal communications, since (as Eco also pointed out) symbolic signals can be sent in the absence of their referents. Although human beings also communicate through "animal signs" and animals too are capable of limited symbol use, which has resulted in some examples of what could be called lying in the animal world, humans rely on symbols far more than any other species, "and therefore lying is essentially a human problem." Rappaport considers it a fundamental one for human society: "The survival of any population of animals depends upon social interactions characterized by some minimum degree of orderliness, but orderliness depends upon reliable communication. If the recipients of messages are not willing to accept the messages they receive as sufficiently reliable to inform their actions, their responses are likely to tend toward randomness, becoming increasingly less creditable, leading to yet more random responses, reducing orderliness still further. When the communication system can accommodate lies it becomes a problem to assure the recipients of messages that the information they receive is sufficiently reliable to act upon" (p. 79). Some means of ensuring reliable communications is thus necessary, and Rappaport's theory is that this "antidote to lie" is sanctification. He is careful to define his concept of sanctity: certain propositions, such as the one that the ghosts of one's ancestors persist as powerful beings who can influence our lives in this world, "being without material referents are not in their nature falsifiable, nor can they be verified, and yet they are taken to be unquestionable. I take sanctity to be the quality of unquestionableness imputed by the faithful to such unfalsifiable propositions" (p. 79).

We are dealing, it should be noted, with "a quality of discourse rather than of the objects, real or putative, with which discourse is concerned" (p. 79). But—and this is one of the factors that gives sanctity its role in society—it is also a quality that is not necessarily limited to "ultimate sacred propositions" but may rub off onto or be extended to either material referents or the affairs of humanity. The sanctification of messages is their certification, and it "increases the willingness of recipients of symbolically encoded messages to accept the messages they receive as sufficiently reliable to act upon" (p. 79).

The theory is particularly applicable to the story of Ser Cepparello, whose place as the first of the one hundred tales puts it into the doubly valent position of being part of the framing system and of its content.[14] Among its many possible interpretations (and it is an extremely rich tale), it could also be partially read as the story of a man who invokes the sanctity of deathbed confession to certify as preposterous a set of lies as any ever uttered, each of which is in its turn based upon another hallowed code—that of the sins that were conventionally accepted as confessable and absolvable. The story is narrated by Panfilo, who claims to have chosen it as an example of miracles, and concerns a loan collector called Ser Cepparello (Sir Little Log), who is sent by a wealthy merchant to collect on some loans the merchant has outstanding in Burgundy. Ser Cepparello (known in Burgundy as Ser Ciappelletto—garland—thanks to an etymological mistake on the part of the French) has been especially selected as the only man "sufficiently villainous to match the villainy of the Burgundians" and thus to be able to carry out his task. Boccaccio's description of him is a model of exaggeration:

> This Ciappelletto was a man of the following sort: a notary by profession, he would have taken it as a slight upon his honour if one of his legal deeds (and he drew up very few of them) were discovered to be other than false. In fact, he would have drawn up free of charge as many false documents as were requested of him, and done it more willingly than one who was highly paid for his services. He would take great delight in giving false testimony, whether asked for it or not. In those days, great reliance was placed in France upon sworn declarations, and since he had no scruples

50

about swearing falsely, he used to win, by these nefarious means, every case in which he was required
to swear upon his faith to tell the truth. He would take
particular pleasure, and a great amount of trouble, in
stirring up enmity, discord and bad blood between
friends, relatives and anybody else; and the more ca-
lamities that ensued, the greater would be his rapture.
If he were invited to witness a murder or any other
criminal act, he would never refuse, but willingly go
along; and he often found himself cheerfully assaulting
or killing people with his own hands. He was a mighty
blasphemer of God and His Saints, losing his temper
on the tiniest pretext, as if he were the most hot-blooded
man alive. He never went to church, and he would
use foul language to pour scorn on all of her sacraments, declaring them repugnant. On the other hand,
he would make a point of visiting taverns and other
places of ill repute, and supplying them with his custom. Of women he was as fond as dogs are fond of a
good stout stick; in their opposite, he took greater
pleasure than the most depraved man on earth. He
would rob and pilfer as conscientiously as if he were
a saintly man making an offering. He was such a prize
glutton and heavy drinker, that he would occasionally
suffer for his over-indulgence in a manner that was
highly indecorous. He was a gambler and a card-sharper
of the first order. But why do I lavish so many words
upon him? He was perhaps the worst man ever born
(pp. 70-71).[15]

While lodging with a pair of Florentine brothers, both usurers in Burgundy, Ser Cepparello or Ciappelletto becomes
very ill. He overhears the usurers worriedly discussing the
situation. If they throw him out, people will accuse them
of heartlessness, and if he dies in their house unshriven,
as such a sinner is certainly likely to do, people might
equally use that as an excuse to seize their money and
perhaps to do them physical injury. Ser Cepparello calls

the brothers in and tells them not to worry but to summon the most saintly friar they can find to hear his confession and administer Extreme Unction to him. He then proceeds to invent a farrago of innocence in which he confesses to such sins as having drunk his water avidly and having felt greedy for wild herb salads during periods of fasting. Among the worst, brought forth with an incredible show of weeping and penitence, he includes spitting in church and having cursed his mother when he was a little boy. The friar is so deeply impressed by Ser Cepparello's purity and innocence that on the latter's death (that same day) he assembles all his colleagues, solemnly installs the body in their church and holds Ser Cepparello up to the townspeople as an example of saintliness. The people believe it all and strip the body in their eagerness to obtain relics of the saint, who is duly buried in the friar's church and whose body is said to perform many subsequent miracles. Perhaps, Panfilo says, he genuinely repented with his last breath and went to Heaven; more likely he went elsewhere, but in either case the story is to be taken as an example of God's loving kindness, as He grants the prayers of many who invoke "Saint Ciappelletto," in spite of his possible damnation.

Ser Cepparello tells his lies, he claims, in order to use sanctity to protect his hosts from the "civic disorder" that would certainly ensue if it were to be known what manner of evil sinner they have been harboring. The knowledge would be just the sort of excuse the good citizens of the town would like to have for breaking into the usurers' house and robbing them of their possessions, if not of their lives. The fact that the whole elaborate hoax—the appealing vitality of its *joie de mentir* notwithstanding—is set up to protect a pair of usurers, who as such were repellent not only to Boccaccio but to a sanctification system that regarded usury as sinful, adds a further preposterous dimension to the tale and undermines the social, as well as the religious, function to which sanctity is put in this case.[16] All of this is perfectly obvious to the book's two audiences (the real one and the fictive one of the *cornice*).[17] Sanctity is invoked to preserve the good reputation of a thorough-going rogue and the property of his anti-social usurer hosts. It is thus flagrantly misused on earth, whatever the outcome for Cepparello's immortal soul, which Boccaccio is careful to refrain from predicting: "It was thus, then, that Ser Cepparello of Prato lived and died, becoming a Saint in the way you have heard. Nor would I wish to deny that perhaps God has blessed and admitted him to his presence. For albeit he led a wicked, sinful life it is possible that at the eleventh hour he was so sincerely repentant that God had mercy on him and received him into His kingdom. But since this is hidden from us, I speak only with regard to outward appearance, and I say that this fellow should rather be in Hell, in the hands of the devil, than in Paradise" (p. 81).[18]

The anti-social aspect of the misuse of sanctity is further underlined by a detail in the story: Ser Cepparello has repeatedly succeeded in efficiently perverting the civic justice of the times, which is clearly based on the certification of messages by their sanctity. "In those days, great reliance was placed in France upon sworn declarations, and since he had no scruples about swearing falsely, he used to win, by these nefarious means, every case in which he was required to swear upon his faith to tell the truth" (p. 70).[19] Like the description of the plague in the *cornice*, whatever its other functions within the extremely complex whole may be, the opening story of the *Decameron* points out the failure of the religious system to perform its proper functions from a civic point of view.

Together with the shift in emphasis from God and Fortune to man's intelligence and the necessity of the harmonious resolution of social problems (as seen by such critics as Greene and Padoan), a large part of the revolutionary impact of the *Decameron* is rooted in its deliberate desacralization of the institutional habits of the Church and its clergy, as well as of its hierarchy of saints. This comes not from a lack of religious feeling in Boccaccio but from his awareness that the institution in its current state has forfeited its sanctity through its own behavior and must now be either genuinely reformed or cleared out of the way to leave room for another and more reliable system of sanctification and certification that will enable society to function again with some degree of orderliness, at the same time preserving those of its values that are worthwhile. There is little doubt that any "new" system Boccaccio might have envisioned would have been a Christian one, but there is equally little doubt that the treatment of things ecclesiastic in the *Decameron* deliberately and systematically deprives that institution of its claim to sanctity. This treatment, which, as we have seen, is built carefully into the *cornice* as well as being evident in anti-clerical stories and jokes, goes beyond the usual contemporary outrage at Church mores.

Rappaport draws an analogy between sanctity and the evolutionary principle called "Romer's rule," which is that the first effects of evolutionary changes are conservative because they make it possible for an extant way of life to persist in spite of changed conditions (the example given is that of the lobefinned fish who became more or less amphibian so as to migrate from one drying up body of water to another). "Similarly, sanctity may have permitted the persistence of some previously existing mode of social organization, or even the survival of the associations of organisms termed 'societies,' in the face of the threat posed to orderly social life by an increasing ability to lie" (p. 80). The social role of sanctity is to stabilize the conventions of particular societies by certifying directives and authorities, but once these have broken down, as they clearly have in the *Decameron*, sanctity itself may become harmful by certifying a social system that is no longer effective, and it becomes necessary to desacralize that system and to change it. Sanctity in Boccaccio's world, as is clear from the documents and literature of the times, had for some time been used to certify the Church in its political struggles and also to cover up the bad behavior of the clergy of all ranks:

matters had not improved at all since Iacopone da Todi
had addressed a poem to Pope Boniface VIII from jail,
accusing him of living in scandal as naturally as a salamander lives in fire and predicting that he would go to
hell.[20] It was clear that the time for desacralization had
come, and Boccaccio thus did not limit himself—as had
Dante, who firmly believed in the sanctity of the system—
to pointing out the many cases of non-compliance with the
rules.

The social role of liturgy is crucial to any religious system.
Rappaport defines liturgy as both the formal acts and word-
ing of the rituals themselves and the non-varying sequences that make up ritual cycles and series—a definition
that serves equally well for the Catholic liturgical calendar
or for the ritual cycles, say, of the Maring of New Guinea.
Liturgy "preserves convention inviolate in the face of the
continual violations of usage and in this respect may be
without functional equivalents" (p. 90). *Behavior* may vio-
late the conventions, but the act of taking part in liturgy
is an act of acceptance of the rules and conventions certified
by that liturgy. It is essentially a social act, and it is surrounded by a sense of morality. While Boccaccio has taken
care to include his Christian beliefs in his work, there is
evidence of a definite exclusion of Church liturgy. This is
done in two ways: first by using the church of Santa Maria
Novella purely as a gateway to and from the liminal world
and second by taking care to leave ecclesiastic ritual out of
the protagonists' life during their two-week absence. On
the first Sunday, no mention is made of mass or prayers;
on the second there is merely a fleeting one of what could
be a purely conventional custom: ". . . and after sauntering
for a while upon the dew-flecked lawns, they made their
way, the hour of tierce being nearly half spent, to a nearby
chapel, where they heard divine service. Returning to the
palace, they breakfasted in gay and festive mood" (p. 587).[21]
There are at least twenty mentions of meals or refreshments
in the various introductions and conclusions of the days
in contrast to this one reference to what the Church liked

to refer to as spiritual nourishment. At the same time, Boccaccio took great care to show that his protagonists observed the prescribed Friday and Saturday fasts, and that they refrained from telling stories on those two days, which correspond to those between the Crucifixion and the Resurrection. Once again Christianity is emphasized while the role of the ecclesiastic institution is seriously weakened, if not omitted.

The second way in which Boccaccio attacks the liturgy in the *Decameron* is by his repeated emphasis on the unholy behavior of those in Holy Orders, whose office is an integral part of Roman Catholic ritual. His constant repetition of scathing remarks or diatribes about them in the *cornice* and the large number of stories in which they figure in derogatory ways go beyond chance and realism, even though the stories circulating about the clergy during the period were based on fact, as even a cursory acquaintance with Church history shows. Twenty-one of the hundred tales in the *Decameron* attack the clergy, and the number would be twenty-three if one included the tales of Nastagio degli Onesti, which makes fun of typical religious *exempla* in sermons, and that of Ghino di Tacco's cure of the greedy Abbot of Cluny's stomach disorders by a bread and water diet. There is at least one anti-clerical tale in each day, and there are five in the first and third days.[22]

According to the customs of Boccaccio's time, consecrated clergy were not to function as normal individuals within a society, who participated in its rituals and thereby accepted its rules. Rather they were living representatives of that ritual itself. They could be termed "liturgical," as their vows and special costume set them apart from other men. They not only claimed to live by different rules but were legally subject to their own, separate legal systems and order of justice, which they considered superior just as they considered themselves superior to the rest of humanity.[23] It was considered that their celibacy in part so certified them, and thus breaking this vow was far more than just a violation of an accepted rule: it could be read as an attack on the rule itself, and because of the clergy's special status, an attack on the very liturgy of which they were a part. "Liturgical performance is the basic social act for humans, for social contact or even covenant is implicit in its very nature" (Rappaport, p. 90). Thus the misbehavior of the clergy was, in a sense, an attack on society, even though it was not considered an attack on the ultimate sacred propositions that were the source from which sanctity flowed to the Church. This latter could be defined as a "lower order institution" that was definitely "directly involved in the regulation of social systems" (Rappaport, p. 95). Boccaccio's constant reminders of this clerical misbehavior are thus also aimed at the liturgy itself, and it is not merely his understanding of human nature and his storytelling genius that cause him so often to choose sexuality as the grounds on which he shows the clergy's ritual unworthiness.

The general behavior of the actual clergy (Boccaccio's descriptions may exaggerate reality somewhat, but they are based on it) was also dangerous to the Church in another way. Though sanctity is initially a conservative brake in times of transition, it is also a concept that can function to facilitate social change, although it does so in a roundabout fashion. Insofar as ultimate sacred propositions are not in any way material and do not refer to material things, they are also not in themselves tied to any particular institution. Their sanctity spills over to other and more specific, perhaps materially oriented, directives or practices, creating a hierarchy of liturgical orders (which Rappaport refers to as "lower order sentences"). These latter are vulnerable, and may become open to questioning. The oversanctification of anything highly specific, in view of its referential nature, at first serves to stifle change but later becomes dangerous, as, being more material, it is more open to disproof. "If adaptive systems are to remain flexible, the degree of sanctity accorded to directives [or institutions] should be inversely correlated with their material specificity" (p. 96). Rappaport sums up the whole system as follows:

1. The regulatory structures of societies are sanctified by their relationship to ultimate sacred propositions enlivened in rituals.
2. But . . . the persistence of ultimate sacred propositions is contingent upon their acceptance by those subject to the regulatory structures that they sanctify.
3. There is, thus, a closed cybernetic loop, which implies that if the operation of the regulatory structure, which may include both discrete authorities such as chiefs and kings [or clergy], and specific directives, does not produce conditions satisfactory to those subject to it for long periods of time, it may be deprived of its sanctity.

This is to say that if authorities wish to maintain their sanctity they must keep the operation of the regulatory structures they administer in responsible working order. If they do not, they may find themselves deprived of sanctity (p. 98).

The *Decameron* deprives both the clergy and the institution they represent of sanctity precisely because the regulatory structures they administer have proved no longer to be in working order, and have in fact broken down completely in the face of the social crisis produced by the plague.

The concept of God had remained on the whole unchanged, but the degree of sanctification that flowed from it to the Church was being radically reassessed by society, both due to the fact that society was in a period of transition and due to the customs and bad behavior of the clergy. Their material specificity, in view of this behavior, could indeed be said to be demonstrably higher than their claims of superior spirituality, as Boccaccio repeatedly points out in his tales and in his storytellers' comments. His bitterness very probably stems from the fact that the clergy's behavior could conceivably threaten the sanctity of the ultimate propositions in which Boccaccio himself deeply believed, as well as from the realization that it had undermined the Church's very necessary social roles in keeping order and in acting as a conservative social force.

Boccaccio, as an examination of the stories themselves shows, was in many ways very conservative. If a rather progressive view of economics creeps into stories such as that of Federigo degli Alberighi through the comment at its very end that he lived happily ever after, *"having become a better manager of his affairs"* ("miglior massaio fatto"—V, 5, 43), the main thrust of the story praises a liberality that is clearly not a part of either humanist ethics or the bourgeois point of view (the term "bourgeois" can certainly be used for the city-dwelling merchants of Boccaccio's times). The values in Boccaccio's minor works are also clearly not "progressive" ones but those learned at the court in Naples, and they were very important to him, as was the world in which they were rooted and which was breaking down on all fronts. Beneath the surface unity of the *Decameron* there is a very definitely ambiguous attitude that is in itself a reflection of the fact that its author lived in a time of transition and was aware of the crisis of the society in which he lived. The very emphasis on humanity-in-the-world as opposed to God-as-reflected-in-the-world is an indication of this crisis point and made the Church's failure in its social role all the harder to bear.

Boccaccio, however, was fundamentally a practical-minded man and a realist. The Church's loss of sanctity and thus its ability to certify rules and conventions that would preserve the social order was as irrevocable as the passing of a great part of that social order. The best that could be done for civilization under the given conditions was to attempt to save those values that should and could be saved and to try to build a worthy civilization in the place of that which was so patently collapsing around Boccaccio and around his ten protagonists. This is the purpose of the whole liminal structure in the *Decameron*, and Boccaccio's attacks on the Church can be read as an attempt to clear the ground.

The medium he chose for carrying out this task was discourse, a logical enough choice. Sanctity is a quality of discourse rather than of the referential world, and its destruction must therefore take place on the same plane. Boccaccio's conscious use of discourse can be traced on several levels: First of all, he chose writing, a weapon to be respected in those days, when a tyrant such as Visconti could remark that Petrarch's pen was worth an army to him. Boccaccio, himself a humanist and a man with experience both in the world of the courts and in that of the merchants, was fully aware of the power of the word and he used it deliberately and sapiently.[24] Second and most importantly, the vehicle for the protagonists' learning experience is itself discourse. They gather in their liminal retreat and learn about their world not through symbolic actions, or to only a very small extent through symbolic actions (their general way of living and the solemn song and *carola* at the end of each day), but by telling and listening to stories, many of which, in their turn, emphasize storytelling as a medium, for they are presented as tales that well-known people used to tell. In other cases stories have definite functions in the plot, as in that of Madonna Oretta (VI, 1) or that of Bergamino, who reproves Can Grande della Scala for his parsimony by telling him how Primasso reproved the Abbot of Cluny for his lack of liberality (I, 7).

Boccaccio also called attention to the importance of the word and of discourse in more formal ways. It is no accident, as the critics have noted, that both the first and the fifty-first of his hundred stories are about verbal power. The first (Ser Cepparello) is in fact a story in which a fictitious being created by words (Saint Ciappelletto) has a marked effect on society in spite of the fact that such a being is a lie and exists only on the plane of discourse. The fifty-first story is, in a way, its opposite: it deals with the inability of poorly used words to create an illusion. This is the story of a knight who, in the course of a longish walk, offers to take Madonna Oretta riding on the back of a fine tale and makes such a poor job of recounting it that she begs him to set her down as his horse's trot is too jerky. Since medieval thought sought order and symmetry whenever possible, the position of the story as the first in a possible second half of the book lends added importance to its theme of the need of skill in discourse.[25]

Tales that deal with the power of discourse have a direct semantic link with the *cornice* and can therefore be discussed in some detail here. The most interesting of these are I, 1 (Ser Cepparello), and VI, 10 (Frate Cipolla).[26] Both are highlighted by their position: the tale of Ser Cepparello, the first in the book, has obvious primacy and that of Friar Onion is the closing one in a series, each of which deals with a quick response or a witty saying that saved its protagonist from some form of unpleasantness. It is also the only example of Dioneo keeping to the day's official theme, instead of using his freedom to depart from it, which serves to underline it even more. Dioneo himself emphasizes this point: "Charming ladies, although I have the privilege of speaking on any subject I may choose, I do not propose to depart from the topic on which all of you have spoken so appositely today. On the contrary, following your footsteps I intend to show . . ." (p. 505).[27]

Both stories deal with hallowed ecclesiastic institutions that had been blatantly misused and that were the object of severe criticism by contemporary society. In both cases the destruction of the sanctity of those practices is very obviously carried out by discourse. The story of Ser Cepparello is the story of a false "saint" who has been created entirely by his own lies and by the credulity of the holy friar who hears his confession. The latter used to be much criticized, but those who blamed the monk missed the point: he believes Ser Cepparello not because he is simple-minded but because he is holy and firmly believes in the holiness of his system. The sanctity of the latter renders Cepparello's confession unquestionable. In keeping with Rappaport's definition, Cepparello's lies are able to endow Ciappelletto

61

with sanctity because of the absence of a material referent. Ser Cepparello's thoroughgoing wickedness is known only in Italy, not in Burgundy, where he can operate freely because no one has ever heard of him. The story is based on an idea that is not original: in Sulpicius Severius's *Life of St. Martin*, the tomb of a thief is venerated as that of a saint and in Juan de Mariana's *History of Spain* there is an incident in which heretics create pseudo-miracles in order to induce the populace to worship the tomb of one of their company (Branca, *Decameron*, p. 1003). Boccaccio uses the idea in a new and interesting way, however, perverting it from its original use, which was to inspire horror at the impiety of the infidel, and blending it with the very popular theme of the hypocrite in order to attack an institution that was already having problems of credibility—witness the later restriction of the power of canonization to the pontifical Curia.

The story of Friar Onion[28] is similar to that of Ser Cepparello in that it, too, emphasizes the role of discourse and the internal audiences's willingness to swallow what are obvious lies because of its belief that they are certified by the sanctity of the system. Friar Onion belongs to the begging order of St. Anthony and in the course of his yearly rounds visits the town of Certaldo, where he has always collected large amounts of alms because of his ability with words: "he was such a lively and excellent speaker that anyone hearing him for the first time would have concluded not only that he was some great master of rhetoric, but that he was Cicero in person, or perhaps Quintilian" (p. 506).[29] One year he decides to impress his audience and increase his take by promising to show a wonderful and exceptionally holy relic: one of the angel Gabriel's feathers, left behind during the Annunciation. The friar plans to use a parrot's feather, as these exotic creatures are totally unknown to the simple-minded rustics of Certaldo. A pair of wily practical jokers in the audience, friends of his, decide otherwise, however, and steal the feather from his baggage, substituting some coals in order to see if he can save the situation. Friar Onion, unaware of this, introduces his relic with great fervor. Upon opening the box and seeing the substitution that has taken place, a change in material referents that could well have spelled his ruin, he immediately passes it off as a miracle, claiming that God Himself caused him to pick up the wrong casket and show the coals on which St. Lawrence was martyred because that Saint's feast day is imminent. The people accept this explanation and he not only collects more money and goods than ever before but has a wonderful time with the laying on of coals, drawing huge black miracle crosses on all the peasants' Sunday clothes and claiming that the miraculous mineral constantly renews itself.

The whole confidence trick is made possible by the audience's belief in the holiness of relics in the first place and by the razzle-dazzle of Friar Onion's holy patter, one of the funniest speeches in all literature.[30] In his youth, he says, he was sent by his superiors "to those parts where the sun can be seen" and duly set forth:

> So away I went, and after setting out from Venison, I visited the Greek Calends, then rode at a brisk pace through the Kingdom of Algebra and through Bordello, eventually reaching Bedlam, and not long afterwards, almost dying of thirst, I arrived in Sardintinia. But why bother to mention every single country to which I was directed by my questing spirit? After crossing the Straits of Penury, I found myself passing through Funland and Laughland, both of which countries are thickly populated, besides containing a lot of people. Then I went on to Liarland, where I found a large number of friars belonging to various religious orders including my own, all of whom were forsaking a life of discomfort for the love of God, and paying little heed to the exertions of others so long as they led to their own profit. In all these countries, I coined a great many phrases, which turned out to be the only currency I needed.

Next I came to the land of Abruzzi, where all the men and women go climbing the hills in clogs, and clothe pigs in their own entrails; and a little further on I found people carrying bread on staves, and wine in pouches, after which I arrived at the mountain of the Basques, where all the waters flow downwards.

In short, my travels took me so far afield that I even went to Parsnipindia, where I swear by this habit I am wearing that I saw the feathers flying—an incredible spectacle for anyone who has never witnessed it. And if any of you should doubt my words, Maso del Saggio will bear me out on this point, for he has set up a thriving business in that part of the world, cracking nuts and selling the shells retail.

But being unable to find what I was seeking, or to proceed any further except by water, I retraced my steps and came at length to the Holy Land, where in summertime the cold bread costs fourpence a loaf, and the hot is to be had for nothing. There I met the Reverend Father Besokindas Tocursemenot, the most worshipful Patriarch of Jerusalem, who, out of deference to the habit of the Lord Saint Anthony, which I have always worn, desired that I should see all the holy relics he had about him. These were so numerous, that if I were to give you a complete list, I would go on for miles without reaching the end of it. But so as not to disappoint the ladies, I shall mention just a few of them.

First of all he showed me the finger of the Holy Ghost, as straight and firm as it ever was; then the forelock of the Seraph that appeared to Saint Francis; and a cherub's fingernail; and one of the side-bits of the Word-made-flash-in-the-pan; and an article or two of the Holy Catholic faith; and a few of the rays from the star that appeared to the three Magi in the East; and a phial of Saint Michael's sweat when he fought with the Devil; and the jawbone of Death visiting Saint Lazarus; and countless other things.

And because I was able to place freely at his disposal certain sections of the Rumpiad in the vernacular, together with several extracts from Capretius, which he had long been anxious to acquire, he gave me a part-share in his holy relics, presenting me with one of the holes from the Holy Cross, and a small phial containing some of the sound from the bells of Solomon's temple, and the feather of the Angel Gabriel that I was telling you about, and one of Saint Gherardo da Villamagna's sandals, which not long ago in Florence I handed on to Gherardo di Bonsi, who holds him in the deepest veneration; and finally, he gave me some of the coals over which the blessed martyr Saint Lawrence was roasted. All these things I devoutly brought away with me, and I have them to this day (pp. 511-512).[31]

Various devices in the speech make it both funny to the reader—educated and trained in logic and rhetoric, as is the *cornice* audience—and credible to the rustics, rendered uncritical by their belief in the system, their own simplicity, the personal charm of the speaker, and the speed of the words, whose rhythm in the Italian is quite remarkable (the overall effect is in some ways akin to that produced by a first class auctioneer). Friar Onion cites Florentine street names such as Borgo de' Greci and Parione as examples of exotic places, states obvious truths as if they were miraculous, and refers to well-known symbolic trappings of the Roman Catholic faith. These are designed to generate instant recognition and thus feelings of familiarity and hence trust in the mind of the internal audience, composed of uneducated peasants whose reactions are determined by their lack of analytical training and their blind faith in the sanctity of the Church and all those officially connected with it, as is Friar Onion.[32]

The *cornice* audience, on the other hand, is clearly meant to see through the speech. One result of the story, for them as for the *Decameron* reader, is the desanctification of relics as well as that of begging friars. The representative of the latter is shown to be a cynical rascal when seen in the frame of his calling as a priest, but he is also presented as an engaging, witty, and talented human being who thoroughly enjoys a good joke.[33] The effect is to leave the onus of the rascality on his action while presenting the person in a light that seems rather admirable than otherwise according to contemporary customs.[34]

The desanctification of relics is carried out in an especially interesting way, because it quite deliberately underlines material referents, whose absence is one of the prerequisites of sanctity. Boccaccio thus draws attention to the flaw inherent in the very concept of relics—and of other forms of idolatry for that matter.[35] According to Rappaport's definition, sanctity is "the quality of unquestionableness imputed by the faithful" to propositions that "being without material referents are not in their nature falsifiable" and that can also not be verified (p. 79). When Boccaccio's friar claims to have seen the Holy Ghost's finger, or the rib of the Word-Made-Flesh, or the garments of the Holy Catholic Faith, not to mention the jawbone of Death (usually represented as a female skeleton) visiting St. Lazarus, he is not only dazzling his rustic audience with the mention of relics whose invention is based on psychologically familiar concepts and may not be much more ridiculous than some other relics to which they have been exposed. Boccaccio is here indulging brilliantly in his sense of fun, but also using the speech to point out the falsity of the whole system for the benefit of his initiands by having the friar invent false and obviously ridiculous material referents for items of a sacred proposition.[36] The gross and rather coarse materialization of sacred symbols in Boccaccio's jokes forcibly reminds the reader and the *cornice* audience that "sanctity . . . should be inversely correlated with . . . material specificity."

Friar Onion's endowing of the Holy Ghost with a flesh-and-blood finger, or his contaminating the idea of the Word-Made-Flesh with "Adam's rib" in all her frailty by the truly sacrilegious joke "the word-made-flesh-come-to-your-

window"[37] are rendered doubly shocking by the fact that
it is a member of the ecclesiastic order who carries out the
sacrilege, just as it was a member of the ecclesiastic order
who enabled Ser Cepparello's confession to turn him into
a saint. Credulous or incredulous, the clergy are instruments in the destruction of their own institution. The content of the stories thus shows itself to be perfectly in keeping with the comments of the storytellers on this subject,
and with the demonstrated failure of the Church to deal
with the social crisis engendered by the plague. As in the
built-in religious commentary in the frame tale, however,
there is a careful separation of God and Church. We have
seen it explicitly stated in the story of Ser Cepparello, and
it is implicitly stated by making the "spokesman" in the
story of Fra Cipolla a member of a class (the clergy) that
has already been publicly discredited as deceitful and hyp-
ocritical. The conclusion to be drawn is that it is the ecclesiastic institution and not the Godhead that must go, and
in both cases the whole elegant operation is carried out on
the plane of discourse. Saint Ciappelletto's extended lies
and Fra Cipolla's baroque ones show the initiands in un-
mistakable terms that the institution the two of them represent has become desacralized *not* because of any lack of
belief in the ultimate sacred propositions from which it
derived its authority and credibility, but because its own
representatives are undermining the quality of unquestionableness that has extended to it from those ultimate
sacred propositions. They do so with *words*: in I, 1, the
incredibly exaggerated set of lies is represented alongside
a supposed "material referent" (Ser Cepparello) who ex-
plodes any possibility of sanctity that might accrue to him.
(It must be remembered that, as the avowed protagonist
of a fiction, Ser Cepparello himself exists only on the plane
of discourse.) In VI, 10, it is the generation of supposedly
material referents (doubly on the plane of discourse—the
relics are patently fictitious) that exposes the questionable-
ness of the whole Church practice of using these contra-
dictorily material bits of the sacred to make money.

~ CHAPTER III ~

The Significance of
the Signifier

THE DESCRIPTION of the plague that opens what may be called the *Decameron* proper is very carefully constructed and rhetorically elegant. It was probably modeled either on Thucydides (from Lucretius via Macrobius) or on Paolo Diacono (with overtones of Isidore of Seville), in spite of the realism of the facts, which are not so different from the ones given by those of Boccaccio's contemporaries who, like him, had witnessed the epidemic.[1] The second of the two questions that arise from the long and prominent description of disaster at the beginning of a self-avowedly "happy" book, which is said to be written for the mere entertainment of housebound ladies tormented by love, is thus why it should be so very "literary." Vittore Branca, in keeping with his theory of the progression from vice to virtue, has suggested that Boccaccio purposely used the formal rhetorical device of *imitatio* to highlight the gravity of the situation (*Boccaccio*, pp. 302-303). Šklovsky, who sees no artistic unity in what he calls "the separate parts of the *Decameron*," dismisses the question with the somewhat vague statement that the description is "artistically designed" (p. 196). Other critics, especially those who read the book as a triumph of art over life or of culture over nature, have seen no particular significance in this factor.[2] Actually, however, the literary quality of the text is one of the key aspects of the *Decameron* and should be seen as an important component, bearing semantic value. It should be studied as a stylistic subcode, and as an instance of what Umberto Eco calls "overcoding."[3] That is true of the whole work, not only (though perhaps especially) of the description of the plague. It must be kept in mind that at that time the social and civic importance of the man of letters was generally acknowledged, as Petrarch's career amply demonstrates. Consequently, when a writer indicates in any way that he is assuming the role of poet or humanist he may well be calling attention to the gravity and importance of what he has to say.

Boccaccio's own interpretation of the role of literature is best expressed in the *Genealogia Deorum Gentilium*, a later work that may nevertheless be used as a guide to the *Decameron* because its point of view is the same as that expressed in defense of poetry in the Introduction to the Fourth Day. In this passage Boccaccio openly states that it is poets who have made their epochs flower, and that they have found more to sustain them among fables than many a rich man among his treasures (IV, Intro., 37-38; McWilliam, p. 330). A reading of the *Genealogia* makes it possible to account for the literary tone of the description in inverse terms to those in which Šklovsky posed the question when he wrote, "But the plague had actually happened, Boccaccio's father died of it. Why did the writer, in order to represent what he had lived, feel the necessity [of using] what he had read about? What he had read helped him to see what he saw in Florence in 1348" (p. 195). The relationship between reading (or writing) and seeing should be reversed. Boccaccio was firmly convinced of the serious intent hidden in fable and showed the seriousness of his belief by stating that even the Holy Ghost and Christ Himself spoke in fables.[4] The title of Chapter X of the famous Book XIV of *De Genealogiis* confirms that "it is foolish to believe that poets did not hide meanings beneath the bark of fable" (p. 966), and Boccaccio goes on to refer to poets as both philosophers and (in the case of Dante) theologians (p. 968). His defense is absolute:

Let these ignorant chatterers [the attackers of poetry]
then be still and let stuck-up men be quiet, if they can.
It is to be believed that famous men nurtured on the
milk of the Muses, who have spent time with and been
tempered by sacred studies at the altars of philosophy,
have always put profound meanings into their poems.
There is even no crazy little old woman, who—sitting
up at night around the fire of her home, inventing and
telling stories of ogres, fairies, and witches and such
like, out of which those stories are very often made—
does not include, under the pretext of tale telling and
according to the possibilities of her weak intellect, some
meaning that is not at all to be laughed at, through
which she wants either to inspire terror in little children or to please young girls or to make fun of old
people or at least to show the power of Fortune.[5]

Boccaccio further states that poets hid the truth beneath
fictions "so that those things which, if openly expressed
would have been held to be of little account, when sought
after with hard work by the mind and understood in different ways would be held more dear."[6]

All of this is clear evidence that Boccaccio's texts were
frequently a product of a conscious encoding operation and
legitimates a decoding effort on several levels. We may
seek "the truth beneath the veil" not only on what is apparently the content plane in the description of the plague
and in the *cornice*, but also in the form of the expression.
The polished rhetoric of the description of the plague, a
sort of "artificiality" on the expression plane, denotes "ex-
emplarity" on the content plane (the terms "expression
plane" and "content plane" are Eco's). It is thus useful to
explore both as far as possible and also to examine Boccaccio's use of the cultural codes[7] of his time not only for
the meaning or message they may convey but as indices
of the seriousness of his intent.

The Preface to the *Decameron* (*Proemio*) is itself a model
of sapient writing. It opens, according to the precepts of

medieval rhetoric, with an aphorism: "To take pity on people in distress is a human quality" (p. 49).[8] It then proceeds
to introduce Boccaccio the narrator and his sufferings as
one who loved above his station, in proper courtly love
fashion. The style throughout is closer to the grand (*genus
grave*) than to the middle (*genus modicum*), and proper ac-
knowledgment is made of the poetic deities who preside
over the literary world that is being entered. The first is
God, "who being infinite decreed by immutable law that
all earthly things should have an ending"[9] (including the
narrator's love, which gradually died away to a memory).
The second, however, is the god of Love. The lovesick
ladies for whom the work is being written are told to thank
him for having freed Boccaccio from his bonds, thus ena-
bling that author to write the book. The fact that the two
are used together is an indication of a literary intent. Both
are allusions to known codes and are interesting. The idea
of the god of Love and his bonds belongs to the worldly
and elitist *amour courtois*; the idea of writing specifically for
ladies probably comes from the same source. The allusion
to God Himself and the terms in which it is couched may
at first seem strange within the context, but it would quickly
alert any reader familiar with Petrarch's *Canzoniere* and *Se-
cretum*, both of which are the story of the extremely serious
conflict between his desire for the blessings of this world
and those of the other world.[10] *Amour courtois* was, from
the Florentine point of view, an artificial and a primarily
literary phenomenon, and Petrarch was the most famous
man of letters of his day, so that the value of the *Decameron*
as literature is being underscored. The Preface goes on to
say that, mindful of the helpful distractions through which
his friends saved him when he was in danger of dying of
love, Boccaccio will now endeavor to provide distraction
for others suffering from love, and that those who most
need this help are ladies, whose life provides no other
distractions. As Branca notes, "the gracious picture of idle
women dreaming of love . . . was part of a long literary
tradition dating from Ovid (Heroides, XIX, 5ff.)"—p. 979.[11]

So once again Boccaccio has underlined the fact that his work is literature.

To the reader who knows the great esteem in which Boccaccio held *poesia*[12] and bears in mind the fact that he says he is setting out to tell "a hundred stories or fables or parables or histories or whatever you choose to call them" (p. 47),[13] the repeatedly underlined code of literature throughout the Preface takes on increased meaning. The Preface serves the double purpose of emphasizing the importance of the work and pointing to the dignity of the form the author has chosen. One further detail reinforces the argument: the opening rubric of the whole work states, "Here begins the *book* called Decameron" (p. 45, italics mine).[14] There are several connotations for "book" and they enter into an extremely complex semantic system, which bears the added complication of not being stable, but the obvious connotation *poesia* with the secondary connotation "containing a hidden meaning" that Boccaccio ascribed to it is no less clear for that.[15]

The Preface serves several functions. Not the least is to set off some of Boccaccio's implicit statements *about* the book from the argument itself. In this sense the Preface, together with the author's Epilogue, serves as part of a complex framing system. But it also serves to set off the contents of this first frame, and to point to everything from the end of the Preface to the beginning of the Epilogue (with the partial exception of the introduction to the First Day) as a special and integral world. Within this world there is again an apparent frame, the actual *cornice* that tells how ten young people meet by chance in a church during the plague and decide to leave Florence and go to the country where, for a period of two weeks, they lead a leisurely and elegant life.[16] Every day except for Fridays and Saturdays each one tells a story, and these hundred tales form the main part of the *Decameron*. The structural function of the *cornice* is rather different from that of the Preface, however: whereas the latter, the Introduction to the Fourth Day and the Epilogue are separated from the *cornice* and the stories much in the same way that a picture frame is separate from the canvas it encloses, the *cornice* is inextricably intertwined with the stories, not only because it is brought back into focus at the beginning and end of each day but because the name of the narrator is mentioned at the beginning of each tale and seventy-four of the hundred open with some comment on the group's reaction to the previous story.[17] The reminder that the *Decameron* is *poesia* also recurs throughout by reason of the fact that every one of the stories—with the single exception of V, 7—opens with a metanarrative reference by the teller, such as "the story I plan to tell," which should be read in the light of the *De Genealogiis Deorum Gentilium* passage quoted above. Almansi could have cited these reflexive comments in support of his remark that the *Decameron* "forces the reader to be continuously aware of the fact of its being literature, part of the genre of storytelling" (p. 5). "Literature" should not, however, be equated only with "the genre of story telling": the word should be taken on a *genus grave* level. Storytelling was both an acknowledged court pastime and an equally élite literary tradition, as the subtitle of *Il novellino*, "The Hundred Ancient Tales or Book of Stories and Elegant Noble Talk," bears out.[18]

The Introduction follows the Preface and comes inside the rubric "Here begins the First Day of the *Decameron*, wherein first of all the author explains the circumstances in which certain persons, who presently make their appearance, were induced to meet for the purpose of conversing together" (p. 49).[19] It opens on a solemn note, with the warning that the work must have "a grave and unpleasant beginning" and continues immediately, within this opening sentence, to bring in the plague: "such as the painful memory of the recent deadly plague."[20] It is a sign of the latter's importance that it thus has a certain pride of place in the *Decameron*. The passage comes after the rubric announcing the first day, rather than being incorporated into the Preface, which further underlines the plague's function as an integral part of the text rather than as background material.

The first paragraph[21] of the Introduction also contains pointers indicating that "this is literature": most critics agree that there is a clear echo of Dante in Boccaccio's encouragement to the ladies he is addressing to read on because his grim beginning is like a steep and rugged mountain, beyond which lies a pleasant and charming plain. Intertextuality is by now a well-known concept and in this case it is a sign-function. The choice of Dante as "signifier" here is in itself a "signified"; it serves to denote the seriousness of the intention. The same paragraph contains a transparent allusion to Proverbs XIV. 13: "And just as the end of mirth is heaviness" (p. 49),[22] which is an aphorism with a known rhetorical function. The second paragraph moves into the marvelous description of the plague, whose literary echoes have already been pointed out. From a purely formal point of view, its very length is impressive: it constitutes over forty percent of the Introduction. The narrator's opening justification for beginning with the plague and the description of the protagonists' meeting (one-third of which is devoted to Pampinea's speech about the plague) make up the remainder. Again, the reader is being alerted to the importance of the subject and the seriousness of the book's purpose. The style never deviates from the *genus grave*.

Boccaccio opens his description of the pestilence with the utmost solemnity and an allusion to two cultural codes that were taken very seriously: "I say, then, that the sum of thirteen hundred and forty-eight years had elapsed since the fruitful Incarnation of the Son of God, when the noble city of Florence, which for its great beauty excels all others in Italy, was visited by the deadly pestilence" (p. 50).[23] There is no sign of irony or doubt in the sacred formula used for the date, even though a case could be, and often has been, made for irony in the immediate continuation of Boccaccio's sentence: "which was visited upon mortal men either through the influence of heavenly bodies or because of God's righteous wrath at our iniquitous ways."[24] The second marker of Boccaccio's gravity is the allusion to the nobility and beauty of Florence, a serious matter to the Florentines, who were economically powerful and in many ways cosmopolitan, but basically still insular and parochial.[25] It is not a subject on which he could have been playful, given his father's importance in Florentine affairs and his own contributions to public life.

That same gravity underlies the introduction and the description of the protagonists. At the height of the plague, a group of young women meet in a church that is not only "venerable" but was among the most famous in Florence. Its fame was due in part to the exceptionally high quality of those who preached there (including Passavanti), and it had only recently been enclosed by the "third circle" of the city walls.[26] All of the young women are designated as (a) real, (b) of noble blood, (c) beautiful, and (d) well bred (Intro., 49). The last three attributes were chosen as befitting characters belonging to the "high" style used for epic and tragedy rather than to the "low" style.[27] All the ladies have pseudonyms that are literary in origin; several occur in Boccaccio's earlier works.[28] The names of the servants are also literary: they are typical of Greek comedy.

The constitution of the group of protagonists again invokes an important and well-known cultural code that proves to play a key role in the *Decameron* both on the expression plane and on the content plane. Numerology was of great cultural significance and importance in Boccaccio's time: "number was sanctified as a form-bestowing factor in the divine work of creation. It acquired metaphysical dignity. This is the imposing background of numerical composition in literature" (Curtius, p. 504). The numerology in Boccaccio's work has only recently begun to come under more serious investigation.[29] It is used in the *Decameron* to form a coherent semantic system that will be discussed in Chapter IV. For the moment I wish merely to show its use as an s-code employed in the formal construction of the work. Its importance is expressed in two ways: through the cultural significance of the numbers chosen, which function as well-known signs in both secular and sacred codes, and through the very complexity of the system Boccaccio himself builds with them.

The group that meets in the Church of Santa Maria Novella consists of seven young women who are later joined by three young men. The importance of the number seven both in biblical exegesis and in cosmological arithmetic is obvious: to cite only some of its possible meanings, it represents perfect order (the ternary and the quaternary), the cardinal and the theological virtues or the Liberal Arts (formed of the trivium and the quadrivium).[30] There are also the seven opposing capital sins, the seven planets, the seven days of the week, the seven Directions of Space (the center is the seventh). Victoria Kirkham has shown that Boccaccio used subtle and complex numerological schemes in his minor works. The number seven in these represents the goddess Diana, a meaning that would be in keeping with the *cornice* ladies' chastity.[31] The number three has a similar importance: it is not only the number of the Holy Trinity but also the male number, and the marriage number in Orphic cosmogony. The sum of ten is of course also exceedingly important: God himself is triune and therefore a ten (3×3 and 1×1). In decimal systems ten signifies the return to unity, and because of this in some systems it signifies the totality of the universe. It is the number of perfection in almost all systems, which further adds significance to the one hundred stories of the *Decameron*, whose numerical relationship to the *Divine Comedy* has often been noted.

The protagonists' ages are also mentioned, again invoking the numerological code. None of the ladies in the group is older than twenty-eight or younger than eighteen (Intro., 49). The former is a "perfect" number in the Pythagorean system because it is the sum of the numbers from 1 to 7; the latter should be taken as the product of 6 and 3.[32] Six is both a "perfect" number ($1 + 2 + 3$ as well as $1 \times 2 \times 3$) and significant in itself, being the product of the first of the odd numbers (male) and the first even number (female).

It is also the number of the days of creation.[33] None of the three men is older than twenty-five (Intro., 78), the square of five, which perpetually repeats itself when multiplied by odd numbers and is not only a number frequent in the Bible but is also considered to be the number that represents the world and its inhabitants, being made up of the female two plus the male three.[34] The astrological approach currently being explored by Kirkham and Smarr in the minor works would also give a pattern here of a connection between Venus (three) and Mars (five). A parallel code, the geometric one, is referred to as well: the ladies sit almost in a circle (Intro., 52), again a highly symbolic form as it can represent the sun (hence also God) and perfection. It also has a relationship with the number ten, so presumably the ladies are an incomplete circle (or number ten) without the men. Finally, the fact that the author's defense of his work comes in the Introduction to the Fourth Day is also significant: four was obviously an important number, representing the elements. It was also extremely significant in the Pythagorean system: "Justice *was* the number 4, on the ground that justice essentially involved a reciprocal relationship between persons, and that reciprocity was embodied in a square number."[35]

The opening rubric, "Here begins the book called *Decameron*, otherwise known as Prince Galahalt, wherein are contained a hundred stories, told in ten days by seven ladies and three young men" (p. 45)[36] further underlines the importance of the numerological code: not only are four numbers mentioned in the four brief lines, but they form a "perfect" system: $100 = 10 \times (7 + 3)$. One other factor is immediately made clear: only days on which stories are told "exist" within the formal structure. The same is true for all the internal rubrics: each begins "The x day of the *Decameron* ends: the y day begins," and there is no break in the numerical sequence for days on which the protagonists abstain from storytelling. The intricacy of the structure is a fascinating testimonial to the formality of Boccaccio's intent and the subtlety of his mind.

The group's bearing and attitude, as well as their elegant life and the descriptions of the country villas to which they retire, clearly designate them as belonging to an educated and literate aristocracy. The ladies are described as "intelligent, of noble blood, beautiful and adorned with elegant manners and pure charm."[37] The amusements available in the first "garden of pleasure" they visit, along with singing, round-dancing, and the playing of lute and viol, include chess, draughts, and backgammon, which were among the "preferred pastimes of the most elegant society of the fourteenth century" (Branca, *Decameron*, p. 1002). Later (III, Intro., 15) the reading of romances is added to the amusements. The aristocratic background of the young people, the fact that all of them own country property, the description of the villa and garden and the amusements available to them work together to create what Lotman calls the space of a cultural text, forming a cultural model of the "direct" type, whose point of view coincides with that of Boccaccio (as shown by the literary and hence elitist code he himself uses) and with that of his designated audience. Lotman illustrates his concept with the following diagram in which EX stands for external space and IN for internal space:

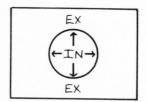

He continues:

> Since the internal space is closed . . . and the external space is open, it becomes natural to interpret the opposition "internal–external" as a spatial transcription of the antithesis "organized (having a structure)–not organized (without structure)." In the various texts of

the culture it can be differently interpreted, showing itself for example in oppositions like:

my, our people (clan, tribe)	vs.	foreign people (clan, tribe)
sacred	vs.	profane
culture	vs.	barbarity
intelligentsia	vs.	people
cosmos	vs.	chaos

In such cases the presence of organization in each of the oppositions is essential on the one hand and so is its absence on the other. Organization functions as the strong member of the opposition: it includes the marked trait, while its antithesis is limited to underlining its absence. Organization is conceived as inclusion in a closed world (p. 65).[38]

This concept functions to a marked extent in the *cornice* of the *Decameron*: not only in the opposition between the chaos generated by the plague and the extremely orderly and tranquil life of the group but in the formality of the social structure created through the setting up and the daily rotation of the queen- or kingship, explicitly done because "nothing will last for very long unless it possesses a definite form."[39] Boccaccio's rotating rulership is doubly based: the election of a king or queen was typical of the courts of love (an allusion to a literary convention) and also took place among actual groups formed for entertainment purposes, who went through the city playing and singing, with garlands on their heads, led by a crowned king (Branca, *Decameron*, p. 1000). Lotman's concept can also be applied to the deliberately formal way in which the circular model itself is repeated in the now complete circle in which the ladies and gentlemen sit to begin telling their tales. A further, doubly based formal detail is the use of laurel to crown the queen: this act can be construed in two ways: laurel, frequently used to weave garlands and crowns, is expressive both of victory, as in Caesar's wreath, and of poetry.

In the latter meaning the crowning of Pampinea (I, Intro., 97) could also (though not solely) constitute a metaliterary act.

The settings chosen for the tale-telling themselves belong to a known literary tradition. The stories are told in a series of three gardens, and as Edith Kern demonstrated, these are carefully modeled on a familiar literary garden-of-love tradition and perhaps more especially on the *Roman de la Rose*.[40] Kern pointed out that the first garden has no distinctive features, whereas the second is surrounded by square walls and has a fountain in its midst, while the third is circular—a rare quality borrowed from the *Roman de la Rose*, just as the form of the second garden is. Kern's thesis (a naturalist one) is that the group progresses from a traditional garden of love to a more remote and sensuous earthly paradise bearing all the marks of being sacred to Venus and then to an even more remote and perfect "Sanctuary of Venus Genetrix," signaled by the teeming fish in the clear waters. Kern did not, however, see the purely "formal" aspect of the series, which is a clear progression from a garden of no particular form, to a square form with a center, to the more perfect circle formed by the Valle delle Donne. The series of gardens thus in itself constitutes a sign-function whose content implies a perfecting in terms that apply to the most serious forms of literature.

The contrast between the characters in the stories and the stylized figures of the protagonists of the *cornice*, as well as their equally stylized existence, is also a sign-function. The ten young people and their life are described in terms so general as almost to make them lose their humanity. Unlike the characters and life in the stories, they have the same quality as those figures labeled "Temperance," "Fortitude," or "The Prophet So and So" to be found in bas-reliefs or in frescoes, where they were also sometimes used to divide (or frame) the narrative sequence. Boris Uspensky has convincingly argued that increased conventionality of representation in painting and/or literature was meant as "enhancement of the semiotic quality of the representation: the description is not a sign of the represented reality . . . but a sign of the sign of this reality."[41] Boccaccio's ten young people of good family and their life style are "exemplary" in much the same way as the frescoes that were intended to remind the church-going public of lessons learned from the pulpit.[42] They and the work in which they appear have an equally serious function. By thus emphasizing the "semiotic" quality of his frame tale, Boccaccio is seeking to draw our attention to the protagonists' life and behavior as elements in an important text.

The ten young noblewomen and men are all given literary names and only three of them—Filomena, Neifile, and Fiammetta—are in any way physically described. The descriptions are in the most conventional and literary terms: Filomena is "well shaped and attractive," Neifile's eyes are "lovely and sparkling like the morning star." Fiammetta, whose description is the most detailed, is also an echo of several of Boccaccio's previous ladies from the *Caccia di Diana*, the *Filocolo*, the *Commedia delle Ninfe Fiorentine*, the *Amorosa Visione* and the *Canzoniere*. She has "long golden curls that cascaded down over delicate, pure white shoulders, a softly rounded face that glowed with the authentic hues of white lilies and crimson roses, a pair of eyes in her head that gleamed like a falcon's and a sweet little mouth with lips like rubies" (p. 401).[43] Not that descriptions of physical beauty are frequent in the *Decameron*: very few lovely feminine bodies are described. The most notable is that of Cymon's lady, Iphigenia, and the description is really more allusion than description, "wearing so gossamer a dress that it concealed almost nothing of her pure white body . . . praising her hair, which he judged to be of gold, her forehead, her nose and her mouth, her throat and arms and especially her bosom, still not very pronounced."[44] Tenuous as it is, this description is nevertheless far less conventional than that of Fiammetta. A further contrast in tone is furnished by the gross realism of descriptions like that of the physically ugly kitchen maid Nuta in the story of Fra Cipolla, who is "fat and coarse and small and misshapen, with a pair of paps that seemed like two baskets of manure and a face that looked like a Baronci's, all sweaty and greasy and smoke grimed."[45]

The details of the contrast between the overall realistic atmosphere of the stories and the stylized (what Uspensky would call the "semiotic") quality of the *cornice* are interesting in the minuteness of their consistency. The days spent by the ten protagonists are monotonously similar: the young people rise at dawn, walk a little way, refresh themselves—always with excellent wines and sweet-meats—linger in a pleasant garden, sing, dance, dine, rest, gather to tell their stories, elect the next day's sovereign, amuse themselves at chess, checkers, and backgammon, or by reciting from or discussing romances, sup, dance again, and end each day with an amorous *canzone*. The monotony is only seemingly broken by the two occasions on which the protagonists pursue the almost tame animals around them, by their move to another villa, and by the episode of the Valley of the Ladies; all the details of their daily life remain unchanged in their out-of-the-world rhythms and their somewhat abstract quality. The only exceptions are Dioneo's irreverent proposal of a series of bawdy songs instead of the approved courtly *canzoni* at the end of Day V and the comical irruption of the realistic world through the much discussed quarrel between the servants Licisca and Tindaro as to whether Sycophant found his bride to be a virgin or "wise," as Licisca claims most brides are. Otherwise, in the *cornice*, characters and actions seem almost interchangeable as we follow the seven blushes of the seven ladies upon being chosen queen and the seemly rejoicing of all the others from day to day. The villas are relentlessly upper class, each with its ornate and well disposed rooms, its cool well, and its cellar of excellent and costly wines. Even the meals are abstract and stylized: in contrast to the roast cranes, fat pigs, and plump capons that abound in the stories, aside from the "excellent comfits and wines" with which the young people refresh themselves every morning, we are told on the first day that they partake of "delicately prepared dishes" and after that the formula varies little: they eat "with laughter and merriment," "with very great delight," "gaily," "tranquilly and with gaiety."[46] *What* they eat remains consistently abstract. Similar formulas are used twice a day for all ten days, but the reader cannot imagine these young aristocrats actually enjoying their food as they dine in their privileged space.

The Introduction to the Fourth Day has a special place in the *Decameron*. Unlike the Proem and the author's Epilogue, which serve as a more or less "external" frame setting off all that lies between them as an integral world, Boccaccio's defense of his *Decameron* seems an interruption, breaking into the apparently idyllic world of his protagonists and reminding his readers that "this is literature" in a very marked way. This metanarrative factor has its own value on the expression plane: its position underlines its meaning.

As in the Proem, allusions to literary codes are frequent. The Introduction opens with a cliché: Boccaccio had "always assumed that only lofty towers and the tallest of trees could be assailed by envy's fiery and impetuous blast" but, he continues, he was mistaken, as the blast of envy attacked "even these little stories of mine, which bear no title and which I have written, not only in the Florentine vernacular and in prose, but in the most homely and unassuming style it is possible to imagine" (p. 325).[47] It is no declaration of humility on the part of *Johannes tranquillitatum* as he was nicknamed, but an obeisance to a well-known literary tradition of affected modesty that had passed from classical Roman literature into the writings of the Christian Middle Ages. Its aim was the *captatio benevolentiae*, and examples abound in the writings of Ausonius, Sedulius, Fulgentius, Sidonius, Ennodius, Fortunatus, and others who loved to accuse themselves of thinness, artlessness, crudity, paltriness, and a rustic style. As Curtius drily remarks, "a constant literary formula must not be regarded as the expression of spontaneous sentiment."[48] A close following of an eminently literary tradition, however, may rightly be regarded as an affirmation of literary intent, a marking of the code.

In opening his defense against the accusations he claims have been leveled at him (that he likes women too much, that he is too old to be thinking of pleasing women, that he is frivolous and should keep company with the Muses rather than frittering away his time among the ladies he is addressing, that he should worry about earning his bread rather than writing nonsense, and that he has misrepresented the facts), Boccaccio immediately has recourse to the famous tale of Filippo Balducci, a variant, as we have seen, of a very well-known story. In many versions of the Filippo Balducci tale, women are referred to as "demons" in order to underline the unnatural power of love as viewed from a misogynist perspective. Thus Boccaccio is using yet another well-known cultural phenomenon of his time, religiously inspired misogyny, and very clearly manipulating it so as "to change semantic systems . . . to change the ways in which culture 'sees' the world" (Eco, p. 274). At the same time, he is also putting his theories of the hidden truth in fictions to active use and thereby reaffirming his faith in *poesia*.

The example of Filippo Balducci's son is Boccaccio's answer to the accusation that he likes women too much. His answer to the second charge, that he is too old to wish still to please them, is equally literary: the very well-known code of the *dolce stil nuovo* is invoked through the names of its most famous exponents, Cavalcanti, Cino da Pistoia, and Dante himself. Petrarch is not mentioned, according to Branca because he is "too highly venerated as a hero of the most aristocratic culture" (*Decameron*, p. 1201), but equally probably because he did not belong to the *dolce stil nuovo*. In connection with the use of this code, it should be remembered that *dolce stil nuovo* poetry usually portrayed women as quasi-angelic beings (*la donna angelicata*), who at times served as intermediaries between the poet and God.

The allusion thus lends dignity and importance to the text and to its destined audience.

Boccaccio's somewhat ambiguous reply to the accusations that he should keep company with the Muses (no one can spend *all* his time with the Muses, and the Muses are, after all, women; furthermore women, not Muses, have inspired his verses) also contains an open affirmation that his text is worthy literature: the Muses "have helped me, and have shown me how to write; and maybe they have come to keep me company several times as I wrote these events and stories, humble as they are; perhaps they came to honor and serve women's likeness to themselves, so that, writing these things, I am not distancing myself either from Mt. Parnassus or from the Muses as far as many people may believe."[49] The message could not be more clear, and generations of critics have quoted it as the statement of the conscious artist Boccaccio most certainly was.

His reply to the last accusation is also subtly encoded on a literary plane. To those who tell him that he should be thinking about earning his food he replies first of all by using a *double entendre* that he has worked into the accusation. Translated literally it reads:

But what shall we say to those who feel so much compassion for my hunger that they advise me to earn some bread? [The modern English slang usage here shows itself to be strikingly apt.] Certainly, I don't know, except that, when I try to think what their answer would be if I were driven to asking them for some, I imagine that they would say: "Go seek some among fables." And indeed the poets found more of it among their fables than many rich men among their treasures and many of them, pursuing fables, caused their times to flower, whereas, on the contrary many others, while trying to get more bread than they needed, died unripe. What else? Let these men send me away if I ask them for some—not that, thanks be to God, I need any yet—; and even if I were to be in need, I

know how to suffer scarcity and abundance, as the
Apostle teaches; and therefore let no one worry more
about me than I do myself.[50]

The play of known literary systems in this passage is
remarkable. The use of "bread" is a reference to "the bread
of the angels" (human and divine wisdom), and probably
comes straight from Dante's *Convivio*. The origin may well
be eucharistic. The statement that many died unripe because they tried for too much bread is another allusion to
Dante, this time to the *Divine Comedy*. The line echoes Paradiso XIX, 48, which says of Lucifer, "because he did not
wait for light, he fell unripe."[51] The ripeness metaphor
forms a clearly recognizable semantic network in the *Divine
Comedy*, based on the image of Christ the Husbandman.
Finally, Boccaccio wraps up his angry reply to this particular accusation, which touched him on the raw both because of his well-known poverty and because of his hatred
of avarice, by paraphrasing St. Paul (Philippians IV. 12).
The whole is framed by the topos of the poor but honest
poet-scholar, the same that inspired sonnet VII of Petrarch's *Canzoniere*, "La gola e'l sonno e l'oziose piume . . ."
("Greed and sleep and slothful beds . . ."). Boccaccio may
call his work "these little stories," but he brings up big
guns to defend them.

His final reply is to the presumed accusation that he has
not been faithful to the truth in his report. Its tone is tongue-
in-cheek and quite different from the main body of his
defense:

Finally, I would be greatly obliged to the people who
claim that these accounts are inaccurate if they would
produce the original versions, and if these turn out to
be different from my own, I will grant their reproach
to be just, and endeavor to mend my ways. But so
long as they have nothing but words to offer, I shall
leave them to their opinions, stick to my own, and say
the same things about them as they are saying about
me (p. 330).[52]

In this case the language is not formal or literary, and the tone is actually flippant, but on the content plane there is the affirmation that "this is fiction" with its Boccaccian connotation of *poesia*. The inversion is itself a rhetorical device, coming as it does at the end of a four-prong defense, every one of whose points has been literary in form. The importance and seriousness of Boccaccio's work is thereby doubly affirmed. Almost every detail in the *cornice*—even the fact that every day ends with a *canzone*, the poetic form Dante characterized as the most noble[53]—proves to be evidence of a carefully constructed system, a macro-sign-function whose expression plane is the literary quality of the text and which denotes that this is a profoundly serious work.

The Author's Epilogue repeats many of the arguments of the Introduction to the Fourth Day. In spite of an increased levity in the overall tone, the basic affirmations bear out the seriousness of the work. The Epilogue is again in the vocative, and the young women for whom the work is purportedly written are this time called "most noble young ladies."[54] This mode of address may be designed as a reminder that the book is meant to be read by a higher class of society; it may be an allusion to the fact that the work is dedicated to those ladies who love and whose nobility is enhanced thereby, according to courtly love tenets; or it could conceivably even be directed in part at the author's own characters, the very ladies who are worthy to take their turn as monarch for the day.

Both the opening and the closing sentences give thanks to God:

> I believe that with the assistance of divine grace (the bestowal of which I impute to your compassionate prayers rather than to any merit of my own) those objectives which I set forth at the beginning of the present work have now been fully achieved. *And so, after giving thanks, firstly to God and then to yourselves,*

the time has come for me to rest my pen and weary hand (p. 830).

. . . for the time has come for me to bring all words to an end, *and offer my humble thanks to Him who assisted me in my protracted labor and conveyed me to the goal I desired*. May His grace and peace, sweet ladies, remain with you always (p. 833).[55]

The formal ending (part of the outermost frame of the book) is thus in its turn framed by pious thanks to the author of the book of the world, thanks which become more serious in the second and concluding passage cited by their specific exclusion of the ladies, who are this time separately consigned to God's grace rather than being included in Boccaccio's formal gratitude.

After his initial statement, he reopens the defense of his work by confronting the possible charge of licentiousness. His reply is that nothing is so unseemly that it may not be said, provided that it be couched in proper language. This is in keeping with an established medieval literary tradition that is mentioned in more than one *ars poetica* (Branca, *Decameron*, p. 1564), and thereby serves as an allusion to *poesia*. It may also serve as an indirect allusion to the story of Filippo Balducci and the "geese." In that example, words were ill-advisedly used in an attempt to disguise facts; in claiming here that there is no fact that may not be presented in suitable words, the author reminds us of the power of discourse and also of his own story with its previously discussed connotations of both *poesia* and religious *exempla*.

The defense continues along two lines. Boccaccio claims that "if any of the stories is lacking in restraint, this is because of the nature of the story itself, which, as any well-informed and dispassionate observer will readily acknowledge, I could not have related in any other way without distorting it out of all recognition" (p. 829).[56] The statement is at the same time a reminder of the autonomy of fiction and an allusion to the author's own mocking comment in the Introduction to Day IV that those who claim that his reporting is incorrect should bring the facts to refute him.

Boccaccio's defense of his language is equally interesting: he claims that he has done nothing more than use words such as mortar, hole, and pestle, which are not only said all day long by both men and women but represent objects that are freely painted without arousing any objections, such as St. George's lance, and the nails in the feet of Christ crucified. Even Christ and Eve, Boccaccio points out, are painted as men and women. Despite the ambiguity created by the tongue-in-cheek tone (which will be further discussed in Chapter V), the character of the two cultural codes alluded to once again indicates the dignity of the work. The religious code—ambiguously used here as elsewhere—has its own high-level cultural connotations, which are in fact the very quality that makes it so effective when it is used in a carnivalesque way, as it often was by all social classes at the time. The art of painting was also a matter of extreme pride and gravity, as Giotto's reputation (and Dante's allusions to him as a master in the *Divine Comedy*) show. The use of the religious code is deftly underlined by the comment, in the following paragraph, that one should speak of the Church "with a chaste mind and a pure tongue (albeit you will find that many of her chronicles are far more scandalous than any writings of mine)" (p. 830).[57] It is typical of Boccaccio's ability to have his cake and eat it: the same undercutting technique is frequent in his stories.

After the reminder that the Church is no more seemly than the *Decameron* (a reminder that could be reversed and read in more positive terms), the very carefully constructed final justification of the work continues. The author further reminds the readers that the book is set not among clerks and philosophers nor yet in schools, and during a time when hardly any action was considered unseemly. The major themes of the *cornice* are all brought into one clause in the Italian:

They [the stories] were told in gardens in a place designed for pleasure, among people who, though young
in years, were nonetheless fully mature and not to be
led astray by stories, at a time when even the most
respectable people saw nothing unseemly in wearing
their breeches over their heads if they thought their
lives might thereby be preserved (p. 830).[58]

The presence of the plague all around the *Decameron* is
forcibly brought back to the reader's attention by the last
words.

Boccaccio then moves from a defensive to an offensive
position, comparing his stories to wine, to fire and to arms,
all in themselves beneficial if correctly used but extremely
harmful if misused. Wine is said to be harmful to those
who suffer from fevers, and yet excellent for other men—
a biblical example (Proverbs XX. 1 and XXXI. 6-7). Wine,
fire, and arms, however, are also classical components of
the epic tradition. They recall the importance of Homeric
armor and the customary sacrifices and libations to the
gods. The allusion is thus to the two noblest known forms
of *poesia*.

The peroration of the defense against the accusation of
licentiousness opens with a double allusion: "No word,
however pure, was ever wholesomely construed by a mind
that was corrupt" is an elaborated paraphrase of St. Paul's
omnia munda mundis (*Ad Titum*, I, 15). The continuation of
the sentence is very probably an echo of some lines in a
famous *canzone* by the poet Guido Guinizelli, "Al cor gentile
ripara sempre Amore": "And just as seemly language leaves
no mark upon a mind that is well ordered, any more than
mud will contaminate the rays of the sun, or earthly filth
the beauties of the heavens" (p. 830). ("The sun strikes the
mud all day long; it remains vile, nor does the sun lose its
heat.")[59] Guinizelli was the founder of the *dolce stil nuovo*,
the poet whom Dante had called "father to me and all
others, who, better than I, wrote fair and graceful love
poetry."[60] Even the Bible, Boccaccio then continues, the

90

most sacred and worthy of reverence of any book ever written, has been used by perverse men to lead themselves and others to perdition. Once again, he is bringing up very big guns to defend his humble tales. He closes with the important statement that for the right people and in the right times his stories cannot but be useful and honorable, and advises religious hypocrites to abstain from reading them.

The serious tone of the Epilogue then becomes very light. After stating that it is only natural that not all his stories be masterpieces, since only God invariably achieves perfection and even Charlemagne, the creator of paladins, was unable to create enough of them to form an army (allusions to both religion and sacred epic poetry), Boccaccio again takes refuge in his pretext that the *Decameron* is meant as mere amusement for idle ladies in love. His comments become increasingly flippant: he puns on the adjective "heavy" (which in the middle ages, as now, could mean "serious") by saying that he is so light that he floats in water and once again defends his jokes on the grounds that they are in no way dissimilar to those to be found in sermons. Finally he says that although some have accused him of having a poisonous tongue because he tells the truth about the clergy, he forgives them for their defense of this class, made up of good persons who flee all discomfort for the love of God, enjoy grinding in mortars without letting it be known, and would be excellent company if they did not stink of goat. He then "confesses" that since all worldly things are subject to change, his tongue, recently certified as sweet by a neighbor, may indeed have turned sour, even though most of his stories had been written when she so certified it. The extreme flippancy is somewhat problematic: it may be in part due to the author's medieval desire for symmetry, which causes him to match his Epilogue to his Proem. The latter also contains the equally flippant statement that the ladies who are to be diverted by his tales should thank God and also Love, who has set him free to write for their amusement. Boccaccio's awareness that some of his material is extremely sensitive may also have led him to build in this kind of shield. The tone of the Introduction to Day IV, which is, as it were, "inside" the outermost frame, is altogether more serious. At the same time, the flippancy and especially the comments about the clergy actually match the tone of the stories, drawing Boccaccio into his own work as a narrator even while he claims to be a mere recorder. The last words of the Epilogue, in any case, are the serious and formal thanks to God quoted on pages 32 and 89.

The *Decameron* ends as it opened, with a final rubric. It is instructive to compare the two and see in what elements the work is embedded:

> Here begins the book called *Decameron*, also called Prince Galahalt, in which are contained one-hundred stories told in ten days by seven women and by three young men.

> Here ends the tenth and last day of the book called *Decameron*, also called Prince Galahalt.[61]

The common elements are the number ten and the word "book," the title *Decameron* and the nickname Prince Galahalt. I have deliberately translated "cognominato" as "also called" even though its more usual meaning is "nicknamed." It is a *hapax legomenon* or word used only once (actually it is used twice) in the *Decameron* (usually Boccaccio uses the less latinized "detto"), and may well serve not only to embed the *Decameron* in formal latinisms but to reflect the medieval opposition between name (given at baptism, as an auspice) and nickname (given later, as a judgement based on experience). My use of the word "also," based on *cum* as the root of *cognominato*, is "linguistically allowable but not very likely."[62] It is the context that has caused me to risk using it here. "Decameron," of course, reflects St. Ambrose's exegetical commentary on the Creation, the *Hexaemeron*. There has been a good bit of discussion on the "Prince Galahalt," frequently read as a warning by critics, based on its obvious echo of Dante's famous verse in *Inferno* V.[63] It is internal evidence that suggests the opposition between name and nickname: in the Preface Boccaccio had stated that the ladies who read his stories would find them not only amusing but instructive, for they would learn what they should do and what they should avoid doing. This, as we have seen, is entirely in keeping with medieval interpretations of the lessons to be found in authors such as Plautus and Terence, whom Boccaccio himself mentioned in the *De Genealogiis* (IX, 9, p. 960). In the Author's Epilogue Boccaccio said, "And if anyone should study them [the stories] for the usefulness and profit they may bring him, he will not be disappointed. Nor will they even be thought of or described as anything but useful and seemly, if they are read at the proper time by the people for whom they were written" (p. 831).[64] The Introduction to the Fourth Day clearly shows that Boccaccio's auspice was not taken up by most of his readers: in his final defense of his book he picked up the challenge of their criticism and answered it by the use of the nickname "Prince Galahalt" in his opening and closing rubrics. "No word, however pure, was ever wholesomely construed by a mind that was corrupt." From such minds his book got its nickname; for the others it retains the only title found in the internal rubrics: *Decameron*, very possibly with encoded connotations of re-creation after the plague, based on the title's similarity to the *Hexaemeron*.[65]

CHAPTER IV

Codes, Systems, and Cultural Models
in the *Cornice*

THERE ARE semiotic systems within the *Decameron cornice* that are carefully structured s-codes, deliberately designed as sign-functions by the author, and others that were not so designed but that reflect the changing cultural models of the time. The former provide evidence about Boccaccio's purpose in writing the book and about its function as an aesthetic text. They are thus worth studying both for their message and from the point of view of how narrative systems communicate. The latter should be examined as indications and explanations of the tension in the *Decameron* between traditional and "revolutionary" values, between a past that Boccaccio may well have regarded with nostalgia and a present that was in crisis, the beginning of the sociocultural period known as the Renaissance.

CODES AND THEIR MODIFICATION IN THE *Cornice*

The *Decameron* provides a clear instance of Umberto Eco's definition of an aesthetic text. It deliberately manipulates certain expression systems so as to lead to a reassessment of their content, and this in turn leads to a process of code changing and ultimately produces a new (and more secular) awareness about the world.[1]

The structure of the book itself is what Eco might call "a violation of norms" on the expression plane. Previous collections of short stories either had no frame tale as in the case of the *Novellino*, or had a form of Chinese box structure like the *Arabian Nights* and—even more strikingly—*The Panchatantra*, in which a tale contained another tale that contained yet another tale in itself. The carefully architectonic structure of the *Decameron* may at first seem not only "abnormal" but unnecessary, like the repetition in Gertrude Stein's "a rose is a rose is a rose is a rose," given by Eco as an example in which "the puzzling redundancy of the lexical level stands for a semantic complication on the definitional one" (*Semiotics*, p. 272). The existence of the *cornice* and the obvious care Boccaccio took with its form should be read in the same way and calls for a reassessment of the content.[2]

The first step is to examine and identify that structure, which traditionally has been seen as a two-unit one, consisting of a frame tale (the *cornice*) and a hundred stories. A close study of the details of the framing system, however, will show that what we really have is a series of five concentric "worlds." The first is the world inhabited by Boccaccio's book and its addressees. His use of the vocative to his readers in the Introduction to Day IV makes it clear that this world is to be considered part of his text.[3] The second world is the one in which Boccaccio claims his text is rooted and in which it is to function, according to the tale told by the author: it is the world of lovesick ladies for whom he claims to be writing. The third is Florentine society during the plague. The fourth is the special society set up by the ten protagonists in their country retreat, and the fifth and innermost world is that of the hundred stories themselves. Each of these worlds is connected formally and explicitly with what I shall call a "tale"[4] told by the author. Boccaccio tells us that his book was received in a certain way and should have been received differently; he tells us that he is writing the book to amuse lovesick ladies; he tells us that his description of the plague is necessary: "Believe me, if I could decently have taken you whither I desire by some other route, rather than along a path so difficult as this, I would gladly have done so" (p. 49).[5] Having told us about the plague, he then tells us how ten young men and women left the city of Florence and how they spent their two-week sojourn in the country telling ten tales on each of ten days. This constant emphasis on "telling" carries the connotation that the book is an extremely social one (in the fourth sense given by *Webster's Dictionary*: "Of or relating to human society, the interaction of the individual and the group or the welfare of human beings as members of society").[6] The highlighting of *communication* evident on the expression plane in fact forms a subcode (dialogue with the readers, direct address to a presumed audience of ladies, group activity of tale telling, group commentary on the previous story and repeated reflexive remarks such as "the story I am about to tell").

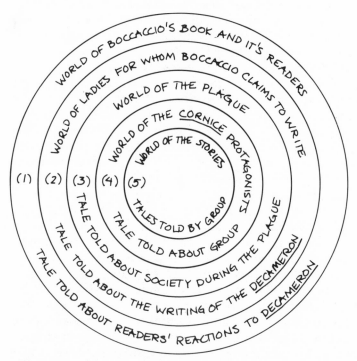

The structure of the *Decameron* is shown in the diagram.

The concentric form is familiar to any student of medieval literature, where the enclosing of something precious in a walled garden or in a castle surrounded by a series of moats and walls is habitual. The Castle of the Noble Spirits in *Inferno IV* with its sevenfold walls and gates, and the castles, gardens and hedges of the *Roman de la Rose* immediately come to mind. The pervasiveness of such structures is normal enough in view of the medieval conception of the universe, in which nine heavens whirl harmoniously around the still world at their center, all enclosed in the limitless and omnipervading Mind of God.

Geometric figures themselves were considered to be a code, whose most accepted content was theological. One of the standard metaphors for God was *"Deus est sphaera cuius centrum ubique"* (God is a sphere whose center is everywhere). He was also represented as a circle—like that figure in having no beginning or end—and as a triangle. Thus the image of a triangle within a sphere could be easily "read" as representing the mystery of the incarnation, as the following verses from the *Roman de la Rose* illustrate:

> For just as soon as she perceived she bore
> That comfortable weight, she knew that it
> Must be that marvelous, eternal sphere
> Whose center would be fixed in every place
> But whose circumference would nowhere be;
> She knew it was the mystic triangle
> Whose angles superpose in unity
> So that the three are one and one is three.
> Triangular the circle is, or else
> The triangle is round, that found a home
> Within the Virgin.[7]

The whole structure of Dante's *Paradiso* is likewise a play on circularity and eccentric/concentric movement. This is clearly shown by the crucial reversal in Canto XXVIII, when Dante, after passing through the ever-widening sweep of the nine heavens on his way to the Empyrean, sees the nine orders of angels in the form of fiery circles whirling around an intensely bright Point, the Light of God. The final vision of the celestial rose repeats that same structure and both show that the material universe is illusory in "real" (i.e. heavenly) terms. The message is clear: *God*, not man, not the world, is at the center of the circle.

Boccaccio was certainly aware of the geometric code that was an accepted convention among those who believed in the "Book of the World." He used it to some purpose. When his seven young women met in the Church of Santa Maria Novella, they sat down "almost in a circle" that was incomplete without the young men, but when they began to tell their stories, they "all seated themselves in a circle on the green grass."[8] Circular seating is of course a frequent detail in medieval literature and appears in Boccaccio's own earlier works, but he calls special attention to it in the *Decameron*. When the young men first appear in the church, they do not complete the circle, for Pampinea gets up and goes toward them. Their subsequent departure for the country is arranged standing on that spot, and the circle thus is perfected only later, when the protagonists are gathered in their liminal space for their real purpose, that of examining the values of their society through story telling.

The geometric code assigned divine content to the circle as a sign function. Other codes of the times, such as the architectural one, made a practice of using enclosure to give a semantic content of "value." One has only to think of the way that code was used in the *Roman de la Rose*. In the *Decameron* structure and in the grouping of the protagonists, we also have a carefully constructed circle that emphasizes the value of its content. This content is the stories, and the stories center on the world. The Ptolemaic universe placed the world at the center of nine concentric circles, but the accepted religion made it clear in symbolic terms that this was an illusion. For Dante, man had a clearly defined purpose in his earthly life, and that was to ensure his ultimate *leaving* of the earth. In order to do so, he was to substitute God for the world as the center of his spiritual existence and to subordinate all aspects of his life on earth to that purpose. Boccaccio's structure is therefore very significant. When he put the world as a social arena at the center of his carefully constructed circle, he truly manipulated the expression plane of this sign function so as to cause "a reassessment of the content." The circle itself became a social rather than a sacred one and led to a change in the code, producing "a new type of awareness about the world" in the *Decameron*'s contemporary readers, who reassessed its importance. "Insofar as the aesthetic text has a self-focusing quality, so that its structural arrangement becomes one of the contents that it conveys (and maybe even the most important one), the way in which the rules are rearranged on one level will represent the way in which they are rearranged on another" (Eco, *Semiotics*, pp. 272-273). The universe of Boccaccio's readers was not the same as that of Dante's, and this is one reason why the latter has so often been called emblematic of the medieval period at its highest flowering and the former emblematic of the burgeoning humanism. One may disapprove, as De Sanctis did, but one cannot deny the difference, as De Sanctis saw when he named the *Decameron* "the human comedy" in opposition to the divine one.

A similar pattern may be found in Boccaccio's use of numerology. Dante had used the perfect number one hundred to build a poetic universe that was to be a reflection of the material universe that in its turn reflected the mind of God. The great admiration inspired by the *Divine Comedy* reinforced even further the "divine" connotations of its key numbers—three, ten, and one hundred—all of which had already acquired a semantic value of divinity and universality thanks to a process of overcoding.[9] When Boccaccio therefore used the numbers ten and one hundred to structure his universe of stories, some noble, some bawdy, some apparently trivial, some comic, some tragic, but all definitely worldly, he was again manipulating a sign function so as to cause a reassessment of its content.

Some critics have argued that the use of the ten and one hundred structure was merely in emulation of Dante, meant to impress the reader with the perfection of Boccaccio's literary and worldly universe or chosen without a great deal of thought. The very subtle numerological structure in the *Decameron* and the importance of numerological systems in Boccaccio's work in general make such hypotheses unlikely. A close examination of the *cornice* shows a complex system (or s-code, in Eco's terminology) based on the number five working alongside what is apparently the main ten- and hundred-based s-code.[10] The number five is essentially a "social" number: it was traditionally regarded as the world number, the sum of the female two and the male three. Boccaccio's use of it to inform his structure could conceivably therefore bear out Thomas Greene's point that the theme of marriage is at the center of the book, where it functions to render love's desires concordant with social order and to channel the "uncontrollable natural instinct."[11] It certainly underlines the fact that, unlike the *Divine Comedy*, the *Decameron*'s subject is humanity-in-the-world as opposed to the universe-as-a-reflection-of-God.[12]

The number five is subtly built into the *Decameron* alongside the more obviously presented number ten from the very beginning. The opening rubric reads:

> Here begins the book called *Decameron*, otherwise known as Prince Galahalt, wherein are contained a hundred stories, told in ten days by seven ladies and three young men (p. 45).[13]

The use of the numerological code is foregrounded by the use of four religiously significant numbers in the brief opening lines of the book. The title, *Decameron*, derived from what Boccaccio believed to be a Greek root meaning ten days. In the rubric, it serves to flank the number "one hundred" of the stories by two mentions of the number "ten" (*deca merones*—one hundred stories—ten days) but it also introduces a fifth number (the *deca* of *Decameron*). The context within the rubric itself immediately secularizes the numbers, before most of them are even mentioned: "Decameron, also named Prince Galahalt." The ten story-tellers are absolved of any claim to sacredness in the Christian sense of the term, and the fact that Boccaccio mentions only the ten days out of fourteen when stories are told specifically excludes the days that have religious significance for his protagonists, as Neifile states: "Friday is worthy of special reverence because that was the day of the Passion of Our Lord, who died that we might live and I would therefore regard it as perfectly right and proper that we should all do honour to God by devoting that day to prayer rather than story telling. . . . Besides, in deference to the Virgin Mother of the Son of God, they [ladies] are wont to fast on Saturdays, and to refrain from all activities for the rest of the day, as a mark of respect for the approaching sabbath" (p. 228).[14]

In the discussion of the ages of the ten protagonists, there is a similar, and this time more significant, use of the number five alongside the ten and the hundred. The seven ladies are "incomplete" without the three young men, and careful mention is made of the ages of both groups. None of the women is older than twenty-eight or younger than eighteen. The difference is, of course, the perfect number ten. But the numbers eighteen and twenty-eight also carry hidden meanings: one plus eight adds up to nine, or Beatrician quasi-perfection; two plus eight adds up to ten. Twenty-eight is itself a "perfect" number within the Pythagorean system, as it is the sum of the numbers from one to seven ($1 + 2 + 3 + 4 + 5 + 6 + 7 = 28$). Within that same system, however, and also within the Christian code derived from it, three is a more perfect number than seven just as men were considered more perfect than women.[15] The age information given about the young men is also more "perfect." None of them is older than twenty-five, and unlike the case of the ladies, no other number is mentioned in connection with them. Twenty-five gives a seven ($2 + 5$) and thus the men are in a way the equivalent of the ladies. More importantly, 25 is the square of 5, and numbers multiplied by themselves are always more perfect. Five, the world number, is also a special number in another way, bearing within itself its own form of perfection, for it perpetually repeats itself when multiplied by odd numbers (which are masculine).[16]

The fact that the ladies' circle was incomplete without the men could be read in several ways. The 7 added to the 3 gives the 10 of perfection; the 18 of the youngest lady added to the 7 of all the ladies combined gives 25, which in itself adds up to 7, just as the 28 of the oldest lady less the 7 of all the ladies gives 21, which in itself adds up to 3. Boccaccio obviously delighted in the complexity of his Augustinian system, and was no doubt aware of the implication that the perfect 10 of the difference in the ages of the ladies (18 to 28) was incomplete without the 5 of the world. By using the latter in its squared form (through the information given on the ages of the men), and by limiting the number of his men to 3, he seems to be deliberately setting up a human perfection in opposition to the sacred perfection connoted by the hundred.

The 100 stories that are the crucial content of the *Decameron* are told in 10 days, and here again there is a subtle s-code based on the number 5 working alongside the more obvious s-code based on 10. The first stories are told on a Wednesday, since the group first meets on a Tuesday and leaves for the country the next day. No stories are told on the Fridays and Saturdays of the two-week period, so the breaks come after the second and the seventh days. This gives the following pattern: day 1 and day 2, break; days 3, 4, 5, 6, 7, break; days 8, 9, and 10. The first group of days $(1 + 2)$ adds up to three; in the second group, a total of five numbers $(3 + 4 + 5 + 6 + 7)$ adds up to 25; the third group consists of three numbers whose sum $(8 + 9 + 10)$ is 27, or 3^3. The 3 plus 25 plus 27, moreover, add up to 55.[17] Within this system, 5, the world number, is not only the center and the sum but is embedded as it were in a pair of 3s (3 and 3^3). The ultimate and rather daring pattern is the world number 5 at the center, flanked by the traditionally sacred 3s.

The numerological message is thus the same as the geometric message: at the center lies the world, no longer only in the material sense of the religious and Ptolemaic system, but now in a social sense that carries great value. Eco stated that "insofar as it produces new norms accepted by an entire society, the artistic idiolect may act as a meta-semiotic judgment changing common codes" (p. 272). Boccaccio's *Decameron* does just that, implicitly stating: from now on geometry and numbers operate in a *human* world, with connotations that are human as opposed to divine.

THE MESSAGE IN METANARRATIVE FRAMING

The expression systems examined so far have been deliberate uses of conventional codes that Boccaccio manipulated in order to change their content, and these manipulations have been shown in some cases to be extremely subtle. Boccaccio also used other formal systems to signal his intentions, and did so with equal subtlety. One of these is his use of parallel structures and of what I shall call "metanarrative framing." As the diagram at the beginning of this chapter shows, the stories of the *Decameron* are embedded in a fivefold complex framing system. Boccaccio claimed that he set out to write the *Decameron* as one hundred stories that would amuse and distract lovesick ladies. He continuously and consciously reminds us of this fact by bypassing the narrators within the fourth frame of the *cornice*, who are both men and women: ninety of the stories open with vocative addresses to the ladies whom Boccaccio claims he set out to amuse. While the convention of addressing one's remarks to the ladies was common in courts of love[18] and may even have found its literary precedent in the *dolce stil nuovo* or, more specifically, in Dante's famous *Vita Nuova* canzone "Donne ch'avete intelletto d'amore,"[19] within the *Decameron* it functions to remind the reader of the tale that Boccaccio tells about his book. He has further embedded his stories in the *cornice*, which is itself a story. All the tales of the *Decameron* are thus already doubly framed by narration embedded within narration.

The fourth narrative world or frame (that of the ten protagonists) in its turn "frames" the stories told by statements such as "since we tell these tales only for our own amusement."[20] These are what Gregory Bateson called "metacommunicative messages," stating "this is play."[21] They are also essentially the same as the statements Boccaccio *qua* author made about his whole book, a declaration that has been called "concomitantly an admission of estheticism and futility."[22] But there are serious underlying structures at work here. The protagonists' claims that their stories are told merely for amusement implicitly draw attention to that other narrator, Boccaccio, and the apparent paradox of the seriousness of his style in the Introduction works together with the paradox inherent in that type of metacommunicative message to cast doubt on the frivolity of Boccaccio's intentions. A similar doubt is reflected onto the stated frivolity of the protagonists' purpose in telling their tales.

The framing and the "metanarrative layering" systems within the *Decameron* as a whole take on increased importance and meaning when compared to the framing and the metanarrative layering in its opening story. I am here using the term "framing" in the sense in which Erving Goffman used it, meaning the set of expectations that arise from given clues or social situations, in this case clues provided by established literary forms and medieval social and religious conventions.[23] A comparison of the structure of the *Decameron* as a whole with the structure of the first story in it reveals a striking similarity between the two, which may aid in interpreting both.

A first story, especially in a medieval collection, calls for special attention because of its pride of place. Let me therefore again turn to the ambiguous story of Ser Cepparello da Prato (I, 1), which has perhaps generated more controversy than any other in the *Decameron*: critics will no doubt argue for generations to come as to whether Boccaccio's show of piety in it is ironic or sincere, without coming to a definitive answer. This very ambiguous tale is framed by a series of declarations and self-reflexive, metanarrative statements. Its opening sentences are highly portentous and couched in the grand style (*genus grave*): "It is a fitting thing, dearest ladies, that everything done by man should be begun by the admirable and Holy name of Him who was the maker of all things. Therefore, since I, as the first, must begin our story telling, I intend to begin with one of His marvelous deeds, so that, having heard it, our hopes will rest in Him as in that which is unchangeable, and His name will be forever praised by all of us."[24] The story thus opens in frame four, as Panfilo, not Boccaccio, is speaking, but the heavy, ornate, latinate style mirrors the Proem of the other narrator, Boccaccio. The first sentence, in fact, serves as a miniature Proem to the story. The close parallel of structure is underlined by the similarity of the latinate inversion and opening words of each: "Umana cosa è . . ." (Proem, 2); "Convenevole cosa è . . ." (I, 1, 2).

Part of the second sentence ("therefore, since I . . . must begin our story telling . . .") is a self-reflexive and meta-narrative statement that carries the metacommunicative reminder "this is play" (the telling of tales). It also carries all the ambiguities inherent in that message. The same sentence contains a rather weighty exhortation to praise God, which, on the surface, would appear to contradict the reference to storytelling, were this occupation basically "estheticism and futility." There is also a tinge of irony, which does not become apparent until the end of the story. In the narrative order of the *cornice*, there is a parallel reminder of the seriousness of the *Decameron*'s purpose. The corresponding place to Panfilo's second sentence (immediately after the Proem) is occupied by the opening of the Introduction, in which Boccaccio speaks of his book and the sad necessity to begin it with the memory of the plague, which will be like a steep and rugged mountain to be climbed before reaching the beauties of the plain. The author immediately goes on to give the date of that plague in terms that also in effect praise God: "I say, then, that the sum of thirteen hundred and forty-eight years had elapsed since the fruitful Incarnation of the Son of God" (p. 50).[25]

The description of the plague itself in the Introduction,

which culminates in Boccaccio's rhetorically sapient *ubi sunt* passage (I, 1, 48), is structurally paralleled in the story of Ser Cepparello by the lengthy third sentence, with its reminder of the difficulties and dangers to which all that is mortal and transitory falls prey: "It is obvious that since all temporal things are transient and mortal, so they are filled and surrounded by troubles, trials and tribulations, and fraught with infinite dangers which we, who live with them and are part of them, could without a shadow of a doubt neither endure, nor defend ourselves against, if God's special grace did not lend us strength and discernment" (p. 69).[26]

The framing structures in the tale of Ser Cepparello then repeat themselves: God is invoked a second time, again in the ornate and latinate style of the *genus grave*, through the expedient of a long passage stating that He grants prayers according to the purity of the intention of him who prays, not according to the quality of the chosen intercessor:

Nor should we suppose that His grace descends upon and within us through any merit of our own, for it is set in motion by His own loving kindness, and is obtained by the pleas of people who like ourselves were mortal, and who, by firmly doing His pleasure whilst they were in this life, have now joined Him in eternal blessedness. To these, as to advocates made aware, through experience, of our frailty (perhaps because we have not the courage to submit our pleas personally in the presence of so great a judge) we present whatever we think is relevant to our cause. And our regard for Him, who is so compassionate and generous towards us, is all the greater when, the human eye being quite unable to penetrate the secrets of divine intelligence, common opinion deceives us and perhaps we appoint as our advocate to His majestic presence one who has been cast by Him into eternal exile. Yet He from whom nothing is hidden, paying more attention to the purity of the supplicant's motives than to his ignorance or to the banishment of the intercessor, answers those who pray to Him exactly as if the advocate were blessed in His sight (p. 69).[27]

Ambiguous as the passage may be, the *presence* of God and the implicit presence of the Church and the apparatus of religion are undeniable, regardless of the already discussed use to which both are put within the economy of the story. The immediately following sentence is again self-reflexive and metanarrative: "All of which can clearly be seen in the tale I propose to relate: and I say clearly because it is concerned, not with the Judgment of God, but with that of men" (p. 69).[28]

A similar double structure is evident in the framing of the *Decameron* as a whole. After stating his intention of telling a hundred tales, Boccaccio describes the plague and then gathers his interlocutors in the Church of Santa Maria Novella. From the church they leave for the Tuscan hills and there make the formal decision to tell ten stories a day. The self-reflexive statement that the *Decameron* will consist of these is thus presented twice, just as Panfilo twice makes his metanarrative statements "I propose to begin by telling you . . ." and ". . . in the tale I propose to relate."

The story proper begins after this long preamble (some ten percent of the whole) and opens in terms that are uniquely broad: "Ragionassi che . . ." ("it is said that"). Of all the hundred tales in the book, this first one, which together with the last, may also be said partly to frame the story content of the *Decameron*, is the only one to open with an indefinite subject construction. It thereby tends to throw all of the following tales into the rather general frame of reference that it represents from a grammatical point of view. The generality of the construction also carries social connotations: the hundred tales open with what is said in the world surrounding the *Decameron*, the world about which the protagonists must learn.

The basic format (narration-embedded-within-narration) of the *Decameron* also finds a corresponding format within the story of Ser Cepparello. His "confession" is actually the fiction of Saint Ciappelletto, a story invented by himself. The parallel to Boccaccio's fiction of ten narrators inventing or repeating tales is quite clear. And the tale within a tale within a tale (that of "Saint" Ciappelletto as told by Ser Cepparello to the good friar, in its turn told by Panfilo, who is a character in a tale told by Boccaccio) also contains yet another double narrative frame.[29] Panfilo narrates the story of Ser Cepparello in the third person and effaces himself during most of it, but he cannot resist a direct interjection in defense of the holy friar's belief in the tale spun for him: "but then, who is there who would not have been convinced, on hearing a dying man talk in this fashion?" (pp. 78-79).[30] This interjection by a narrator corresponds to Boccaccio's authorial interventions in the *Decameron*, such as the Introduction to the Fourth Day, in which he also defends his stories.

There is still another correspondence: that between Boccaccio's ten protagonists and the vignette of the two usurers, hidden by a partition and listening to the story of Ser Cepparello's auto-apotheosis:

> The two brothers, who strongly suspected that Ser Ciappelletto was going to deceive them, had posted themselves behind a wooden partition which separated the room where Ser Ciappelletto was lying from another, and as they stood there listening they could easily follow what Ser Ciappelletto was saying to the friar. When they heard the things he confessed to having done, they were so amused that every so often they nearly exploded with mirth, and they said to each other:
>
> "What manner of man is this, whom neither old age nor illness, nor fear of the death which he sees so close at hand, nor even the fear of God, before whose judgement he knows he must shortly appear, have managed to turn from his evil ways, or persuade him to die any differently from the way he has lived?" (p. 79)[31]

Boccaccio's ten interlocutors are equally often torn between amazement and the desire to laugh as they listen to each other's tales. The repetition of the Italian verb forms *udivano* and *udendo* ("listening . . . they heard"), further points up the storytelling parallel.

At the end of the tale, Panfilo again intervenes directly in his persona as narrator: "It was thus, then, that Ser Cepparello of Prato lived and died, becoming a Saint in the way you have heard" (p. 81).[32] It is another metanarrative statement, and it is followed by Panfilo's closing comment on intercessors and the miraculous ways of God. After saying that Ser Cepparello may be in Heaven but is more likely to be elsewhere, Panfilo continues: "And if this is the case, we may recognize how very great is God's loving kindness towards us, in that it takes account, not of our error, but of the purity of our faith, and grants our prayers even when we appoint as our emissary one who is His enemy, thinking him to be His friend, as though we were appealing to one who was truly holy as our intercessor for His favor" (p. 81).[33] This ambiguous passage corresponds to the one quoted on pages 107-108, and the two allusions to God and the religious apparatus of the Church serve to frame the story proper. In similar fashion, the content proper of the *Decameron* is framed by its protagonists' departure from and final return to the Church of Santa Maria Novella, gateway from and back to the world of the plague.

One final metanarrative statement is made after this: it is *Boccaccio*'s authorial statement "and there the narrator fell silent" (p. 81).[34] This is the only metanarrative statement made directly by Boccaccio *qua* narrator within any of the hundred tales he told us he was setting out to tell and finally framed by his own Author's Epilogue.[35]

The structural correspondences between the tale of Ser Cepparello and the *cornice* are, as the following diagram shows, too clear and detailed to be the result of coincidence: We are evidently again dealing with an expression system whose content plane is open to interpretation.

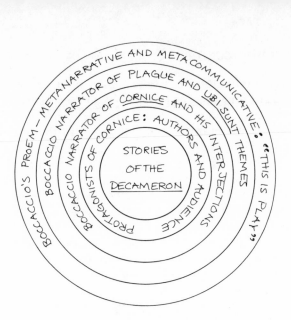

DECAMERON

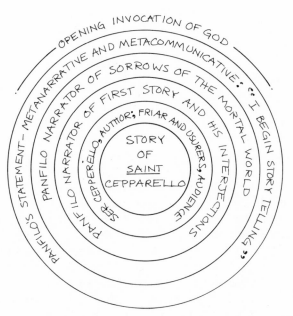

"THE STORY OF SER CEPPARELLO"

The story of Ser Cepparello is the story of how the false Saint Ciappelletto came into being and was duly worshipped by a hysterical populace. The topic, as Branca points out (*Decameron*, p. 1003), is not new, and fits nicely into bitter contemporary polemics against the proliferation of both authorized and unauthorized saints. The second story in the *Decameron* is that of Abraham the Jew who becomes a Christian on the grounds that any religion that succeeds in flourishing despite the manifest corruptness of its Establishment must indeed be a great one. The third story is by no means original but the well-known tale of how Melchisedech the Jew, upon being asked by the Saladin which of the three great current religions is the best, replied with the story of the three identical rings. As an opening trinity, the stories are clearly a protest against the great influence and corrupt religious customs of the Church. The use of the number three is most probably both formally intended and ironic. Boccaccio's protest against Church corruption, as we have seen, stems from a sense of mission. Other systems in the *Decameron* have also very clearly shown that its focus is on humanity-in-the-world rather than on God-as-reflected-in-the-world. The fact that the structure of the story of Ser Cepparello/Saint Ciappelletto so closely reflects that of the *Decameron* in general is a clue to the careful reader, who is expected to see the similarity between the inventions of a corrupt society based on religion (for which the plague represents a sort of deathbed) and the corrupt Ser Cepparello's deathbed invention of himself as a saint. The framework in the *cornice* and in the first tale, like all the other systems and structures I have examined, both social and literary, contradict the author's metacommunicative message about the *Decameron*: this is not play.

Renaissance and Medieval Cultural Models

The true center or message of the *Decameron* lies in the stories. That is obvious, and I have been concerned with tracing the complexity of the structures that support their centrality rather than with showing that they are central. Further evidence of the care with which Boccaccio constructed his work is provided by the marked conventionality of the storytelling protagonists, which has multiple connotations. Some have already been pointed out: the protagonists are conventional because they are meant to represent a more general (although elite) class, and also in order to underline their exemplary function. In terms of the very carefully encoded structure of the book as a whole, their conventionality also has another meaning. It is designed to be seen in contrast to the characters in the stories. The protagonists of the *cornice*, in spite of their conversations and frequent witty remarks to each other (all of which, with the occasional exception of a sally of Dioneo's, are in the patrician style of their class and times)[36] have, as we have seen, much the same quality as certain figures in bas-reliefs or frescoes. Boccaccio knew and respected the painters of his time, as is proved by his comparing himself to them in his Author's Epilogue and by stories such as that of Forese da Rabatta and Giotto (VI, 5). His framing system for the *Decameron* is in fact not unlike that of a series of frescoes: the narrative text is sequentially divided into scenes, each framed by a piece of *cornice*. It is also structured so as to give the feeling of a representation within a representation, a device commonly used by medieval painters. As Uspensky pointed out, in these cases the background or frame representation tends to be stereotypic and almost always more conventional than the central one, which is more natural. In the stereotypic and conventional figure "the description is not a sign of represented reality, as it is for the central figures, but a sign of a sign of this reality. . . . Accordingly the central figures . . . are opposed to the secondary figures by the fact that there is a lesser degree of semiotic quality or of conventionality in their description . . . the central figures . . . are more lifelike."[37] The contrast between the protagonists of the *cornice* and those of the stories themselves thus further underlines the centrality of the latter.

The same contrast may also be read in a somewhat different sense. Yury Lotman and Boris Uspensky, in their essay on "The Semiotic Mechanism of Culture," argue that "culture's basic function . . . is essentially to be found in the structural organization of the world surrounding humanity. Culture generates structure, and by so doing, it creates a social sphere around humanity which, like the biosphere, makes . . . a social life possible."[38] (Culture itself is defined as *"the non-hereditary memory of a collectivity* which expresses a given system of prohibitions and ordinances"—p. 66.) "The organization of a poetic text" in its turn "reproduces the structure of the world in the poet's consciousness."

Lotman and Uspensky further classify cultures as belonging to two basic types: those in which there is a fixed and necessary relationship between expression and content, and those in which the relationship is considered arbitrary or conventional. The first type, which they call dominantly expression-centered, is apt to view the world as "a text made up of signs" whose content is predetermined and which can be "read," provided that one knows the language. This kind of culture tends toward rigid ritualization of the forms of behavior, and, believing as it does that the relationship between expression and content is not only fixed but reciprocal, it also believes that ritual can influence or "form" content. A content-centered culture, on the other hand, presupposes freedom both in the choice of content and in its relationship with expression.

An expression-centered culture is apt to view itself as a series of *texts*; a content-centered culture as a set of *rules*. The former leads to the ideal of the Book and tends to organize its text in a catechistic form, or as anthologies; the latter leads to the ideal of the Manual, which is considered a generator of texts. The classic examples of expression-centered cultures given are the Middle Ages and nine-

113

teenth-century European realism; that of a content-oriented culture is European Classicism.[39]

One other factor in Lotman and Uspensky's model can lead to insights into the nature of the *Decameron*. A content-centered culture that views itself as a set of rules is apt to set up a system of fundamental antitheses based on the concept "order v. disorder" and consequently on concepts such as "cosmos v. chaos," "ectropy v. entropy," "culture v. nature." An expression-centered culture that views itself as a set of texts ruled by norms will set up its antitheses on a basis of "right v. wrong" (wrong in the sense of erring, not of incorrect), and consequently, of "true v. false" (Lotman and Uspensky's examples also include "Christian v. pagan" and "good v. evil").

In terms of the expression v. content-centered models described above, the *Decameron* seems to be a typical product of an expression- or text-oriented culture, a true offspring of medieval times. A series of minitexts, the *novelle*, are presented in a basically anthological form. These stories frequently end in a proverb presented as a general rule or are themselves presented as useful examples of behavior. The life of the *cornice* is formal and rigidly ritualized.

In terms of the antithetic systems set up by the two kinds of cultures, however, the *Decameron* does not in the least seem the product of an expression-oriented culture. It definitely seems based on an "order v. disorder" or "cosmos v. chaos" system, rather than on a "right v. wrong" or "good v. evil" one. As so many critics have pointed out, the elegant and orderly life of the ten protagonists in their country villas is itself a contrast to the civic and natural chaos raging in the world of the plague. The *cornice*'s courtly order is also in strong contrast to the life of the stories, which certainly does not share its stylized repetition. (None of the attempts I have seen to fit the stories into definite and precise formal patterns of meaning has been successful, including my own.)

The *Decameron* thus expresses not only the opposition between tradition and innovation that is so obvious in the

rich mix of its stories but also that between the medieval
and renaissance tendencies of Boccaccio's transitional cultural matrix, the former very definitely expression-centered
and the latter more content-centered, a civilization that was
certainly to produce its share of manuals.

The contrast between the *cornice* and the stories that are
its content within the structure of the book[40] can also be
studied in terms of Yuri Lotman's spatial models of culture.[41] He classifies the subtexts of a culture into two types,
those that express the structure of the world and those that
express "the place, the seat, the position and the activities
of humans in the surrounding world" (p. 152). ("Subtext"
is his term for works generated within the culture, which
is itself considered to be the main text.) The first group
answers the question: "How is it organized?" and the second that of "What happened and how?" or "What did the
character do?" The answer to the first question has a semantic content that goes beyond mere taxonomy, as it also
expresses an axiological hierarchy via concepts such as
up/down, right/left, concentric/eccentric, inclusive/ex-
clusive (p. 152). The ten protagonists of the *cornice*'s insistence on leaving their retreat before others can join them
definitely expresses an elitist and inclusive/exclusive structure; the *cornice* belongs to the first group. The stories, on
the other hand, clearly belong to the second type, which
is dynamic and characterized by a plot.

Lotman also uses his distinctions as an aid in placing
characters: some of these are tied to their environments
and others (like the hero in Russian folktales) are not. He
goes on to classify narrative heroes according to his subtext
types:

> Fixed heroes are personified circumstances inasmuch
> as they represent nothing but the name of their own
> environment [which may be magic, geographical, so-
> cial, etc.]; and it is more useful to describe them as
> phenomena belonging to structure 4.0.1 [a subtext that
> characterizes the structure of the world and is immo-

bile]. They fit completely into the classifying principles of a given picture of the world, since, from the point of view of such a picture, they are distinguished by their extreme degree of generalization (of "typicalness"). Mobile heroes, on the other hand, conceal in themselves the possibility of destroying a given classification and affirming a new one, or else they represent a structure not in its unvarying essence, but through a polyhedral variability (p. 154).

The distinction could be applied to the individual stories in the *Decameron*, but the results of such a study would in all probability be merely taxonomic. Applied to the differences between the *cornice* and the world of the stories, it is informative. The characters of the former are generic and immobile: essentially they move only from the world of the plague into the world of their storytelling environment and back out: they "do" nothing but tell stories, and none of them changes or develops in any way. With the possible exception of Dioneo, in fact, they are all stereotypes. There is no quest, no trajectory, and no indication that they will change the structure of their world or destroy its classifications. The characters in the stories, in general, could be called "mobile heroes" and certainly express "the place, the seat, and position and the activities of humans in the surrounding world." It is they who "conceal in themselves the possibility of destroying a given classification and affirming a new one" and thus express the changes in society and the rise of the new merchant class that Branca identified with the heroes of the *Decameron* "epos."

The contrast is not illogical. Lotman and Uspensky noted that "changes of culture (especially in times of social revolution) are usually accompanied by a net increase in the semiotic nature of behaviour (. . .); the fight against old rituals may in some cases acquire a totally ritualized character. On the other hand, not only the introducing of new forms of behaviour, but also the reenforcing of the semiotic nature of the old forms may bear witness to a given change of a type of culture."[42] In the *Decameron* we can see both forces at work: its dynamics spring from both reaction and revolution, and it reflects the new forces as well as the old ones that seek to keep them at bay.

The contrast not only points up the central and instructive nature of the stories from a "static" versus "dynamic" point of view but also suggests a further meaning. The connotations are important, both from the structural point of view that indicates the parallelisms between the roles of Boccaccio and of his storytelling protagonists, and from the social point of view, which shows its liminal aspects. Boccaccio wrote the *Decameron* for a serious purpose. He believed that the mission of the poet was an important one, and his defense of storytelling as an instrument of education is completely in keeping with his defense of fables in the *De Genealogiis*. It is legitimate to infer that Boccaccio, like his own protagonists, was learning from the observations and experiences he recounted (it should be remembered that very few of the stories in the book are original). The structure of the book (*cornice* and stories) and the closeness with which the narrative framing system of the *Decameron* as a whole and the story of Ser Cepparello reflect each other also have a semantic content. The protagonists as narrators reflect the author's role. As audience, they reflect the reader's, who thus to some extent enters the liminal world with them, and, temporarily stripped of all other roles in life, examines and learns the values of the society in the separate space and time of the realm of literature. Like his ten young protagonists, gathered together in the limen of their fictionally plague-free space in the country, Boccaccio did not set out to be a revolutionary. He examined his world from what Mazzotta has called "the marginal space of literature"[43] in order to understand it, and perhaps to enable himself to dominate it. But the world he wanted to understand and master was in no way static: not only was it in transition, but the transition itself had reached a crisis point. The *Decameron* reflects both the static society to which Boccaccio probably wished to belong (that of the court of Robert of Anjou and the older medieval virtues as opposed to the new merchant ethics) and the crisis-torn transitional society identified by the historians. Its reflection of the latter may have come about in spite of the author's intentions.

The architectonic structure, the unusual way in which the *cornice* is inextricably intertwined with the innermost core of the book, the stories, may also have a further semantic content. The stately and ritualized life of the ten extremely stylized protagonists frames the opening and the closing of each day of storytelling in much the same way as the decorative motifs and pillars or figures that were used to divide or frame the narrative sequences in frescoes or in sculptured works such as the Perugia fountain or the famous pulpits by Nicola and Giovanni Pisano. It is perhaps a sign of the author's effort to contain the world of the stories, to capture it and to use it for a liminal intent to which, in the ultimate analysis, it refuses to lend itself, an *ante litteram* Pirandellian duel between life and form. In attempting to capture its times for the study and transmission of certain traditional values, the *Decameron* became revolutionary in spite of itself. The static and stylized world could not endure, as is shown by the eruption of the spirit of the bawdiest *novelle* into the Introduction to the sixth day. The Boccaccio of the earlier, court-influenced works, who had taken his protagonists into the liminal space of literature, may himself have internalized and accepted the values of the burgeoning renaissance society that was actually his rather than the more feudal Angevin one reflected in his early works.[44]

Complex and ambiguous as it is, the *Decameron* is certainly a work of art. As an aesthetic text, it focuses on itself, so that its structure is one of the meanings it conveys.[45] The complexity of this structure is an integral part of the text's aesthetic quality, according to Eco's definition. The *Decameron* is a text that carefully organizes many ambiguous messages on several levels in such a way that each affects the others contextually.[46] By playing on and rearranging the codes employed, it recreates them and, at the same time, both recreates and reflects a new world. In all the systems and patterns of meaning examined in this and the preceding chapters, the central message has been the same: the *Decameron* is a social book, describing a "liminal" experience (whose aims are always social) and reaffirming the importance of a view oriented towards humanity-in-this-world. This is, in its own way, revolutionary and places Boccaccio beside Petrarch as a founding father of the renaissance in spite of the fundamentally conservative values transmitted alongside the new ones in so many of the stories.[47]

CHAPTER V

The Function of Framing
in the *Decameron*[1]

THE FIVE CONCENTRIC "WORLDS" of the *Decameron* shown in Chapter IV can also be presented as a series of five "frames," as in the diagram on the following page. The elaborate fivefold structure has a double function. It not only encloses the stories in such a way as to emphasize their value but also serves, in accordance with a long and continuing literary tradition, to guard their author from possible accusations of sedition against the official morals and religion of the times.[2] The series of frames also insulates the reader from the material contained in the stories, which at times becomes very subversive, as we have seen.

Each frame is specifically identified as such within the book itself. The Preface, the Introduction to the Fourth Day, and the Author's Epilogue are all addressed to Boccaccio's readers, and in the Introduction to the Fourth Day he doubly underlines this fact by citing those readers' objections to his work. With the exception of the Preface, however, these pages are addressed to the ladies for whom Boccaccio claims to be writing. They thus focus both outward into the world of the readers of the book and inward into the fiction of the audience of lovesick ladies that is the *Decameron*'s ostensible public. These two worlds constitute frames one and two. The paradox of the act of writing itself—as a further frame between the author, the reader, and reality—is also brought into play by the position of the first rubric:

Here begins the BOOK called *Decameron*, otherwise known as Prince Galahalt, wherein are contained a hundred stories, told in ten days by seven ladies and three young men.

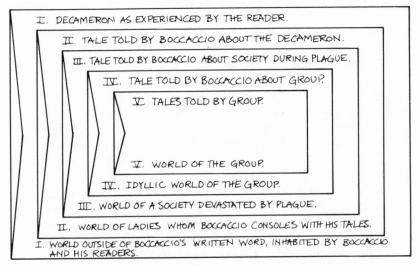

The rubric comes *before* the Preface, reminding us of the *librum experientiae* on which Boccaccio claims to be drawing when he tells us at some length that he wrote the *Decameron* in the first place because of his experience as a man who has suffered and recovered from love.

The section labeled "Introduction" comes after the rubric of the first day:

Here begins the First Day of the *Decameron*, wherein first of all the author explains the circumstances in which certain persons, who presently make their appearance, were induced to meet for the purpose of conversing together, after which, under the rule of Pampinea, each of them speaks on the subject they find most congenial (p. 49).[3]

It thus brings in not only frame three (that of the plague) but also frame four (that of the idyllic world of the group).

Within the innermost frame (that of the stories themselves), each tale is set off under its own number in each
day, and the days are in turn delimited by the author's
recurrent formula: "The ____ day of the Decameron ends:
The ____ day begins, in which . . . is discussed. . . ." But,
again, almost every tale is begun by a brief comment on
the group's reaction to the previous tale, followed, in most
cases, by a moral pointed out by the teller before he or she
plunges *in medias res*, often via the framing formula "so I
say that . . ." and thus the tales bring in frame four as well
as frame five. It is easy to see that considerable slippage
thus occurs even in the formal constitution of the frames.
The best example is in the already cited very first rubric,
where the word "book" indicates the first frame of writing;
Prince Galahalt refers to the second; the title *Decameron*
itself and the statement "told in ten days" refer to the
fourth and the "which contains one hundred tales" (which
is given syntactic pride of place) refers to the fifth frame.
Four of the five major frames are referred to in an extremely
compact space (only three, the frame of the plague, is left
out), and the overall effect is almost to eliminate the fivefold
framing system and to bring the reader and the stories
closer together. This effect is deliberate and typical of Boccaccio's literary artistry. The overt message "this is play"
is thus once again contradicted by the subtle manipulation
of the structural devices employed in the book.

Boccaccio carefully sets up his work in five major overt
frames, but he weakens his own structure by skipping in
and out from one to the other (as will be seen) and by
frequently also raising doubts about the frame he is working in. This is one reason for the ambiguity that the reader
perceives in the book, which is not only full of these "frame
shifts" but also of "frame breaks," factors that, to a considerable extent, account for the duel between "Boccaccio
the escapist" and "Boccaccio the realist" that continues
across the pages of critical literature.

The terms require further clarification. A "frame shift"
is an unexpected change from one of the *Decameron*'s five

major frames to another. A "frame break" will refer to the concept of a psychological frame used by Bateson and by Erving Goffman in his book *Frame Analysis*.[4] Goffman subtitles his book "An Essay on the Organization of Experience" and assumes that one approaches any current situation via the question "what is it that is going on here?" He tries, in his words, to

> isolate some of the basic frameworks of understanding available in our society for making sense out of events and to analyze some of the special vulnerability to which these frames of reference are subject. . . . Definitions of a situation are built up in accordance with principles of organization which govern events—at least social events—and our subjective involvement in them; frame is the word I use to refer to such of these basic elements as I am able to identify. My phrase 'frame analysis' is a slogan to refer to the examination in these terms of the organization of experience (pp. 10-11).

Although Goffman never defines the term, it follows that to "break frame" is to behave in some such way as to place these principles of organization in doubt, and to reopen the question of "what is going on here?" Inappropriate behavior will do this, as will changes of tone in literature when the tone does not seem suited to the ostensible content or subject. A "change of registers" thus signals a frame break.

A reading of the *Decameron* in the light of frame theory shows so many shifts and breaks in frame that one cannot help but think them purposeful. Boccaccio deliberately and consistently used frame shifts and frame breaks (the first can be an example of the second, but not vice versa) to destroy the elaborate fivefold framing system and leave the reader face to face with the world of the stories, which is fundamentally subversive, on a level closer to what Bateson would call the "denotative" or "primary" level (pp. 21ff.). The reader is thus drawn into the liminal experience along with the protagonists. This happens throughout the book, not only in the first rubric. It can best be shown by examining the major frames in terms of their overt functions and studying the ways in which the author subverts these.

The ostensible "keying" of the *Decameron* as make-believe in the Preface obliges the reader to accept it as "only entertainment" and thus relieves Boccaccio of a certain responsibility.[5] He states that he is writing only for those ladies who are in love, and immediately continues:

> I intend to narrate a hundred stories or fables or parables or histories or whatever you want to call them, told in ten days by a worthy band of seven women and three young men who gathered during the plague-stricken time of the recent epidemic and some songs sung by the above mentioned women for their pleasure. In which stories pleasant and sad examples of love and other exciting happenings can be seen, which took place in both ancient and modern times; from which the already mentioned ladies, who will read these tales, will be able to derive both pleasure from the amusing things recounted in them and useful counsel, insofar as they will be able to recognize what should be avoided and likewise what should be followed: which things I do not believe can come about without their affliction passing.[6]

But this is not so simple and straightforward as it seems. Giovanni Boccaccio, author, picks up his goose quill and writes that he is going to tell one hundred tales in order to console and succor such noble ladies as are afflicted by love. The reader is thus faced with Giovanni Boccaccio, implied narrator, making a statement about Giovanni Boccaccio, virtual author, and this statement is framed by the fact that a real Giovanni Boccaccio has, in fact, picked up his goose quill. The situation is further complicated by the references to frames two, three, and four in the passage, as well as the reference to five, implicit in the mention of the hundred tales to be told. Frame two is brought in by the mention of what proves to be—at this stage of the game—a fictional audience that is still potential rather than actual (a shift in time frame): "the already mentioned ladies who will read these tales." The fictional audience will become actual in the first line of the Author's Introduction, where the ladies are addressed in the vocative as "most gracious ladies," but for the moment both the sending of the message (writing) and its receiving (reading) are put into the future as regards frame two, while a message is obviously being sent and received (by another sender to another audience) in frame one. Frames three and four appear with the mention that the hundred tales were told during the recent plague by an honorable group of young people, a change in point of view from past experience on the part of the narrator to future experience on the part of the reader who has not yet met the protagonists.

Meanwhile, one effect of the statement "I intend to tell one hundred stories or fables or parables or histories or whatever you want to call them, told in ten days by a worthy band of seven women and three young men during the plague-stricken time of the recent epidemic," is to reduce the distance between frames one and five from the very beginning. Another effect is to underline the difference between Boccaccio, the author, and Boccaccio, the narrator: "narrative can be cast in a double perspective: it can be conducted from the temporal perspective of one or more characters who participate in the action, and, simultaneously, from the point of view of the author. The author's temporal viewpoint differs substantially from that of the characters because he knows what they cannot know: he knows how this particular story will end."[7] Each perspective constitutes a frame.

A careful examination of the Preface in these terms reveals that its framework is not clear-cut. The metacommunicative messages conflict, and the psychological frames no longer efficiently exclude certain messages while including others, for the excluded messages keep slipping in as they do throughout the whole *Decameron*. The lack of clear-cut distinctions is equally evident in other ways: the Preface opens rhetorically as well as thematically on a majestic note more suited to high tragedy than to the telling of a hundred tales: "To have compassion for the suffering is human." It continues on this noble note throughout the description of Boccaccio's past love, which is done in a highly elegant and latinate style and in terms suited to the literature flowing from Andreas Capellanus's *De arte oneste amandi*. This is in itself not new for the times, and could be regarded as not constituting a "frame break" around the year 1350.[8] But at the close of the Preface the rather Ovidian picture of sad and leisured ladies dreaming of love suffers a shock; it ends with the wish that God grant that Boccaccio's tales be both useful and entertaining to them, for which they are to thank Love, who by freeing Boccaccio from his bonds has enabled him to attend to their pleasure. The last sentence is almost flippant in its rhythm, being formed of three short clauses separated by commas and followed by one longer clause with no particular rhythmic pattern: "And if that happens, may God grant that it will, let them thank Love, who has conceded to me the power to think of their pleasure by freeing me from his bonds."[9] It is in forcible contrast to a preceding long and rolling period that describes how Boccaccio's love finally passed, according to the will of Him who made all earthly things to have an end. This sentence ends with a marked hendecasyllable. The reader is thus left in doubt as to just how the *Decameron* is rekeyed.

Boccaccio also characterizes his material in mixed terms: "stories or fables or parables or histories or whatever you want to call them." "Stories" is a generic term covering all types of subject matter; "fables" is more specialized, as in the French *fabliaux*; "parables" were considered didactical or allegorical, and "histories" were of illustrious personages, usually based on reality.[10] These constitute rather specific genres, different semiotic subsystems within narrative, and as such are really different frames.

The Preface thus introduces all kinds of frame play, which

will be typical of the whole work and serves specific purposes that can be traced in spite of the apparent ambiguity that is its most apparent result. Frame one (that of the book and its readers) next overtly appears in the Introduction to the Fourth Day, after the *cornice* has been established and the first thirty stories told.[11] Most of the Introduction to Day IV is metanarrative and is thus in itself a reflexive frame break as it takes narrator and reader outside the fictional world the author has created. It is also a veritable juggler's exhibition of frame shifts and breaks, as is the Author's Epilogue. The Introduction opens in frame two, drawing a circle around narrator and supposed audience by the use of the vocative "dearest ladies" (this vocative is consistently used throughout). Almost immediately, however, there is a switch to frame one, in which Boccaccio makes the metanarrative statement that he has sought to avoid envy by writing his "little tales" in Florentine, in prose, and in "a very humble and low keyed style." This is what Goffman would call a "self-referencing reflexive frame break" (p. 388). Boccaccio goes on to list the various objections to the tales by different readers and through this device the audience in frame one is being discussed with that in frame two, effectively breaking down the barrier between them. The first of these objections is interesting in terms of frame: "Judicious ladies, there are those who have said, after reading these tales, that I am altogether too fond of you, that it is unseemly for me to take so much delight in entertaining and consoling you, and, what is apparently worse, in singing your praises as I do" (p. 375).[12] In this passage, the frame-one audience objects to the fiction that Boccaccio has set up in frame two, but the objection is discussed with the very fictional audience to whom the objection is directed. (The passage is in the vocative.) These frame-two characters then abruptly slip into frame one as Boccaccio calls on the ladies to defend him (still in the vocative), even though their forces will be insufficient to do so alone:

By gusts of such a kind as these, then, by teeth thus

sharp and cruel, distinguished ladies, am I buffeted, battered, and pierced to the very quick whilst I soldier on in your service. As God is my witness, I take it all calmly and coolly; and though I need no one but you to defend me, I do not intend, all the same, to spare my own energies. On the contrary, without replying as fully as I ought, I shall proceed forthwith to offer a simple answer to these allegations. For I have not yet completed a third of my task, and since my critics are already so numerous and presumptuous, I can only suppose that unless they are discredited now, they could multiply so alarmingly before I reached the end that the tiniest effort on their part would be sufficient to demolish me. And your own influence, considerable though it may be, would be powerless to prevent them (p. 326).[13]

He then helps defend himself by telling the tale of Filippo Balducci and his son, a deliberate mingling of frames to which he calls attention by the metanarrative statement that the story will not be complete as he does not wish to compete with the company of frame four:

But before replying to any of my critics, I should like to strengthen my case by recounting, not a complete story (for otherwise it might appear that I was attempting to equate my own tales with those of that select company I have been telling you about), but a part of one, so that its very incompleteness will set it apart from the others (p. 326).[14]

He addresses the story of Filippo Balducci directly to his frame-one audience. The Italian reads, "and, speaking to my assailants, I say that. . . ." The story he chooses to tell (which is actually not in the least incomplete) performs a further telescoping function between frames one and five, for of all the one hundred and one tales of the *Decameron* it was perhaps the best known and most widely diffused in the contemporary "real" world.[15] It ends with another metanarrative statement to the effect that the partially told story will suffice.[16] The tale is thus enclosed by two metanarrative sentences, which themselves constitute a further frame that emphasizes the major frame shift.

This is just the beginning of an extended series of shifts. Boccaccio next says that he will turn to his frame-one audience: "I wish to address those to whom I have told it," but he continues addressing the ladies of frame two in the vocative and then adds in frames one and five by comparing his own avowed natural love for women with the fictional Filippo Balducci's:

> To these charges I openly plead guilty: it is quite true that I am fond of you and that I strive to please you. But what, may I ask, do they find so surprising about it, when you consider that a young man who had been nurtured and reared within the confines of a tiny cave on a bleak and lonely mountainside, with no other companion except his father, no sooner caught sight of you than all his desires, all his curiosity, all the leanings of his affection were centred upon you, and you alone? (pp. 328-329).[17]

Next Boccaccio takes up the objection of those who think he is too old to think of women, and again he telescopes frames one and five by the simple device of a change of register that constitutes a shift to frame five. He says that a leek's white head belies its green tail, and this sort of language is as typical of the stories as it is atypical of the language used by Boccaccio in the other frames; it is also an image used in I, 10, a story with a certain importance of position within the *Decameron*. In the same sentence he goes on to say, in rather elevated language, that he is not ashamed to be in the company of authors such as Cavalcanti and Dante, a juxtaposition of very different registers that comes close to constituting a frame break (on the syntactical level the frames are separated by a colon and a parenthetical phrase of the "jokes aside" type). Another shift follows with the statement that, if it were not going outside of the established mode of discourse ("the accustomed way of talking"),[18] Boccaccio would give historical examples to show that many great men have loved. This case is especially interesting: it not only assumes that frames one and four are the same (the "established mode of discourse" referred to is the tales of frame five) but serves to draw attention to the historical roots of many of the stories, which most of the contemporary readers would instantly have recognized, and which have been proved conclusively by Vittore Branca.

The next objection to be taken up is the already discussed one of those who believe Boccaccio should spend his time with the Muses on Mt. Parnasus instead of wasting it talking nonsense with women. It will be remembered that he answers that no one can live with the Muses all the time and that when one cannot be with them it is logical to delight in beings similar to them, like women. His further contention that, though women inspired him, the Muses helped him, juxtaposes women and Muses on an equal level, which mingles two very different registers and thus constitutes another notable frame break.

Boccaccio's reply, to those who think he should be earning his bread (quoted in Chapter III), is a masterly use of connotation to confront two systems of values, or two possible frames.[19] The trick involves some juggling on the paradigmatic axis:[20] there is a substitution of one metaphoric use of "bread" (money) for another (spiritual nourishment), derived, as we have seen, from the idea of the Symposium, and probably with Dante's *Convivio* in mind. In the further reference to Dante, "whereas on the contrary many, by trying to gain more bread than they needed, died unripe" (38), an echo, as we saw, of *Paradiso* XIX, 48, these objectors are sent to Hell in an elegant way that works together with other Dantesque references and phrases as a lovely example of *intertextualité*.[21]

One last objection remains to be dealt with in the Introduction to Day IV and Boccaccio does so in a way that not only highlights two very important parts of his overt frame system (frames three and four, those of the plague and of the ten protagonists' retreat) but also brings their reality into question. Those who object that his description of the life of the *cornice* is not accurate are challenged to produce the original facts so that the two versions may be compared. Boccaccio, the implied narrator,[22] is here refuting an objection to the facts in frame four by a reference to Boccaccio, the author, as a writer of fictions in frame one. The confrontation between the objectors and the author is ridiculous, given the fact that both are dealing in fictions. The whole Epimenides paradox is reposited thereby.[23] Furthermore, the status of the objectors themselves comes into question: they too may well be fictions, and we no longer know if their place is in frame one with the book's readers or with the ladies in frame two, the first posited frame of fiction, which is thereby placed in some doubt.

Finally, Boccaccio again uses metaphor (in itself a frame, as Bateson has shown) to turn his fictional world upside down: "For whatever happens, my fate can be no worse than that of the fine-grained dust, which, when a gale blows, either stays on the ground or is carried aloft, in which case it is frequently deposited upon the heads of men, upon the crowns of kings and emperors, and even upon high palaces and lofty towers, whence, if it should fall, it cannot sink lower than the place from which it was raised" (p. 331).[24] The idea of wind carrying the dust high over the heads of the greatest in the land would have given almost any medieval audience, more accustomed than we to this type of paradigmatic acrobatics, the clue for a simple substitution: to be on high is to sit in judgment, which is a far cry from the key of mere entertainment posited in frame two. God and nature then having been invoked to set the proper noble register, Boccaccio gathers up his audience, deftly pulls it into frame two by the use of the vocative "oh lovely ladies" and then into frame four: "but we must return, for we have wandered enough, oh lovely ladies, to where we started, and follow the order that we began."[25] It is as though he were reminding the ladies to get back into frame, except that it is the ladies of frame two who are invited into frame four.

The last act of the overt frame one is the Author's Epilogue. Again Boccaccio replies to objections that could be raised this time by audiences in both frames one and two. "There will perhaps be those among you who will say that in writing these stories I have taken too many liberties, in that I have sometimes caused ladies to say, and very often to hear, things which are not very suitable to be heard or said by virtuous women" (p. 829).[26] By the use of the Italian construction "to have ____ say" and "to have ____ do," the metanarrative statement is clearly made from frame one by Boccaccio, author, which is tantamount to accepting the *Decameron* as fiction, destroying the claims to reality made for frames three and four. The answer comes, in a sense, from frame five and gives the stories an existence of their own: "the facts of the stories required it," and Boccaccio could not have told them without changing their "form," which term is here used in its full scholastic sense. The defense is continued by a play between denotative and connotative language that seems to contrast two very different frames of reference.

And even if the stories do, perhaps, contain one or two trifling expressions that are too unbridled for the liking of those prudish ladies who attach more weight to words than to deeds, and are more anxious to seem virtuous than to be virtuous, I assert that it was no more improper for me to have written them than for men and women at large, in their everyday speech, to use such words as *hole*, and *rod*, and *mortar*, and *pestle*, and *crumpet*, and *stuffing*, and any number of others. Besides, no less latitude should be granted to my pen than to the brush of the painter, who without incurring censure, of a justified kind at least, depicts St. Michael striking the serpent with his sword or his lance, and St. George transfixing the dragon wherever he pleases; but that is not all, for he makes Christ male and Eve female, and fixes to the cross, sometimes with a single nail, sometimes with two, the feet of Him who resolved to die thereon for the salvation of mankind (pp. 829-830).[27]

First a series of expressions with obscene double meanings straight out of level five is given: "hole, spindle, mortar, pestle, sausage"; their use is then justified by the fact that painters show similar objects, such as swords and lances, in their paintings. This comparison constitutes a linking of metaphors that basically belong to quite different paradigms in any system other than that of obscenity. Again frames are being juggled, and this is extremely significant, since Boccaccio uses sex as a metaphor for the natural world as opposed to the artificial one created by the Church. The metaphoric play is then extended in what would constitute out-and-out blasphemy were it not for the protective frame of factual reality in which it is enclosed (what Goffman would call a "fabricated downkeying"): painters are said to paint Christ as a man and Eve as a woman and even to paint the nails in Christ's feet.

Having said all this, the author suddenly takes refuge in frames three and four, saying that these things were not told in church, to which one must always refer with respect even though its history contains scandals far worse than those in his tales, but in gardens among gay young people, and during the plague when all forms of behavior were allowed, including the inversion of wearing one's breeches on one's head. (There may be a reference to IX, 2, here.) There is also a neat possible reversal of frames: if church history is full of scandals worse than those of the tales, then the necessity of treating all church matters with respect becomes a fiction, or, at the very least, the stories in frame five are raised to the level of history. One is no longer sure how to key them. Boccaccio's next defense is based on just this: he claims his right to set the official key for his stories, and refuses to be responsible for the fact that some people miskey them as obscenity. He has meant them to be useful: "they will not deny usefulness and fruitfulness to those who seek such." This picks up a phrase from the Proem: "they [the ladies who read the stories] will be able to get useful advice." The usefulness is, however, reserved for the proper audience, no longer the ladies of frame two in the vocative, but a far broader one.

The frame then shifts abruptly: Boccaccio claims he had no choice about what stories he included, as he had to write those that were told. This sudden hiding within frame four and denial of the previously admitted fiction is followed by a hypothetical sentence of the if/then type (a classical way of denying), reinforced by a declarative disclaimer: "But even if one wanted to suppose that I had been both the inventor and the writer of those tales, which I was not, I say that I would not be ashamed if they were not all good."[28] The if/then clauses refer to the frame-one audience's suppositions, however, not to Boccaccio's writing. He then adds that no one but God does all things perfectly, and that there is no need for perfection, as he is merely talking to a (frame-two) audience of simple young women, a theme he elaborates at length. (To bring in God at this point and in this way is a frame break that reminds the reader of the social and worldly orientation of the book.) The whole careful reconstruction of the series of frames that has been equally carefully, albeit sporadically, demolished leads into a defense of the many jokes and puns in his tales by a comparison with the sermons of the clergy. Again there is a juxtaposition of two worlds in such a way as partly to equate them and also to extend the world of the stories in frame five into frame one, where a public polemic against the jokes and puns of the clergy had been going on since the previous century.[29] Those who do not like the tales are told to read Jeremiah, the Passion, or the repentance of the Magdalen, and here the frame of the Church is set up in clear opposition to that of the stories, a fact which takes on implications when one remembers that the group departed for the world of frame four from a church, and returned to a church from it, which leaves us with the implication that the Church is a gateway framing the world of the plague.

The last objection Boccaccio conjures up and deals with is that he has been indulging in malicious sayings about the religious brotherhood. He pardons those who say so on the grounds that they are quite right to defend the clergy, who are "decent fellows, who forsake a life of discomfort for the love of God, who do their grinding when the millpond's full, and say no more about it" (p. 833).[30] The first of these phrases echoes the most irreligious, if not anti-religious, story of the *Decameron*, that of Fra Cipolla,[31] and the second is an obscene *double entendre* repeated from the story of Monna Belcolore.[32] Frames one and five are thus once more equated, and the *Decameron* ends here, with the author's pious thanks to God and to his audience of ladies.

> Here ends the tenth and last day / of the book called *Decameron*, surnamed / Prince Galahalt.

The inscription comes *after* the author's conclusion, which is thereby framed as a valid and necessary part of the work. After all the frame play described, the reader is left in some doubt as to "what is going on here."

The Preface, Introduction to Day IV, and Author's Epilogue have been again treated at length because the play of frame shifts and breaks here is the most complex and the most illuminating as to Boccaccio's techniques. It is also the first frame, enclosing all the others, and as such will condition the reader's perception of each of them. Since a frame, by its very existence, marks off a world that has special semantic significance,[33] a series of frames raises the question of whether the semantic spaces are meant to play on each other or not as well as that of their meaning.

The device of a representation within a representation was commonly used by the medieval painters to whom Boccaccio compares himself. Uspensky, as I noted, pointed out that the background or frame representation will almost always be more conventional than the central one, which will consequently be more natural (p. 166). The immediate question that faces us as we turn to the third frame, the description of the plague, is whether it is frame or central episode. Its position hints at frame, for it opens the Introduction, but, as with all Boccaccio's major frames, there is no clear-cut answer. The description itself is prefaced by a long and frame-ambivalent discourse in frame two, in which the ladies are begged not to let themselves be put off by the horrid details, whose necessity is based on the vaguest of rhetorical and possibly Biblical grounds: the description will be like an arduous mountain climb leading to a pleasant plain, and bliss must always be mingled with sorrow. These reasons are perfectly consonant with the rhetoric of the times. The plague is thus actually presented as a frame. But the next statement is a very interesting metanarrative one: Boccaccio declares (in the vocative) that if he could have led the ladies to what he desires in any other way he would have done so, but that, since the reasons for which what is to be read later came about could not have been shown otherwise, he forces himself to write, constrained by necessity. The somewhat stilted prose and the play of tenses, which I have reproduced exactly and in order, creates an interesting play of time frames: the use of the present for Boccaccio's desire and the writing that ensues creates a synchronic point of view in which time seems to stop, enclosing Boccaccio and his readers on one plane. This enchances the importance of what is about to follow. It is an internal point of view, as opposed to the external one constituted by the verbs in the past, which represent the author contemplating what he has done. The statement also sets up a reason for the description that is opposed to the purely literary and rhetorical ones mentioned earlier. The description, which continues for about five fairly straightforward pages, is bracketed by metanarrative statements, for it ends with Boccaccio's comment that, filled with pity at describing so much misery, he will leave out as much of it as he properly can. Both metanarrative statements are, however, on the face of it, untrue: there is no necessity for the long description on the narrative plane, which could perfectly well have started out with a statement like "At the height of the late terrible plague ten young people met in the church of S. Maria Novella." The statements therefore create a frame that points to the plague description as being significant on some other plane, what Barthes calls a "connotator," or sign of another denoted system (p. 91). This is so clear that the whole description of the plague is suddenly seen to be a frame break (between frames two and four as a continuum) as well as a frame in itself.

In examining the description of the plague, it is necessary to ask whether its qualities point to its being of central or background importance in Uspensky's terms. As usual, the answer is ambivalent. The passage has been rightly praised for its realistic and moving eloquence; still, it is not original, but modeled as we have seen on Thucydides or on Paolo Diacono.[34] Branca suggests that it is an example of *imitatio* deliberately used to highlight the gravity of the subject. This would give the passage some elements of conventionality. Nevertheless, it is clearly keyed as reality, not as stereotypic conventionality. In the latter, it will be remembered, there is "an enhancement of the semiotic quality of the representation" (Uspensky, p. 162). This does not hold true for the description of the plague, but it definitely holds true for the *cornice*. "Accordingly the central figures . . . are opposed to the secondary figures by the fact that there is a lesser degree of semiotic quality or of conventionality in their description . . . the central figures . . . are . . . more lifelike" (p. 163). The plague is thus, despite what Uspensky would call its "semiotic" qualities as literary imitation, more realistic; the figures of the *cornice* are more conventional and better suited to a frame (or background), and the true central, or most realistic, figures—judging by Uspensky's canons and in line with the liminal, learning experience theory of this study—turn out to be the figures in the stories themselves. This is borne out by the work of Vittore Branca, who has shown that very many of the figures thought to be fictional, such as Cepparello in I, 1, and Salabaetto in VII, 10, actually existed. This evidence, too, points to the presence of a story beyond the story: a system somewhat like that of a narrative text sequentially divided into scenes like the frescoes of the time, each framed by a piece of *cornice*: "For example, in painting, a flat decorative background . . . contrasting with the three-dimensional figures in the central part gives the effect of live actors in front of painted scenery" (Uspensky, p. 156). In Goffman's terms, the plague and the stories are "downkeyed" toward reality.

In the pages describing the group and its life in the *cornice*, the frame play becomes a little more noteworthy than in the description of the plague. Frame four (that of the ten protagonists) is the only one not set off by a formal framing device such as the label "Preface" or "Introduction"; Boccaccio plunges into it in the same sentence that contains his metanarrative statement about the description of the plague:

> The more I reflect upon all this misery, the deeper my sense of personal sorrow; hence I shall refrain from describing those aspects which can suitably be omitted, and proceed to inform you that these were the conditions prevailing in our city, which was by now almost emptied of its inhabitants, when one Tuesday morning (or so I was told by a person whose word can be trusted) seven young ladies were to be found in the venerable church of Santa Maria Novella, which was otherwise almost deserted (p. 58).[35]

The tension on this level is between the conventionality of the characters and Boccaccio's metanarrative statements about them. The whole of frame four is framed in its turn by that old standby "as I heard from a trustworthy witness" (I, Intro., 49), which distances the author from the core of the *Decameron* (frame five) and also sets up a fiction-purporting-to-be-truth in contrast with the fiction-purporting-to-be-fiction in the Preface. (The Epimenides paradox that is a leit-motif of the work thereby reappears.)

The storytellers are conventional paragons of conventional virtues with very "semiotic" (in Uspensky's sense of the word) names about which the critics are still arguing. As was seen in Chapter III, the relations among them are likewise stylized versions of the extant doctrines of love. Boccaccio, however, comments that he will not give their real names because he does not wish the envious to speak ill of them. Though we do not know whether this is the author or the implied narrator speaking, it does contrast with the "semiotic" quality of the life of the group as described (and of the few physical descriptions given, which are again straight out of the love doctrines). This produces a frame ambiguity that continues throughout all the pages devoted to the group (the Introduction and the openings and conclusions of the various days). Much of the narrative is in direct discourse, so as to give a greater impression of actuality, but the tone of the speeches is as artificial as is the system of self-governance. The same is true of the descriptions of nature, which are very like the contemporary frescoes of "The Garden of Pleasure." The world of the plague has disappeared: Pampinea mentions it once when she first suggests a retreat to the country; then it is hardly seen anymore, even though the first distance given is two miles from the town (89).

There is one interesting detail:

> Pampinea's proposal was greatly to everyone's liking, and they unanimously elected her as their queen for the first day, whereupon Filomena quickly ran over to a laurel bush, for she had frequently heard it said that laurel leaves were especially worthy of veneration and that they conferred great honour upon those people of merit who were crowned with them. Having plucked a few of its shoots, she fashioned them into a splendid and venerable garland, which she set upon Pampinea's brow, and which thenceforth became the

outward symbol of sovereign power and authority to all the members of the company, for as long as they remained together (p. 65).[36]

When Filomena the wise thus crowns Pampinea, the first queen, with laurel, the act is a metaliterary one: the queen sets the story-telling, and the implication makes a statement about the stories. It is only one of several ways in which frame four alludes to or shifts to frame five. The most obvious frame shift is found in the openings of the conclusions to the various days. It is grammatically based: all these conclusions open with references to the previously told stories, and in seven of these "the story" is a subject in the first sentence.[37] Of the remaining three, the conclusions to VII and VIII contain the phrase "After _____ had finished his/her story" in the first sentence, and that to IX opens with the impersonal construction "let her who will still laugh at this story imagine how much it was laughed at,"[38] which also shifts frame to the audience of ladies in frame two. There are not many other frame shifts in these parts of the *cornice*, whose pattern is usually rather carefully repeated, though once Filostrato suggests that the group should imitate Alibech in putting the devil back into Hell (III, concl., 2).

Most of the exceptions are clustered around the end of Day V and the beginning and end of Day VI, at the center of the work. At the end of Day V, Dioneo, whose character is itself an exception within the group, refuses at first to sing the usual type of courtly *canzone* and suggests a whole series of obscene ones whose titles form a litany from a different register. There is also a series of frame shifts and frame breaks in the opening and conclusion of Day VI. This day is the only one that *opens* with a picture of the group discussing and laughing at the stories, and this shift into frame five is reinforced almost immediately by the episode of the quarrel between Tindaro and Licisca as to whether "Master Bludgeon entered Black Hill by force and with bloodshed or peacefully with the great pleasure of those

inside"[39] on Master Sycophant's wedding night. At the end
of the day Dioneo is chosen king and makes a self-reflexive
comment that there are better kings on the chessboard than
he. The comment is "engrossment-breaking" for it reminds
the reader that the "kingship system" on level four is keyed
as make-believe. The allusion to the *droit de seigneur* of real
kings (if the ladies would give him "real" obedience as a
king, he would have them enjoy that without which no
feast can be truly happy) reinforces the keying and also
serves as a change of register that causes a shift to frame
five. When Dioneo gives Licisca the ironic title "Donna"
in announcing that she had inspired his topic, a shift is
again obvious. The ladies then protest at the theme (tricks
played on husbands by their wives): it is as if they were
afraid of being drawn into the innermost frame, that of the
stories. Dioneo must reassure them by obviously making
frame again:

> "Ladies, I know as well as you do that the theme I
> have prescribed is a delicate one to handle; but I am
> not to be deterred by your objections, for I believe that
> the times we live in permit all subjects to be freely
> discussed, provided that men and women take care to
> do no wrong. Are you not aware that because of the
> chaos of the present age, the judges have deserted the
> courts, the laws of God and man are in abeyance, and
> everyone is given ample licence to preserve his life as
> best he may? This being so, if you go slightly beyond
> the bounds of decorum in your conversation, with the
> object, not of behaving improperly but of giving pleas-
> ure to yourselves and to others, I do not see how
> anyone in the future can have cause to condemn you
> for it.
>
> "Besides, it seems to me that this company of ours
> has comported itself impeccably from the first day to
> this" (p. 515).[40]

His reminder that their behavior has been exemplary re-
assures them and brings the narrative back into frame four.

But the reference to the plague as a frame within which ordinary behavior is inverted not only breaks the rule made in the Introduction that no one was to mention anything unpleasant from the outside world, which is in itself a frame, but also constitutes a shift to frame three. The conclusion of Day VI also contains the episode of the *valle delle donne* and at its end comes the frame-shifting statement by Pampinea "on this very day we have tricked you" and Dioneo's answer, "What, are you beginning with deeds before getting to words?"[41]

The conclusion to the tenth day would be expected to recapitulate the four innermost frames of the *Decameron* and in fact does so: the last story is discussed, then Panfilo reminds the group that it has been absent from plague-stricken Florence for fifteen days, living an exemplary life in spite of the lascivious stories and the good cheer, but that it might be difficult to continue this state of affairs for much longer, and that it is subject to interruption by out-siders (a frame-breaking fear that was also mentioned as a reason for moving on day two). The evening is then spent in the usual manner, and next day the group returns to Florence and disperses from the church in which it had gathered. The church thus forms a closing bracket for the experience of "the green world," a conceptual frame around the inner citadel of the *Decameron* that is repeatedly broken by the stories.

If it is true that Boccaccio deliberately demolished his elaborate frame system through breaks and shifts in order to leave his frame-one audience face-to-face with his frame-five stories and thereby draw them into the liminal expe-rience, there should be examples of frame breaks and frame shifts through which the stories reach back out to frames four through one. These breaks do exist and are in fact many and varied. An example from the more formal point of view is the use in a story of a *canzone* that has been found on its own in various manuscripts and was therefore prob-ably an extant one known to the times.[42] This connects frame five with frame one. Further examples can be found in the actual construction of the stories. The invariable pattern is that of an opening paragraph of commentary or moral or both, which also serves as a constant reminder of the presence of the narrators. The net effect is that the company of frame four seems to be pulled into frame five. It is usually left there: only twenty-nine of the stories end with a frame-making device like a reminder of the presence of the narrator or a moral; the other seventy-one end within the narrative itself. Another device serves to redirect the stories to the audience of frame two (the ladies for whom the book is ostensibly written): ninety of them open with a vocative such as "dear ladies" or "valorous ladies," bypassing the narrating group by leaving out the three young men.[43] Finally, the work is formally divided into ten days, and there is no change in the rubric ("The _____ day ends, the _____ day begins")[44] between the second and third and the seventh and eighth days, in spite of the group's decision to omit storytelling on Fridays and Saturdays. The rubrics thus belong entirely to frame two, Boccaccio's tale about the *Decameron* and his reasons for writing it.

The other frame breaks fall into two categories: those that shift frame between four and five (usually, but not always, set up to pull the narrators into the world of the stories), and those that shift frame back out to one and two. Shifts in the first category are of various types. There are some outright metanarrative comments made by one of the group, such as Lauretta's comparison of her story and that of Pampinea:

> Fairest ladies, it is in my opinion impossible to envisage a more striking act of Fortune than the spectacle of a person being raised from the depths of poverty to regal status, which is what happened, as we have been shown by Pampinea's story, in the case of her Alessandro. And since, from now on, nobody telling a story on the prescribed subject can possibly exceed those limits, I shall not blush to narrate a tale which, whilst it contains greater misfortunes, does not how-

ever possess so magnificent an ending. I realize of
course, when I think of the previous story, that my
own will be followed less attentively. But since it is
the best I can manage, I trust that I shall be forgiven
(p. 136).[45]

Similar examples are the frequent comments by a narrator
that his or her story cannot match the quality of those
already told. By thus commenting in frame terms on the
stories, the narrators of frame four acquire a certain degree
of reality at the expense of that of the stories themselves:
"It should be noted that when a character comments on a
whole episode of activity *in frame terms*, he acquires a peculiar reality . . ." (Goffman, p. 400). This serves to blur
the distinction between the narrators and the stories that
was set up by making frame four so stylized and artificial,
but it should be noted that it occurs only within the formal
framework of frame five and thus begins the chain reflection of that frame back toward frames two and one without
seriously impairing the stylized quality of frame four. The
best example is Dioneo's statement "I shall tell you a little
tale . . . which, albeit much of it will strain your credulity,
should nevertheless prove entertaining in parts" (p. 580).[46]

There are also many examples of shifts brought about
by the use of frame-five stories as signifiers in frame four.
A typical case is Filostrato's already cited suggestion that
the group imitate Alibech. A more complex example is
Dioneo's praise in III, 4, 2, of Filomena's prayer (at the end
of III, 3) that the *cornice*'s characters may have many nights
like those enjoyed by the lovers in the tale. Similar prayers
that frame-five results will operate in frame four are frequent. (A reversed version of the same frame-shifting device is Filostrato's announced envy of Guiscardo and Ghismonda's love in IV, 2: "I would think it a small price to
pay if I were to give my life in exchange for one half of the
bliss Ghismonda had with Guiscardo. Nor should any of
you consider this surprising, because I die a thousand deaths
in the course of every hour that I live, without being granted

the tiniest portion of bliss in return" (p. 342),[47] after which he makes frame again with the reflexive comment "But leaving my affairs to take care of themselves for the moment . . ."). The many discussions of stories by the group mentioned within the openings of following stories, as well as the frequent use of the adjective "useful," are frame breaks that underline the impression that the group is there to learn: thus the two examples of stories within stories (I, 3, and I, 7) are not only clearly teaching devices but they also tend to blur frames. What Uspensky would call the highly semiotic quality of the audience in frame four could therefore be explained not only by its being a sign of the "real audience" in frame one, which is to learn from the stories as we have seen, but also as a device that functions to abolish the distinction between frames. The idea of a story within or about a story is itself a frame-reflexive device.

Devices from the second category (which shift frame back out to frames one and two) are also plentiful. When the narrators break into their own stories with general comments on the life of their times, they are essentially dealing with frame one. It is one of the most effective devices for demolishing the whole frame system and reminding the reader of the book's purpose. There are several of these comments, which may be long, as in the diatribe against the clergy in IV, 2, or brief, as in the parenthetical comment on Rome "which as it was once the head is now the tail of the world." The most remarkable example in frame terms is Lauretta's long interruption of her story:

> Now, it so happened that whilst this fellow, by spending not a penny, was busily increasing his fortune, there arrived in Genoa a worthy courtier, Guglielmo Borsiere by name, who was refined of manner and eloquent of tongue, altogether different from the courtiers of today. For to the eternal shame of those who nowadays lay claim, despite their corrupt and disgraceful habits, to the title and distinction of lords

145

and gentlemen, our modern courtiers are better described as asses, brought up, not in any court, but on the dungheap of all the scum of the earth's iniquities. In former times, their function usually consisted, and all their efforts were expended, in making peace whenever disputes or conflicts arose between two nobles, negotiating treaties of marriage, friendship or alliance, restoring tired minds and amusing the courts with fine and graceful witticisms, and censuring the failings of miscreants with pungent, fatherly strictures, all of which they would do for the slenderest of rewards. Whereas nowadays they spend the whole of their time in exchanging scandal with each other, sowing discord, describing acts of lewdness and ribaldry, or worse still, practising them in the presence of gentlemen. Or else they will justly or falsely accuse one another of wicked, disgusting, and disreputable conduct, and entice noble spirits with false endearments to do what is evil and sinful. And the man who is held in the greatest esteem, who is most highly honoured and richly rewarded by our base and wretched nobles, is the one whose speech and actions are the most reprehensible. All of which is greatly and culpably to the shame of the modern world, and proves very clearly that the present generation has been stripped of all the virtues, and left to wallow abjectly in a cesspit of vices.

But to return to what I had begun to say before my righteous anger carried me somewhat further astray than I had intended . . . (pp. 104-105).[48]

The interruption is doubly underlined by the frame-making comment "but to return to what I had begun to say."

The use of proverbs, very frequent in the *Decameron*, also connects frames one and five. Often a general frame-one proverb or saying is used in a story, as is the case for "the paternoster of St. Julian." More interesting cases are those in which a frame-five story is said to become proverbial and subsequently work as a signifier in frame one, like the proverb at the end of the story of Alatiel (II, 7): "And that is why people said 'A kissed mouth doesn't lose its luck, but renews itself like the moon,' " or the expression "to put the devil back into hell": ". . . and they coined a proverbial saying there to the effect that the most agreeable way of serving God was to put the devil back in Hell. The dictum later crossed the sea to Italy, where it survives to this day" (p. 319).[49] There are also reflections from frame five to both frames four and one in comments such as that in X, 7, 2, that the Ghibellines in the group did not relish the praise of King Charles of Anjou. Among the functionally most important are those that seek to show that the stories recount actual facts, either through numerous frame setting formulas such as "there was, in our own city" or "as worthy persons told me" or by open assertions, such as Fiammetta's that not to tell the absolute truth in stories detracts from the pleasure of the listeners: "I shall venture to add a further tale to those we have already heard about him. I could easily have told it in some other way, using fictitious names, had I wished to do so; but since by departing from the truth of what actually happened, the storyteller greatly diminishes the pleasure of his listeners, I shall turn for support to my opening remarks, and tell it in its proper form" (p. 701).[50] This kind of statement, of course, brings in the Epimenides paradox again. In this connection it should be mentioned that, with the exception of Boccaccio's already discussed direct remarks, he maintains a strictly external point of view in frames three, four, and five, apparently disappearing from the work. Even his own metaliterary remarks are disguised, like the one in IX, 5, 2, that the group neither praised nor laughed much at the preceding story. There is one exception, however, when he speculates that the ladies sighed as much for Alatiel's good fortune in having so many wedding nights as for pity: ". . . but who knows what their motives may have been? Perhaps some of them were sighing, not so much because they felt sorry for Alatiel, but because they longed to be married no less often than she was. However, leaving this question aside . . ." (p. 191).[51] The speculation is introduced by the general phrase "who knows what caused those sighs," in which the pronoun opens the frame to the widest possible audience.

So far I have dealt with the shifts and breaks operating in the major frames of the *Decameron*. Space does not allow a detailed examination of the actual stories, but as one of the main points of this chapter is the ambiguity generated by Boccaccio's use of frame shifts and breaks, at least two stories, the first and the last, will be briefly looked at. In a sense the first and the last enclose all the other stories in the reader's mind and they may thus be considered important parts of the framing system. The first tale, that of Ser Cepparello, turns on the frame of confession, part of whose psychological essence rests on the implied statement "all statements within this frame are true," the exact opposite of Bateson's model. As it turns out, that particular frame is what Goffman calls a fabrication, and the situation of the two usurers is saved only by the containment (Goffman's term for successful deception within a certain frame) of all those who believe in the sacred truth of confessions. At the same time, the events in the story are framed by a set of pious statements, at the beginning and at the conclusion, on the mysterious ways in which God's mercy works. The question as to whether this is ironic will probably never be settled, and the story's ambiguity is largely due to the framing statements.

The last tale, that of the supremely patient Griselda, has also given rise to mixed reactions, ranging from Petrarch's unstinted admiration to some modern readers' baffled rage that the *Decameron* could end this way after seeming so often to argue for a more dignified status for women in terms ranging from the bawdy story of Madonna Filippa da Prato (VI, 7) to that of Tancredi and Ghismonda (IV, 1).[52] Griselda is the low-born wife of the Marquis of Saluzzo, who, urged by his subjects to marry and produce heirs, chooses her because of her beauty and good manners. Before marrying her, he exacts her promise to obey

him absolutely in all things. He then has her stripped naked
in public and dressed again in noble garments before the
public wedding ceremony. She proves to be a perfect and
noble wife and soon her reputation for virtue of all kinds
and his for wisdom in having chosen her spread far beyond
the confines of the marquisate. Griselda bears her husband
a female child and, in order to test her, he first treats her
with great harshness, and then tells her that his subjects
are dismayed at her low birth, especially now that she has
proved herself fertile. She bears all this with humble patience, and even when he sends a servant to fetch the child,
supposedly with orders to kill it, she bows her head and
gently agrees that her husband's will be done. She then
bears a son, and the same thing happens. Griselda does
not even complain to her own ladies-in-waiting. Several
years later, Gualtieri pretends that the Pope has annulled
the marriage and, again publicly, commands her to return
to her sheepherder father with the same dowry that she
brought to her wedding. Griselda nobly restrains her tears
and asks only that he give her a shift in exchange for the
virginity she brought to the marriage, rather than driving
her naked from the house. Shortly thereafter, he commands her to act as maid in preparing a reception for his
new bride. Again she agrees with the utmost docility, and
greets the presumed new bride as her lady with a fair mien,
even praising the girl when Gualtieri solicits her opinion.
He thereupon condescends to explain to her his wisdom
in doing all that he has done in order to teach her to be a
good wife, and reveals that the girl is their daughter, and
that their son is still alive. Everyone is now content, and
they live happily ever after, Gualtieri presumably basking
in his reputation for wisdom.

It is a puzzling story. On the surface, as Petrarch's reaction to it shows, it is a perfect medieval *exemplum* (indeed,
I can think of few tales better calculated to encourage women
to eschew matrimony and embrace the holy life in a con-
vent). But if, as De' Negri suggests, Boccaccio was using
Ser Cepparello's exaggerated wickedness to poke fun at

149

the genre, it is just as likely that he was doing the same in this equally exaggerated tale of the virtue of Madam Griselda (this is a point that De' Negri may not have considered sufficiently when he analyzed the story's stylistic and artistic merits as a "mystery" in a "liturgical mode" [p. 189]). In this sense, both the first and the last tales of the *Decameron* may carry a lesson on exaggeration. The first has a built-in warning in the clear balance between the incredible virtue of the self-created saint and the equally hard-to-believe wickedness of his creator; in the second, the lesson need not be so obvious, for the initiands should by now have learned a great deal and the exaggeration itself may serve as a metacommunicative message stating "this is not true."[53] It is very tempting to speculate that what Dioneo characterizes as Gualtieri's "senseless brutality"[54] and the exasperatingly senseless patience of his wife are meant as a lesson to counteract Filomena's and Elissa's arguments on the superiority of men in the Introduction, but there is not enough evidence to support such a theory.

In terms of framing, the story of Griselda is the opposite of I, 1, in that, instead of being bracketed by two framing statements, it is bracketed by two notable frame breaks. As soon as the story of Torello and the Sultan ends, Dioneo opens his turn by laughing and saying that the good man who was waiting to lower the ghost's rigid tail wouldn't have cared a snap for Messer Torello's liberality. The obscene allusion (to VII, 1, 27ff.) is not only out of place within the day's grandiloquent theme but makes no real sense, except perhaps as a clumsy effort to contrast the abstract pleasures of liberality with certain other pleasures. The most likely interpretation is that it is meant to be a frame break that will begin to undermine what is to come. Since the story of Griselda is also that of the "senseless brutality" of the Marquis of Saluzzo, it is in part a theme that breaks the frame for the day, as is Dioneo's custom, and also breaks the frame of the kind of tale that we have come to expect from him. It is couched in sufficiently high-minded and eloquent terms to have persuaded Petrarch to translate it into Latin and circulate it throughout Europe. Yet this pearl of a medieval *exemplum* has a rather odd ending:

> What more needs to be said, except that celestial spirits may sometimes descend even into the houses of the poor, whilst there are those in royal palaces who would be better employed as swineherds than as rulers of men? Who else but Griselda could have endured so cheerfully the cruel and unheard of trials that Gualtieri imposed upon her without shedding a tear? For perhaps it would have served him right if he had chanced upon a wife, who, being driven from the house in her shift, had found some other man to shake her skin-coat for her, earning herself a fine new dress in the process (p. 834).[55]

After two high-flown, elaborately antithetical rhetorical questions, Boccaccio does not close frame five (the core of the *Decameron*) with the expected third rhetorical question. The story ends with the comment that it would not perhaps have harmed the marquis to have met a lady who, on being thrown out in her shift, would have found another man to so shake her bush that something nice would have come of it ("una bella roba"—there is a pun on dress involved). The change of theme and register blows the noble frame of the tenth day stories wide open, and frame ambiguity once more proves to be the keynote of the *Decameron*. Again, consciously or unconsciously, the material within the stories rebels against the courtly values aimed at by the author and narrator/protagonists in setting the theme.

~ CONCLUSION ~

THE RICH AMBIGUOUSNESS of the *Decameron* is perhaps the only quality about which critics will not continue to argue. All texts are the offspring of the worlds in which they are born and into which they are reborn each time they are read. By their very nature as texts, their communication is governed both by the sender and by the receiver. Senders and receivers are in turn influenced by their cultural models. A text born in a transitional period and read over six hundred years later, during what may well prove to be another transitional crisis, therefore offers doubly interesting semiotic possibilities.

> . . . those models which may be seen projected into or reflected out of the work are historical, in the sense of culture bound, period specific, and not explicative but rather *implicative*. . . . they do not explain the work but, on the contrary, build further implications into it, and are interpretants in the Peircian sense,—signs or sign systems used to translate a discourse into another, to transform the first text into a second text. . . . By offering several different (but not randomly chosen) models, criticism can suggest possible paths of reading, translating, reorganizing, making use of, and interpreting the text without imposing a single center of perspective or constraining the text into one closed set or frame of reference. The critic can, in this manner, open the text to the extratextual, to cultural reality, and still render it incomplete and expose the critical discourse itself as a new assemblage of semiotic possibilities.[1]

This is of course true of any text, but it seems especially true of the *Decameron*, perhaps because it is so very definitely what Thomas Greene called "a polyvalent and poly-

152

vocal text"[2] which is in turn due at least in part to the fact that its cultural matrix was equally polyvalent. The whole unusually varied history of *Decameron* criticism stands as evidence of the extraordinary richness of this book's interaction with its successive centuries of readers.

The foregoing chapters are meant to add to the ongoing discussions and enrich them. My intention is more to build further implications into the text than to attempt to present definitive answers to all the problems examined. These pages are thus to be read as polyvalent hypotheses. Literary criticism stands in a relationship that can best be described as symbiotic with the works it examines, and any reductive approach to a text is self-serving rather than serving that text, as it should.

The *Decameron* reflects the human world, and like that world does not easily lend itself to any one interpretation. The only fact that can be stated with perfect confidence is that the *Decameron* is a political book, in the original sense of the word, deriving from Aristotle's characterization of the human being as a *zoon politikon*, naturally created to live in association with other human beings. *Cornice* and stories alike deal with human interactions on all levels, from the public to the intimate, and in all kinds of situations, from the farcical to the tragic. The fivefold structure of the book can thus be read from a very social point of view as representing (1) the interaction between the *Decameron*, its author, and its readers, based on the latter's presumptive accusation that the book may have a corrupting influence and on Boccaccio's defense of its usefulness to society; (2) the author's claim to be writing because "to take pity on people in distress is a human quality which every person should possess" and to be doing so for a repressed social class, ladies afflicted by love; (3) the pivotal description of a society in a state of breakdown that serves as a justification for the writing of the work; (4) the description not only of a liminal ritual but also of a minicommonalty with a definite social hierarchy and clearly defined systems of government set up within the liminal space, and (5) as a highly varied but intensely human world of social interactions in which not a single story of the hundred deals with only one human protagonist operating on his or her own without interpersonal contacts and obligations of one sort or another.

The book's political or social aim governs all the ideas in this study. As an actively involved citizen of Florence, Boccaccio naturally dedicated the major work of his maturity to the study of society. As an intelligent citizen witnessing the slow erosion, after 1340, of "the easy-going laissez-faire rule of a secure urban patriciate . . . characterized by the confidence, or at least the hope, that men could be persuaded by example and rhetoric to follow the dictate of reason in their quest for the highest good,"[3] and then seeing the economic crisis and finally the breakdown of society in the face of the terrible ravages of the plague of 1348, it was equally logical that he should have written his book for the guidance of future leaders and that he should have done so in terms that can be seen to reflect many universal characteristics of the liminal rituals that come into play among societies at crucial turning points in their development as well as in individual lives and at moments of general crisis. As a firm believer in the power of literature and of the word in general, it was natural that he should have considered discourse a valid weapon in attacking an institution based on discourse, which had failed in its social role. As a humanist living during the great era of Florentine civic humanism, he inevitably had faith in the importance of letters and used them to make an effective contribution to his society. It was equally fitting that, as an urban citizen and a Florentine, he should have used humor to temper that contribution.

The stylistic and structural systems Boccaccio used similarly reflect the book's social aims. Its main device is the use of storytelling among a group. Its fivefold, center-protected structure is like that of a city surrounded by a series of fortifications (Florence had only recently enclosed the church of Santa Maria Novella within its third circle of walls)[4] or of one of the castles that functioned as miniature cities in time of war, protecting not only the lord and his immediate family but also all his dependents, a self-supporting mini-state that encompassed what Leon Battista Alberti was later to describe as a "family."

The less obvious devices and subcodes also have their social side. Parallel metanarrative framing structures are used to convey a warning about the corruption of the Church viewed as a social institution. The contrast in life styles and to some extent in literary styles between the *cornice* protagonists and the protagonists of the stories points up the utility of the varied life of the latter and their central position as the main content of the learning experience. It also reflects the changing and to some extent conflicting cultural models of a society in transition.

Finally, the carefully constructed series of frames and frame breaks that both protects the stories and leads the reader into more direct contact with them emphasizes the fact that the content to be learned by the protagonists of the *cornice* (knowledge of the world) is equally to be learned by the readers of the *Decameron,* who are thus led to share in the training for leadership and responsible civic behavior on the upper levels of society. The latinate syntax and rather difficult vocabulary together make it stylistically clear that the book was by no means meant for an audience on the level of the *popolo minuto,* but for an educated (oligarchic?) group.

The ambiguity that is such a marked characteristic of the book on its various levels is in great part due to the fact that it reflects the transitional and crisis-torn social matrix from which it came. An eighteenth-century or Victorian novel based on the cultural model of the English aristocracy or upper middle class could never be as varied or as ambiguous simply because the life from and into which it was born was not nearly so varied, dynamic, complicated and changing as the society of fourteenth-century Italy and in particular of Florence at the peak of the first stage of the Renaissance.

~ NOTES ~

INTRODUCTION

1. Robert Hollander, *Boccaccio's Two Venuses*, p. 6.

2. The critical literature on the *Decameron* is mountainous and I will not attempt to list it all here. Good summaries may be found in Aldo Scaglione, *Nature and Love in the Late Middle Ages*, especially pp. 48-53 and 173-177; Carlo Muscetta, *Giovanni Boccaccio*, which has an annotated bibliography; Guido Almansi, *The Writer as Liar: Narrative Technique in the Decameron*, especially pp. 1-62, and in the notes in Hollander's book. See also the *Bollettini Bibliografici* in *Studi sul Boccaccio*; Vol. VI (1971) lists "Boccaccio Studies in English" on pp. 211-229. Another source is Cesare De Michelis, "Rassegna Boccacciana—Dieci Anni di Studi" in *Lettere Italiane* 25 (1973), 88-129. One of the best is Enzo Esposito, *Boccacciana: Bibliografia delle edizioni e degli scritti critici*, con la collaborazione di Christopher Kleinhenz. The 1614 entries are indexed by subject as well as author and some reviews are indicated. See also Vittore Branca's bibliographical review article "Boccaccio e le tradizioni letterarie," in *Il Boccaccio nelle culture e letterature nazionali*, pp. 473-496. A collection of essays in English may be found in *Critical Perspectives on the Decameron*, ed. R. S. Dombroski. It includes essays by Foscolo, De Sanctis, Branca, Petronio, Šklovsky, Auerbach, De' Negri, Moravia, Greene, and Mazzotta. The edition of the *Decameron*, translated and edited by Mark Musa and Peter Bondanella, also contains critical excerpts by writers contemporary to Boccaccio and by some modern critics: Foscolo, De Sanctis, Scaglione, Wayne Booth, Todorov, Robert Clements, Auerbach, Marga Cottino-Jones, Ben Lawton, and the editors.

The naturalist thesis has best been argued by Aldo Scaglione. Robert Hollander tends to read the work as a warning against the dangers of the flesh. The aesthetic approach is De Sanctis'; the idea of the paean to intelligence was proposed by Umberto Bosco in *Il Decamerone* and followed up by G. Petronio, *Il Decamerone*. The pure entertainment thesis is Auerbach's, and the theory of the *Decameron* as a mercantile epic is presented in Vittore

Branca's *Boccaccio Medievale*. All references to *Boccaccio Medievale* are to the 1970 edition. A specially revised edition appeared in English as *Boccaccio: The Man and His Works*, trans. R. Monges and D. McAuliffe. The first ten chapters are a detailed life of the author, followed by four abbreviated and revised chapters from the original.

Critics who have studied the *Decameron* as metaliterature include Guido Almansi, *The Writer as Liar*, pp. 29ff.; Giuseppe Mazzotta, "The *Decameron*: The Marginality of Literature," *University of Toronto Quarterly*, 42, 1 (Fall 1972), 64-81, hereafter "Marginality" (the quotation is from p. 64), and Millicent Marcus, who has a similar point of view in "Ser Ciappelletto: A Reader's Guide to the *Decameron*," *The Humanities Association Review*, 26, 4 (Fall 1975), 275-288. A revised version is in her *An Allegory of Form: Literary Self-Consciousness in the Decameron*, pp. 11-26.

3. Critical interpretations are a product of their times, and Boccaccio criticism faithfully reflects the changing intellectual fashions. The more modern of these go from the eighteenth century's approach to the text as history, along with that anti-clerical period's praise of the *Decameron*'s moral freedom, to the Romantic accusations of lack of spirituality and of civic feeling. Further fashions reflect—among others—the positivist school's diligent hunt for sources, the Crocean search for the work's aesthetic unity and the Marxist analysis of the Boccaccian world. There is also the dissection of the stories' grammar carried out by Todorov in 1969 (*Grammaire du Décaméron*). The drawbacks of his approach are studied by R. Barilli in "Semiologia e retorica nella lettura del *Decameron*," *Il Verri*, 35-36 (1970), 27-48. For histories of Boccaccio criticism see V. Branca, *Linee di una storia della critica al Decameron*, and G. Petronio, "Giovanni Boccaccio" in *I classici italiani nella storia della critica*, I, 173-236. A good, brief summary may be found in G. Petronio, "I Volti del *Decameron*," in *Boccaccio: Secoli di Vita*, pp. 107-124. The positivist hunt for sources has produced some useful work, notably A. Lee Collingwood's *The Decameron: Its Sources and Analogues*. Branca cites all known sources for the *Decameron* tales in his edition.

4. For a sampling of opposing attitudes, see Charles S. Singleton, "On Meaning in the *Decameron*," *Italica* 21 (1944), 117-124, and N. Sapegno, "Il Boccaccio" in *Il Trecento*, pp. 281-404; Giovanni Getto, "La cornice e le componenti espressive," in *Vita di forme e forme di vita nel Decamerone*, pp. 1-33, and Carlo Muscetta's

Giovanni Boccaccio. See also Carlo Salinari, "L'empirismo ideologico del Boccaccio," in *La critica della letteratura italiana,* pp. 363-370, and T. K. Seung, "The Boccaccian Tour de Force," in *Cultural Thematics,* pp. 193-225, or Hollander's book.

5. Paul Zumthor, *Essai de poétique médiévale,* p. 11, translation mine.

6. See Branca, *Boccaccio Med.* and Padoan's seminal essay "Mondo aristocratico e mondo comunale nell'ideologia e nell'arte di Giovanni Boccaccio," *Studi sul Boccaccio* 2 (1964), 81-216.

7. I shall use the Italian expression *cornice* to refer to the frame tale usually described by that term, reserving the terms "frame" and "framing system" for more specialized meanings described below.

8. The *cornice* of the *Decameron* has come in for its share of critical attention. It has been seen as a decorative framework that serves to distance the writer from his material and thus allows him to dominate it, as well as an ideal of aristocratic life and manners whose impetus is nostalgic. This theory is Mario Baratto's in *Realtà e stile nel Decameron.* He sees the protagonists' withdrawal to the country as a seeking of refuge that symbolizes retirement from the real world. Baratto's thesis, which is probably grounded in Eugenio Garin's theories on renaissance humanism, is that the *Decameron* is bipolar and that its literary combination of architectonic frame and openness of form in the stories reflects the instability of the world and man's efforts to dominate it (pp. 11-68). See also Cesare Segre: "The '*cornice*' represents, in a variety of ways, the extra-temporality (allegorico-mythical in the *Ameto,* nature-oriented and courtly in the *Decameron*) from which the stories stem. . . . The '*cornice*' represents the world of possibility, of primary evocative disposition: ready to take on a time and a rhythm, to distend itself in a real space and also ready to contain the variety of events and things evoked and to return them to a contemplative serenity" (*Lingua, stile e società,* p. 303, translation mine). Another frequently adhered to theory is seen in R. Ramat's intelligently argued essay on the *cornice* as an ideological opposition of civilized and civic-minded life to the communal dissolution resulting from the plague ("Indicazioni per una lettura del *Decameron,*" in *Saggi sul Rinascimento,* pp. 37-49).

Hans-Jörg Neuschäfer sees the *Decameron* as a showcase for the paradox of man's simultaneous *dignitas* and *miseria.* He contrasts the disorder and misery of the plague with the order and elegance of the life led by the ten protagonists, a contrast that is said to express the dialectic between human limitations and human possibilities, as do the stories. The two worlds would thus reflect each other. It is one of the relatively few views that stress the unity of the whole; until comparatively recently the *cornice* was seen as a means of conferring an exterior artistic unity on the *Decameron*, rather than as an integral part of the work. Neuschäfer also points out that, while the idea of a frame is not new but conforms to medieval aesthetics and derives from a well-established oriental tradition, the *Decameron cornice* is more modern, as it has no plot and no clear-cut ending. The typical frame tale as found in the *Thousand and One Nights* or *Il libro dei sette savi* has a beginning, a plot of which the tales are a functional part, and an end. See *Boccaccio und der Begin der Novelle: Strukturen der Kurzerzählung auf der Schwelle zwischen Mittelalter und Neuzeit*, pp. 122-135.

The fundamental essay on the *cornice* as a purely aesthetic unifying factor is that of S. Battaglia, "Schemi lirici nell'arte del Boccaccio," originally published in 1935, now in *La coscienza letteraria del medioevo*, pp. 625-644. Battaglia also argues that the idea of the *cornice*, already present in the *Filocolo* and the *Ninfale d'Ameto*, is designed to "justify the lyric unity of the work" (p. 637). His view is that the protagonists have fled a society in dissolution for an ideal and idyllic space and that their lack of individuality is due to the author's desire not to disturb the quiet they have chosen—because they deliberately propose to exile themselves from real life—la vita empirica—(p. 638). Battaglia calls theirs a "magic condition." The essay is seminal for the theory of Getto (who holds that the *cornice* lifestyle and other elements of the *Decameron* stem from the author's nostalgia for past times), probably for that of Bárberi-Squarotti (for whom see below) and to some extent for certain aspects of Branca's *Boccaccio Med.* One of the several expansions and variations on Battaglia's theme is Antonio Prete's idea that the *cornice* is a narrative metaphor of the function of art. "La cornice del *Decameron*," in *La distanza da Croce*, pp. 253-294. Lucia Marino has expanded on this in her *The Decameron Cornice: Allusion, Allegory and Iconology*. The book is divided into two parts, "Point of View in the Cornice" and "Allegorical and Metaphorical Dimensions of the *Cornice*: A Humanist Tapestry." The first part argues that "cognitive and esthetic distance are reified in the *cornice*" (p. 49), and in the second Marino (influenced by the work

of Eliade) studies certain symbols and rituals that point to Boccaccio's concept of the nature and social functions of art and its
relation to certain fundamental ethical and civic virtues. She also
examines the *cornice* in the light of medieval virtues-and-vices
cycles.

Vittore Branca, the present-day dean of Boccaccio studies, believes that the *cornice* is an ideal parallel to the structure of the
hundred stories, both beginning in tragedy, misery, and squalor
and ending in happiness, serenity and virtue. He has recently
reaffirmed this belief: the *Decameron* is a typically medieval "representation of an ideal human itinerary that goes from the harsh
and bitter reproof of vices in the first day . . . to the splendid
eulogy of virtues in the tenth day" (Introduction, *Tutte le Opere
di Giovanni Boccaccio*, Vol. IV, *Decameron*, p. xvii. All references to
and Italian quotations from the *Decameron* are taken from this
edition with the kind permission of Arnoldo Mondadori, Editore,
which I hereby acknowledge. With the exception of the rubrics,
they follow the standard system of numeration). F. Neri had a
similar theory. See "Il disegno ideale del *Decameron*," in *Storia e
poesia*, pp. 71-82. Most recently, Joan M. Ferrante, too, has come
to a similar conclusion after analyzing the moral patterns in the
arrangement of the stories. "Narrative Patterns in the *Decameron*,"
Romance Philology 31 (1978), 585-604.

Another critic, Giorgio Bárberi-Squarotti, has suggested that
the *cornice*'s true function is to assert social and legal order after
the apocalypse of the plague. Neither of these two theories is
completely satisfying, however. Branca's in particular does not
account for the fact that the protagonists do not necessarily lead
happy, serene, virtuous lives at the end of the book, but are
returned to the world of the plague and disperse without the
reader's having any idea what becomes of them. There is also
room for doubt that the tales of the Tenth Day, so different in
tone and atmosphere from the others, are meant to be purely a
splendid eulogy of virtue. Almansi has noted "a number of doubtful examples of saintly behaviour in the Tenth Day" (p. 13). Bárberi-Squarotti's idea is somewhat more convincing. His thesis is
that the *Decameron* places the frame characters in a "privileged"
situation, a Robinson Crusoe's island of serene and perfectly functioning laws amidst the storm of events, from which they will
return as the bearers of a new social order. "The relationship
between the *cornice* and the stories then . . . is of a structural and

ideological nature: it is part of the total interpretation that Boccaccio gives us in his work, of the myth of a world to be rebuilt after the collapse, of the palingenesis . . . of the human world, that for him is essentially the reconstruction of the signs of an exemplary ordering of social and civic life through the power of the word which governs and regulates actions" ("La 'cornice' del *Decameron* o il mito di Robinson," in *Da Dante al Novecento, Studi offerti a G. Getto*, p. 158).

We now know that Boccaccio was quite active in the civic life of Florence, and that he must have been very much aware of the financial, economic, and social crises that began in the 1320s and culminated in the uprising of *i Ciompi* in 1378. The discord and struggles between classes and parties and between the greater and the lesser guilds could not be ignored by any citizen of the town. There is no basis, then, for believing that Boccaccio was an ivory-tower poet who envisioned a purely literary palingenesis or that the message of the stories lies in their cataloguing and ordering of the world. (For a complete and comprehensive essay on Boccaccio's life and times, see Branca's introductory "Profilo biografico," in *Tutte le Opere*, Vol. I, pp. 3-197, his *Giovanni Boccaccio—Profilo biografico*, or Chapters I-X in *Boccaccio, The Man and His Works*.)

A useful summary of some of the major schools of thought on the *cornice* may be found in Pier Luigi Cerisola, "La questione della *cornice* del *Decameron*," in *Aevum*, 49, 1-2 (1975), 137-156. Cerisola himself concludes that the *cornice* has no organic function in the book and that it is "extraneous . . . both on the plane of Art and . . . on that of Ethics" (capitalization his). I am indebted to Alberto Mancini for calling this article to my attention.

9. Umberto Eco, *A Theory of Semiotics*, p. 59.

10. I have deliberately limited the sources cited in this book to those works that gave me clear and definite insights into the nature and purpose of the *Decameron* and have tried to avoid the temptations of scholarly excursus into related anthropological and sociological works.

11. Branca suggests that these pages are there because the *Decameron* is ideally a comedy in the medieval sense of the word: they furnish the "fetid and horrible beginning" from which a happy ending is to be achieved. (The quotation is from Dante's letter about the Comedy.) Viktor Šklovsky theorizes that the actual conflict in the *Decameron's* plot, its "semantic drift," is

crystallized in the plague, which determines new social relations (*Lettura del Decameron: Dal Romanzo d'avventura al romanzo di carattere*, p. 281). This explanation is made doubtful by an examination of the patterns of behavior governing the ten protagonists and their servants, as well as by the general lack of social equality in the stories (one has only to think of Cisti the baker, who keeps his impressive human dignity carefully to his own class level). Lucia Marino interprets it as an allegory of bad government in a virtues and vices cycle (pp. 123-140). Most critics have agreed that the description depicts the breakdown of society, its rules and its laws, and leave it at that. Others, including some of the stature of Ugo Foscolo and Giovanni Getto, have essentially avoided the issue by stating that the description exists for purely aesthetic reasons of contrast.

12. The communal society described by Branca and Padoan.

13. This term derives from the work of Erving Goffman and will be discussed in Chapter V.

14. I use the term "code" in the sense that Umberto Eco gave to it: a conventionally agreed upon correlation between signs and contents. See Chapter III, note 7, for a detailed explanation.

15. See Natalino Sapegno's notes in his edition of the *Decameron*. See also Padoan, pp. 120-125, and Franco Fido, "Dante personaggio mancato del *Decameron*," in *Boccaccio: Secoli di Vita*, pp. 177-189, and in *Le metamorfosi del centauro*, pp. 77-90. Michelangelo Picone has also explored the relationship between Dante and Boccaccio and the similarities and contrasts between their respective "poetic systems" ("Codici e strutture narrative nel *Decameron*," *Strumenti critici* 34 [1977], 434-443). His approach is based on the semiotics of culture (of the type introduced by Lotman and Uspensky). Picone uses the *Decameron*'s famous subtitle "surnamed Prince Galahalt," to explain Francesca's behavior, which derives from *amour courtois* as a cultural code: "The character . . . (for example Francesca) tries to rise to successively more perfect levels [of a 'higher Reality,' which constitutes the code by which his or her own life is regulated] through *imitatio*, i.e. the process of adaptation to what is the paradigmatic expression (for example Guinevere) of the pertinent code (for example *amour courtois*). Thus 'history' progressively is raised to the perfection of the model." Boccaccio's approach is said to be similar to Dante's in that his stories also are "signs for a historical reality which may be represented and therefore known through a mechanism that

continuously projects the facts that constitute it against a background of previously established rules. The incidents recounted (*Decameron*) bear the same relationship to the book in its totality (Prince Galahalt) as does Francesca to the Breton romance. The story of character or event *x* or *y* is therefore to be subjected to a direct comparison with a given code, which is the *only* one with respect to which the character or event may be analyzed and judged: that is to say, 'written,' and at this point we will have the 'story,' the actual artistic production." Boccaccio's and Dante's cognitive methods are thus shown to be the same.

Picone also shows that he is aware of the fundamental differences between the two authors: sacred versus profane cognitive systems; symbolic versus realistic approach; hierarchic unity versus multiplicity. His overall approach to the *Decameron* belongs with those of Battaglia, Getto, and Bárberi-Squarotti. In the last analysis the value of the storytelling for the ten narrators lies, according to Picone, in its "cathartic value: it is the only means left to human power to purify and to affirm its own elevated rational existence which is continually in danger of being attacked and corrupted by the power of contingency. The participation of the narrators therefore succeeds in transferring (and thus 'saving') nature into cultural models: in this their operation is more ethic than aesthetic" (pp. 435-436; translation mine). See also Giuseppe Mazzotta's pages on the novella of Master Simon (VIII, 9) as a parody of Dante's Hell ("Games of Laughter in the *Decameron*," *Romanic Review* 69 [1978], 125ff.).

CHAPTER I

1. See Gene Brucker, *Renaissance Florence* and *Florentine Politics and Society, 1343-1378*; Giuliano Procacci, *History of the Italian People*, trans. Anthony Paul, and Marvin B. Becker, *Florence in Transition*, which contains an admirably informative bibliographical note. See also Millard Meiss, *Painting in Florence and Siena after the Black Death: 1350-1375*; Carlo Salinari's essay on the *Trecento* in Vol. I of the *Antologia della Letteratura Italiana*, ed. Maurizio Vitale pp. 441-459; Branca, *Boccaccio Med.*, especially Chapter V; Padoan's "Mondo aristocratico e mondo comunale," and G. Petronio, "La posizione del *Decameron*," *Rassegna della letteratura italiana* 2 (1957), 189-207. Petronio was one of the first modern

critics to point out how closely the *Decameron* reflected its "communal" (as opposed to "medieval" or "humanist") matrix.

2. On this and related problems see Arnold Hauser, *The Social History of Art*, Vol. I, Chap. II, and Vol. II, Chap. I. The point was made by Brucker.

3. The information from Villani is cited by Procacci, *History of the Italian People*, p. 55.

4. Brucker, *Renaissance Florence*, pp. 92-106. The most powerful families had been excluded from public office by the *ordinamenti di giustizia* of 1293, but this still left plenty of room for maneuvering by related and slightly lesser lines.

5. These pages closely follow Procacci (pp. 42-48 and 55-59) and Brucker (*Renaissance Florence*). The death figures are taken from the authorities cited by Branca, *Decameron*, p. 990. The clearest and most detailed account of the class power struggle and the events from 1340 to 1348 may be found in Marvin B. Becker's two chapters, "The Failure of Oligarchs, Despots, and Magnates: The End of the Casual Regimen, 1340-1343" and "Popular Government and the Beginnings of the Stern Paidea, 1343-1348," *Florence in Transition*, pp. 123-230.

6. On this see Becker, Branca's "L'epopea dei mercatanti" in *Boccaccio Med.*, and Padoan, especially pp. 133-186.

7. See Padoan, "Mondo aristocratico," pp. 105-116. He underlines the influence of the Florentine world on the *Decameron*. See also Franco Fido's analysis of *Decameron X*, 9 ("Il sorriso di Messer Torello," in *Romance Philology* 23 (1969), 154-171, and in *Le Metamorfosi del Centauro*, pp. 113-142. The story is studied as an example of the ideal of civilization that Boccaccio built into his text. In America one of the earlier critics to underline the morality of Boccaccio's aims in the *Decameron* was Guido A. Guarino in the introduction to his translation of *De Claris Mulieribus, Concerning Famous Women*, pp. xxff. The problem of the *Decameron*'s "morality" is linked to the dates of its composition, which Branca sets as 1349-1350. Padoan argues that it took place over a rather longer period. He bases his argument on internal evidence in both the *cornice* and various groups of stories, and believes those of the Tenth Day to have been composed early if not first. See "Sulla genesi del *Decameron*," in *Boccaccio: Secoli di Vita*, pp. 143-176.

8. See documents published in W. M. Bowsky, *The Black Death: A Turning Point in History?* The parallels in both details and com-

mentary on the overthrowing of laws and morals are strikingly similar.

9. The expression derives from Turner's work on the liminal stage in ritual, first identified by Arnold Van Gennep and discussed in his *The Rites of Passage*, trans. M. Vizedom and G. Caffee. Van Gennep showed that rites of passage enacted death in one condition and rebirth in another and consisted of three stages: pre-liminal (usually consisting of the moment of separation), liminal (the stage of transition which he calls *marge*), and post-liminal (the moment of re-incorporation into society, *agrégation*). Victor Turner's work on the liminal periods is actually a series of studies with far more universal implications on "the nature and characteristics of transition in relatively stable societies." He uses the term "liminal phenomenon" to distinguish between actual rites among early or still agrarian societies and phenomena which have some of their characteristics but are not part of formal rites of passage. On the whole concept of liminality see "Betwixt and Between: Liminal Period," in *The Forest of Symbols* and *The Ritual Process*. The distinction between liminoid and liminal is best explicated in the article "Liminal to Liminoid in Play, Flow and Ritual: An Essay in Comparative Symbology," *Rice University Studies* 60 (Summer 1974), 53-92, especially on pp. 64-65, 71-72, 73ff., and 85ff. To my knowledge, Mazzotta is the only other critic to mention Turner's work in connection with the *Decameron*: "In the absence of the *Logos* what meaning can literature possibly have? What is its function in this world of death? What does it accomplish in the neutral area Victor Turner calls 'betwixt and between'?" "Marginality," p. 65. The allusion to Turner's work is not developed.

10. Geertz, "Thick Description: Toward an Interpretive Theory of Culture," in *The Interpretation of Cultures*, p. 16.

11. Victor Turner used this term in a somewhat specialized way: "I consider the term 'ritual' to be more fittingly applied to forms of religious behaviour associated with social transitions, while the term 'ceremony' has a closer bearing on religious behaviour associated with social states [by 'state' Turner means here 'a relatively fixed or stable condition'], where politico-legal institutions also have greater importance. Ritual is transformative, ceremony confirmatory" (*Forest*, p. 95; the insert is on p. 93). It is a term that critics have used rather loosely about the *Decameron*. Nino Borsellino, in his essay on the book as theater, talks of the *cornice*

as "a rite" that pulls the whole into an "edenic" condition devoid of all social contrasts; he also calls it "a ritual ceremony" as opposed to drama, which has its own "profane sacredness" that is just as important as "ascetic sacredness" is to Dante. According to Borsellino, the aim of the "ritual" is to affirm life against death, and this world versus the other. He also pointed out that there is in the *cornice* "a rhythmic scansion so closely followed as to confer a liturgical character onto this socially absolute existence." Borsellino, "*Decameron* come teatro," in *Rozzi e intronati—esperienze e forme del teatro dal "Decameron" al "Candelaio*," pp. 45-47, 41. Another who speaks of "sacredness" and "ritual" is Carlo Ballerini, whose long and relentlessly lyric essay "Il recupero della letizia dalla tragedia della peste alla libera vita di Bruno e Buffalmaco," in *Atti del Congresso di Nimega sul Boccaccio*, pp. 51-203, is a reading of the *Decameron* in terms of the affirmation of life (represented by the female principle of rebirth as seen in the seven women whom the men join to form a perfect circle for the storytelling) against death (the plague). The reading is interesting for some details such as the meaning of Santa Maria Novella— the church from which the group leaves and to which it returns— seen in terms of Mary as the symbol of regeneration and rebirth *par excellence*. Nevertheless, these critics (including Bárberi-Squarotti) have all used the terms "rite" or "ritual" generically, without defining them, as does Nicholas Perella in the course of some illuminating remarks on a possible "secular analogue to a primitive or religious behaviour pattern": "Each day for ten days the pastime is repeated, and on each occasion there are references to the time or the position of the sun and, in particular, to the heat of the day. The curious but significant effect of this repetition is to lend a quasi-ritualistic character to a mundane mood and activity. There is built up the sense of a deliberate opposition of the *locus amoenus* (in which the storytelling takes place) against the menace of a hostile moment of nature. The storytelling itself might almost be a magical rite. . . . The pattern remains clear, though Boccaccio has employed it with his own dual purpose: he has made it serve an aesthetic end in the creation of a narrative structure, . . . and he has sought to desacralize midday, which serves his secular ethic in storytelling. The noontime telling of tales has been substituted for the Church-prescribed office for the hour of none. A human space, a totally 'earthly' paradise has shut out the direct rays of that midday sun which has symbolical connections with the Divinity and, what is even more pertinent here, with the 'destruction that wasteth at noonday'—the raging pestilence from which the *lieta brigata* has sought to escape" (*Midday in Italian Literature: Variations on an Archetypal Theme*, p. 38). Lucia Marino also discusses the *cornice* in terms of archetypal rituals, concentrating on the episode of the *valle delle donne* (pp. 99-121). A cogent comment is that of Mazzotta: "they (the brigata) construct a realm of phantasy which suspends the purposive structure of ordinary life and envelops it within the form of the ritual" ("Games of Laughter," p. 117). Mazzotta's thesis is very different from mine, however: in speaking of the fact that stories are told on a Sunday he says: "in their contiguity the two experiences stand in ironic self-reflection: as each is cut loose from the other, the ritual purification is emptied of any content, and storytelling, in turn, is drawn within the boundaries of pure ritual." (There is no evidence in Trexler's work that Sunday afternoons were considered sacred, however.)

12. Filomena, the second elected queen, "first of all confirmed the appointments made by Pampinea, and gave instructions as to what should be done for the following morning, as well as for supper that evening . . . (p. 111)" (Boccaccio, *The Decameron*. Introduction, translation, and notes copyright © G. H. Mc-William, 1972 [Penguin, 1975]. Reprinted by permission of Penguin Books Ltd. All quotations, unless otherwise indicated, are taken from this edition.) ". . . primieramente gli ufici dati da Pampinea riconformò e dispose quello che per la seguente mattina e per la futura cena far si dovesse . . ." Branca, I, Concl., 5. Thereafter brief mentions of the seneschal conferring with the day's ruler or carrying out his duties may be found in II, Concl., 10; III, Intro., 2 and Concl., 4; IV, Concl., 6; V, Intro., 3 and Concl., 2; VI, Intro., 5 and Concl., 4; VII, Intro., 2 and Concl., 2; VIII, Concl., 2; IX, Intro., 6 and Concl., 3; X, Concl., 8 and 16.

13. "But for the fact that the queen sternly commanded her to be silent, told her not to shout or argue any more unless she wanted to be whipped, and sent her back to the kitchen with Tindaro, there would have been nothing else to do for the rest of the day but to listen to her prattle" (p. 483). ". . . e, se non fosse che la reina con un mal viso le 'mpose silenzio e comandolle che più parola né romor facesse se esser non volesse scopata e lei e Tindaro mandò via, niuna altra cosa avrebbero avuta a fare in tutto quel giorno che attendere a lei" (VI, Intro., 15). Contrast

this with another queen's disciplining of Dioneo, her social equal, only a few pages previously: "All the ladies laughed except the queen, who was beginning to grow impatient with him. 'No more of your nonsense, Dioneo,' she said. 'Sing us something pleasant, or you'll learn what it means to provoke my anger' " (p. 479). "La reina allora un poco turbata, quantunque tutte l'altre ridessero, disse: —Dioneo, lascia stare il motteggiare e dinne una bella; e se no, tu potresti provare come io mi so adirare" (V, Concl., 14).

14. "Ma per ciò che le cose che sono senza modo non possono lungamente durare, io, che cominciatrice fui de' ragionamenti da' quali questa così bella compagnia è stata fatta, pensando al continuar della nostra letizia, estimo che di necessità sia convenire esser tra noi alcuno principale, il quale noi e onoriamo e ubidiamo come maggiore, nel quale ogni pensiero stea di doverci a lietamente vivere disporre. E acciò che ciascun pruovi il peso della sollecitudine insieme col piacere della maggioranza e, per conseguente da una parte e d'altra tratti, non possa chi nol pruova invidia avere alcuna, dico che a ciascuno per un giorno s'attribuisca e il peso e l'onore . . ." (Intro., 95-96). Alessandro Falassi has shown that the custom of having a ruler or *capo-veglia* preside over storytelling gatherings is still followed in Tuscany today. "Il Boccaccio e il folklore," in *Boccaccio: Secoli di Vita*, p. 268.

15. ". . . dietro alla guida del discreto re verso Firenze si ritornarono; e i tre giovani, lasciate le sette donne in Santa Maria Novella, donde con loro partiti s'erano, da esse accommiatatosi, a' loro altri piaceri attesero, e esse, quando tempo lor parve, se ne tornarono alle lor case (X, Concl., 16).

16. "Essi eran tutti di frondi di quercia inghirlandati, con le man piene o d'erbe odorifere o di fiori; e chi scontrati li avesse, niuna altra cosa avrebbe potuto dire se non: 'O costor non saranno dalla morte vinti o ella gli ucciderà lieti' " (IX, Intro., 4, translation mine). Marino interprets this as an allegory of fortitude and wisdom (pp. 101-103).

17. "The first phase of separation, the phase which clearly demarcates sacred space and time from profane or secular space and time (it is more than just a matter of entering a temple—there must be in addition a rite which changes the quality of *time* also, or constructs a cultural realm which is defined as 'out of time,' i.e. beyond or outside the time which measures secular processes and routines), includes symbolic behaviour" (Turner, "Liminal,"

pp. 56-57). The plague is listed among the situations that call for symbolic behavior representing detachment. See also the statements on cultural order and the plague in René Girard's article "The Plague in Literature and Myth," *Texas Studies in Literature and Language* 15 (1975), 833-850. (Girard does not discuss the *Decameron*.)

18. "Esso avea dintorno da sé e per lo mezzo in assai parti vie ampissime, tutte diritte come strale . . ." (III, Intro., 6). See also p. 81 in Chapter III, below.

19. "—Donne, quantunque ciò che ragiona Pampinea sia ottimamente detto, non è per ciò così da correre a farlo, come mostra che voi vogliate fare. Ricordivi che noi siamo tutte femine, e non ce n'ha niuna sì fanciulla, che non possa ben conoscere come le femine sien ragionate insieme e senza la provedenza d'alcuno uomo si sappiano regolare. Noi siamo mobili, riottose, sospettose, pusillanime e paurose: per le quali cose io dubito forte, se noi alcuna altra guida non prendiamo che la nostra, che questa compagnia non si dissolva troppo più tosto e con meno onor di noi che non ci bisognerebbe: e per cio è buono a provederci avanti che cominciamo.

Disse allora Elissa: —Veramente gli uomini sono delle femine capo e senza l'ordine loro rade volte riesce alcuna nostra opera a laudevole fine . . ." (Intro., 75-76).

20. There may be an implicit analogy to Turner's concept of *communitas* in the absolute equality of the ten protagonists and the timeless repetitiveness of their daily pattern. "Communitas" is a very special sense of communion and comradeship typical of what Turner envisions as the realm of anti-structure as opposed to the realm of structure. He sees the two as basic tendencies in mankind, leading to a dialectics of history generated by the three stages of communitas. These are the spontaneous, the ideological and the normative stage. The genuine feeling of communitas becomes a memory of that feeling and then an attempted "structure of communitas," which is of course an impossibility. See "Liminality and Communitas" and "Communitas: Model and Process" in *Ritual*; also "Passages, Margins and Poverty: Religious Symbols of Communitas" and "Metaphores of Anti-Structure in Religious Culture," in *Dramas, Fields and Metaphores*. There is little genuine *communitas* in the *cornice* of the *Decameron*, however: given the young people's relationship with their servants and their equal aristocratic provenance, the terms on which they stand to each

other are more likely to derive from a concept of oligarchy. It is sometimes useful to examine what is *not* there, however, and the lack of *communitas* reinforces the *liminal* (not *liminoid*) nature of the whole experience and the fact that the social subversiveness in the book was very probably not consciously woven into it by its author. Boccaccio had no intention of preaching the overthrow of the Florentine social structure, although he did wish to substitute some of the actual values already functional in his society for the ideal values still being propagated in theory by the Church. It is as if he were admonishing literature to catch up with life, and follow Dante with the Humanists.

21. "—Amabili donne, se con sana mente sarà riguardato l'ordine delle cose, assai leggermente si conoscerà tutta la universal moltitudine delle femine dalla natura e da' costumi e dalle leggi essere agli uomini sottomessa e secondo la discrezione di quegli convenirsi reggere e governare, e però, a ciascuna che quiete, consolazione e riposo vuole con quegli uomini avere a' quali s'appartiene, dee essere umile, paziente e ubidente oltre all'essere onesta, il che è sommo e spezial tesoro di ciascuna savia. E quando a questo le leggi, le quali il ben comune riguardano in tutte le cose, non ci ammaestrassono, e l'usanza, o costume che vogliamo dire, le cui forze son grandissime e reverende, la natura assai apertamente cel mostra, la quale ci ha fatte ne' corpi dilicate e morbide, negli animi timide e paurose, nelle menti benigne e pietose, e hacci date le corporali forze leggieri, le voci piacevoli e i movimenti de' membri soavi: cose tutte testificanti noi avere dell'altrui governo bisogno. E chi ha bisogno d'essere aiutato e governato, ogni ragion vuol lui dovere essere obediente e subietto e reverente al governator suo: e cui abbiam noi governatori e aiutatori se non gli uomini? Dunque agli uomini dobbiamo, sommamente onorandogli, soggiacere; e qual da questo si parte, estimo che degnissima sia non solamente di riprension grave ma d'aspro gastigamento" (IX, 9, 3-6).

22. ". . . the floor of the Valley was perfectly circular in shape. . . . The sides of the hills ranged downwards in a regular series of terraces, concentrically arranged like the tiers of an amphitheater, their circles gradually diminishing in size from the topmost terrace to the lowest. . . . a stream . . . flowed swiftly . . . to the center of the plain, where it formed a tiny lake . . . free of all impurities . . ." (pp. 516-517). ". . . il piano, che nella valle era, così era ritondo come se a sesta fosse stato fatto. . . . Le

piagge delle quali montagnette così digradando giuso verso il pian discendevano, come ne' teatri veggiamo dalla lor sommità i gradi infino all'infimo venire successivamente ordinati, sempre ristrignendo il cerchio loro. . . . un fiumicello . . . infino al mezzo del piano velocissimo discorreva, e ivi faceva un piccol laghetto. . . . senza avere in sé mistura alcuna . . ." (VI, Concl., 20, 21, 25, 26, 27).

23. Boccaccio's naturalism is amply documented and explored by Aldo Scaglione, *Nature and Love in the Late Middle Ages.*

24. Edith Kern has pointed out that the symbolism of the fish in the lake indicates that the garden is a garden of Venus ("The Gardens in the *Decameron* Cornice," *PMLA* 66 (1951), 519ff.). For a very different point of view (with which I disagree) see Marshall Brown, "In the Valley of the Ladies," *Italian Quarterly* 18 (Spring 1975), 33-52. Brown sees the bathing as "a slightly seditious act" by which the ladies "reduce themselves, so to speak, to the level of their characters" and the valley of the Ladies as a place where the dangerous female levity can indulge its "natural thought-lessness in a potentially dangerous way." Marino's study of the ritual aspects of the *valle delle donne* (pp. 79-121) is interesting but fails to take the episode's position and thematic connection with the following stories into account.

The frequent negativity of the feminine principle in various cultures is a well-known and amply documented fact in both anthropological and sociological literature.

25. ". . . le beffe le quali o per amore o per salvamento di loro le donne hanno già fatte a' loro mariti, senza essersene essi avveduti o no" (VI, Concl., 6).

26. This has been pointed out by Thomas Greene ("Forms of Accommodation in the *Decameron*," *Italica* 15 [1968], 297-312). The evidence Greene presents includes the number of good marriages in the stories and the fact that even the stratagems and deceits practiced by the many extra-marital lovers underline the social sanctions operative in connection with the institution itself, which is clearly accepted. His theory is that even the stories that end in the fulfillment of passion really show how society absorbs the threats to its structure that passion presents rather than being purely naturalistic. Greene also points out how the ten protag-onists return to their community in spite of the danger and social dissolution and states that the result of the stories of the tenth day is a deeper pacification between the subversive, the irre-

sponsible, the dangerous and the harmony of the community. The study is one of the first to emphasize Boccaccio's belief in the social order. The work of Bárberi-Squarotti, Hollander and Bernardo is based on similar assumptions, which also underlie some of the ideas of Branca, Baratto, and Padoan.

Greene also mentioned Boccaccio's interest in theatrics and in the use of epiphanies, stating that further work was needed in this area. Some of it has been carried out by Mario Baratto (*Realtà e Stile*), by Nino Borsellino, "*Decameron* come teatro," and by A. Staüble, "La brigata del 'Decameron' come pubblico teatrale," *Studi sul Boccaccio* 9 (1975-1976), 103-118. Getto, Padoan, and Muscetta also noted the intrinsic theatricality of many of the stories.

27. Giovanni Getto's attitude is typical ("La cornice e le componenti espressive del *Decameron*," *Vita di forme*, p. 27). Another point of view on the problem is Aldo Scaglione's. After pointing out the different levels between "the content and the frame of the stories," Scaglione rejects (as possible reasons for the moral difference between the two levels) the hypocrisy of keeping up appearances and the practical consideration of not shocking the puritanical part of Boccaccio's public by abolishing the decorum of the screening *brigata*. He advocates the "framework of reasonable honesty and decorous wisdom in which Boccaccio believed" as having suggested to the ten young people that "restraint is imperative if they are determined to coexist in an orderly social organism, were it only for fifteen days" (*Love and Nature*, pp. 88-89).

28. Claude Lévi-Strauss, *Les Structures élémentaires de la parenté*. See also "The Family," in *Man, Culture and Society*, ed. Harvey L. Shapiro. Leslie White's thesis may be found in *The Science of Culture*. For an interesting discussion see Marian Kreiselman Slater, "Ecological Factors in the Origin of Incest," *American Anthropologist* 61 (1959), 1042-1059. Slater argues that both Lévi-Strauss and White are equating function with origin and thus dealing with final cause. Her thesis is that the origins of exogamy lie in the earliest impossibility (determined by age and time of death) of finding mates within nuclear families.

29. See Joan Ferrante, "The Frame Characters of the *Decameron*;" Aldo Rossi, "Dante nella prospettiva del Boccaccio," *Studi Danteschi* 37 (1960), 138 (I am indebted to M. Marcus for bringing this article to my attention) and Getto, *Vita di forme*.

30. Douglas, *Natural Symbols, Explorations in Cosmology*, espe-

cially Chapter 4. The "classification and personal pressure" definition is given in Chapter 7 (p. 136).

31. "Appresso, per ciò che noi qui quattro dì dimorate saremo, se noi vogliam tor via che gente nuova non ci sopravenga, reputo opportuno di mutarci di qui e andarne altrove" (II, Concl., 7, translation mine).

32. "Neifile allora, tutta nel viso divenuta per vergogna vermiglia per ciò che l'una era di quelle che dall'un de' giovani era amata, disse: —Pampinea, per Dio, guarda ciò che tu dichi. Io conosco assai apertamente niuna altra cosa che tutta buona dir potersi di qualunque s'è l'uno di costoro. . . . Ma, per ciò che assai manifesta cosa è loro essere d'alcune che qui ne sono innamorati, temo che infamia e riprensione, senza nostra colpa o di loro, non ce ne segua se gli meniamo.—

Disse allora Filomena: —Questo non monta niente; là dove io onestamente viva né mi rimorda d'alcuna cosa la coscienza, parli chi vuole in contrario: Idio e la verità l'arme per me prenderanno" (I, Intro., 81-83).

33. Emilia is self-sufficient in love (I); Pampinea's love is joyous and reciprocated (II); Lauretta's is also returned but her lover's jealousy makes the relationship problematic (III); Filostrato's love has abandoned him for another (IV); Dioneo loves without knowing whether he is loved in return (V); Elissa's love is not returned (VI); Filomena's beloved is absent on a journey (VII); Panfilo's secret love is secretly returned (VIII); Neifile's love is also happy and reciprocated (IX); Fiammetta loves and is loved, but she is so tormented by jealousy and the fear of losing her beloved that she cannot be happy (X).

34. On Boccaccio's concept of passion see Guido Almansi's essay "The Meaning of a Storm" in *The Writer as Liar*. Marino also makes a good case for an allegorical network implying the necessity of control.

35. Douglas, *Purity and Danger*, 1966.

36. This is of course close to Victor Turner's statements about liminality, which also affirms the existing social order and whose rites are frequent in times of transition and disruption.

37. Bárberi-Squarotti's theory and also certain aspects of the ideas of the aristocratic-idyll theorists like Getto are close to Douglas's theory, though her work does not seem known to those critics.

38. There is in fact a whole group of critics engaged in expli-

cating the possible Christian allegories in Boccaccio's work. They include Aldo Bernardo, Robert Hollander, Victoria Kirkham, T. K. Seung, and Janet Levarie Smarr. Lucia Marino's work also to some extent reflects this attitude.

39. "Ma sí come a Colui piacque il quale, essendo Egli infinito, diede per legge incommutabile a tutte le cose mondane aver fine, il mio amore . . . per se medesimo in processo di tempo si diminuì. . . . Il che se avviene, che voglia Idio che così sia, a Amore ne rendano grazie, il quale liberandomi da' suoi legami . . ." (Pr. 15).

"Dico adunque che già erano gli anni della fruttifera incarnazione del Figliuolo di Dio al numero pervenuti di milletrecento quarantotto, quando nella egregia città di Firenze . . ." (I, Intro., 8).

". . . dico che dall'aiuto di Dio e dal vostro, gentilissime donne, nel quale io spero, armato, e di buona pazienza, con esso procederò avanti . . ." (IV, Intro., 40).

". . . per la qual cosa Idio primieramente e appresso voi ringraziando, è da dare alla penna e alla man faticata riposo" (Concl., 1).

". . . tempo è da por fine alle parole, Colui umilmente ringraziando che dopo sì lunga fatica col suo aiuto n'ha al disiderato fine condotto. E voi, piacevoli donne, con la sua grazia in pace vi rimanete . . ." (Concl., 29).

40. "Convenevole cosa è, carissime donne, che ciascheduna cosa la quale l'uomo fa, dallo ammirabile e santo nome di Colui, il quale di tutte fu facitore, le dea principio" (I, 1, 2).

41. The expression is the poet Mario Luzi's. "Il novellare del Decameron," in Atti del Congresso di Nimega, p. 252.

42. "utile consiglio," "quello che sia da fuggire e che sia similmente da seguitare."

43. "Ciascuna cosa in sè medesima è buona a alcuna cosa, e male adoperata può essere nociva di molte; e così dico delle mie novelle. Chi vorrà da quelle malvagio consiglio e malvagia operazion trarre, elle nol vieteranno a alcuno, se forse in sé l'hanno, e torte e tirate fieno a averlo: e chi utilità e frutto ne vorrà, elle nol negheranno, né sarà mai che altro che utile e oneste sien dette o tenute, se a que' tempi o a quelle persone si leggeranno per cui e pe' quali state son raccontate" (Concl., 13 and 14). Translation and italics mine.

44. No moral is stated for I, 4, 6, 8; II, 4, 5, 6, 8; III, 4, 7, 9; IV,

1, 5, 9, 10; V, 2, 3, 4, 5, 7, 10; VI, 6, 7, 8, 9, 10; VII, 5, 6, 7, 8, 9, 10; VIII, 3, 4, 5, 6; IX, 3, 5, 6, 8, 10; and X, 4, 5, 6, 7, 10. Some of these, like the "morals" of II, 2 or of IX, 1, 4 and 7, are clearly tongue-in-cheek, however.

45. Claude Perrus, "Remarques sur les rapports entre écrivain et public dans le *Décaméron* de Boccace," in *Littérature et idéologies, Colloque de Cluny* II, 296. The importance of the distinction between the fictive audience and Boccaccio's desire to "influence real people in real situations," so as to further the regeneration of the human world of the "Introduction" has also the been pointed out by Marga Cottino-Jones in "The City/Country Conflict in the *Decameron*," *Studi sul Boccaccio* 8 (1974), 152. Cottino-Jones's theory belongs to the "regeneration" line of criticism, as does my own in part: "In fact . . . we may already intimate that, through the personal life experience of the *brigata*, as well as through the aesthetic experience of the *novellare*, that same natural social and moral order that is being recreated, experienced, and narrated by the group in the perfected natural environment outside the city, might be thereafter recreated also in the city, once the *brigata* finds it timely to return there" (p. 155). Cottino-Jones's basic idea is that the stay in the country (which represents a "perfected natural world") functions as a regenerative experience or strength-gathering absence from the city. Accordingly the *brigata*'s return to Florence "strongly suggests that they consider this experience of the natural world essential, inasmuch as it has provided them with the necessary means to face the city again and to potentially shape there a perfected form of social existence" (p. 183). In this she is close to the many other critics (see for example the quotations by Almansi and Marcus in note 2 of Chapter III and that by Franco Fido in note 42 of the same chapter) who see the whole experience as a momentary "absence from history." I disagree: the experience, insofar as it partakes of the liminal, is profoundly social and not outside of history at all. On the tensions and relations between these two worlds see also Wayne A. Rebhorn's book on Castiglione, *Courtly Performances*, especially Chapter III.

46. For examples see IV, 2, 5-7; V, 3, 4, and the long discourse on the decline of morals and customs by Lauretta in I, 8, 7-11.

47. On this concept see H. Berger, "The Renaissance Imagination: Second World and Green World," in *The Centennial Review* 9 (Winter 1965), 36-78. I am indebted to M. Marcus for calling this article to my attention.

48. "The City/Country Conflict," pp. 153-154. See also Bárberi-Squarotti, "La 'cornice' del *Decameron* o il mito di Robinson."

49. ". . . io non so quello che de' vostri pensieri voi v'intendete di fare: li miei lasciai io dentro dalla porta della città allora che io con voi poco fa me ne uscí fuori: e per ciò o voi a sollazzare e a ridere e a cantare con meco insieme vi disponete (tanto, dico, quanto alla vostra dignità s'appartiene), o voi mi licenziate che io per li miei pensier mi ritorni e steami nella città tribolata" (I, Intro., 93).

50. Peacock, *Rites of Modernization*. See also Peacock's *Consciousness and Change: Symbolic Anthropology in Evolutionary Perspective*.

51. "La brigata del *Decameron* come publico teatrale," *Studi sul Boccaccio* 9 (1975-1976), 105, 106. He also underlines the group's fondness for being didactic (p. 108). The main thesis of the article is that the "theatrical" and dialectical relationship between the *cornice* and the stories, whose drift is realistic, expresses the personal and social ambivalence of both the *brigata* and Boccaccio through a theatrical interplay of reality and fiction (pp. 114-119).

52. See Enrico De' Negri's essay, "The Legendary Style of the *Decameron*," in *The Romanic Review* 53 (October 1952), 166-189. See also Salvatore Battaglia's essays "L'esempio medievale," "Dall'esempio alla novella," and "La coscienza del realismo nell'arte del Boccaccio" in *La coscienza letteraria del Medioevo* and his *Giovanni Boccaccio e la riforma della narrativa*, especially pp. 1-81. Francesco Tateo argues that while medieval *exempla* move deductively, from the general to the specific, Boccaccio has structured his so as to move inductively from a human experience to a general rule ("Il 'realismo' della novella boccaccesca," in *Rettorica e poetica fra Medioevo e Rinascimento*, pp. 161-202).

53. Analogues of this tale have been found in the extremely ancient Indian *Ramayana*, as well as in almost all the well-known collections of Boccaccio's time. *Barlaam and Josaphat*, Jacques de Vitry's *Exempla*, the *Leggenda Aurea*, Vincent of Beauvrais' *Speculum*, Cavalca's *Vite dei Santi Padri* and the *Novellino* all contained very similar versions. Several of these books are collections of *exempla* specifically gathered for use in sermons.

54. ". . . tu non sai donde elle s'imbeccano" (IV, Intro., trans. mine).

CHAPTER II

1. The problem is seldom addressed directly. Esposito's bibliography lists only five entries on the subject, one of which is a

double listing of a reprinted article on Boccaccio's "conversion" and its influence on his work on Dante. Many critics deal with Boccaccio's attitude toward religion in the course of their other work, however. Indications of some attitudes may be found in Muscetta, Hollander, Scaglione, and in Almansi's summary of twentieth-century attitudes to the story of Ser Cepparello (*The Writer as Liar*, pp. 25ff.).

2. "Convenevole cosa è, carissime donne, che ciascheduna cosa la quale l'uomo fa, dallo ammirabile e santo nome di Colui, il quale di tutte fu facitore, le dea principio" (I, 1. 2; translation mine).

3. ". . . la mortifera pistolenza: la quale, per operazion de' corpi superiori o per le nostre inique opere da giusta ira di Dio a nostra correzion mandata sopra i mortali . . ."; ". . . quasi l'ira di Dio a punire le iniquità degli uomini con quella pistolenza non dove fossero procedesse, ma solamente a coloro opprimere li quali dentro alle mura delle lor città si trovassero . . ." (I, Intro., 8 and 25; translation mine).

4. ". . . tal fu la crudeltà del cielo, e forse in parte quella degli uomini . . ." (I, Intro., 47; translation mine).

5. "E in quella non valendo . . . ancora umili supplicazioni non una volta ma molte e in processioni ordinate, in altre guise a Dio fatte dalle divote persone. . . ."

"E in tanta afflizione e miseria della nostra città era la reverenda auttorità delle leggi, così divine come umane, quasi caduta e dissoluta tutta per li ministri e essecutori di quelle, li quali, sì come gli altri uomini, erano tutti o morti o infermi o sì di famiglie [sic] rimasi stremi, che uficio alcuno non potean fare. . . ."

". . . secondo la qualità del morto vi veniva il chericato; e egli sopra gli omeri de' suoi pari, con funeral pompa di cera e di canti, alla chiesa da lui prima eletta anzi la morte n'era portato. Le quali cose, poi che a montar cominciò la ferocità della pistolenza, o in tutto o in maggior parte quasi cessarono. . . ."

"e quella con frettolosi passi, non a quella chiesa che esso aveva anzi la morte disposto ma alla più vicina le più volte il portavano, dietro a quattro [sic] o a sei cherici con poco lume e tal fiata senza alcuno; li quali con l'aiuto de' detti becchini, senza faticarsi in troppo lungo oficio o solenne, in qualunque sepoltura disoccupata trovavano più tosto il mettevano."

"E infinite volte avvenne che, andando due preti con una croce per alcuno, si misero tre o quatro bare, da' portatori portate, di

dietro a quella: e, dove un morto credevano avere i preti a se-
pellire, n'avevano sei o otto e tal fiata più."

"Alla gran moltitudine de' corpi mostrata, che a ogni chiesa ogni
dì e quasi ogn'ora concorreva portata, non bastando la terra sacra
alle sepolture, e massimamente volendo dare a ciascun luogo
proprio secondo l'antico costume, si facevano per gli cimiterii delle
chiese, poi che ogni parte era piena, fosse grandissime nelle quali
a centinaia si mettevano i sopravegnenti: e in quelle stivati, come
si mettono le mercatantie nelle navi a suolo . . ." (I, Intro., 9, 23,
32, 35, 40, 42).

6. "Mostrato n'ha Panfilo nel suo novellare la benignità di Dio
non guardare a' nostri errori quando da cosa che per noi veder
non si possa procedano: e io nel mio intendo di dimostrarvi quanto
questa medesima benignità, sostenendo pazientemente i difetti
di coloro li quali d'essa ne deono dare e con l'opere e con le parole
vera testimonianza, il contrario operando, di sé argomento d'in-
fallibile verità ne dimostri, acciò che quello che noi crediamo
con più fermezza d'animo seguitiamo" (I, 2, 3).

7. III, 8, 75. McWilliam has brilliantly translated "arse-angel
Bagriel" (p. 303).

8. ". . . gli fece con una buona quantità della grascia di San
Giovanni Boccadoro ugner le mani (la quale molto giova alle infermità delle pistilenziose avarizie de' cherici . . .)" (I, 6, 9). St.
John the Baptist was depicted on the Florentine gold florin. The
allusion is not original: St. John, archbishop of Constantinople,
was called "Crisostomo" (golden mouth) because of his eloquence, and this had already led to a great deal of general punning
(Branca, p. 1028). The example of St. Julian is also not original;
similar jokes about his providing safe lodgings and warm bed-
fellows were current at the time (see Branca, *Decameron*, p. 1050).

9. "—Usano i volgari un così fatto proverbio: 'Chi è reo e
buono è tenuto, può fare il male e non è creduto'; il quale ampia
materia a ciò che m'è stato proposto mi presta di favellare, e
ancora a dimostrare quanta e quale sia la ipocrisia de' religiosi,
li quali co' panni larghi e lunghi e co' visi artificialmente palidi e
con le voci umili e mansuete nel dimandar l'altrui, e altissime e
rubeste in mordere negli altri li loro medesimi vizzii e nel mostrar
sè per torre e altri per lor donare venire a salvazione; e oltre a
ciò, non come uomini che il Paradiso abbiano a procacciare come
noi, ma quasi come possessori e signori di quello danti a cias-
chedun che muore, secondo la quantità de' denari loro lasciata

da lui, più e meno eccellente luogo, con questo prima se medesimo, se così credono, e poscia coloro che in ciò alle loro parole
dan fede sforzandosi d'ingannare. De' quali se quanto si conven-
isse fosse licito a me di mostrare, tosto dichiarerei a molti semplici
quello che nelle lor cappe larghissime tengan nascoso. Ma ora
fosse piacere di Dio che così delle loro bugie a tutti intervenisse
. . ." (IV, 2, 5-7). Other examples may be found in I, 7; I, 8; III,
3; VIII, 2; VIII, 4; X, 2. They accuse the clergy of "dirty lives,"
lust, stupidity, vanity, weakness, hypocrisy and vengeance-seek-
ing.

10. "E quivi dimorando, senza dire a alcuno perché ito vi fosse,
cautamente cominciò a riguardare alle maniere del Papa e de'
cardinali e degli altri prelati e di tutti i cortigiani: e tra che egli
s'accorse, sì come uomo che molto avveduto era, e che egli ancora
da alcuno fu informato, egli trovò dal maggiore infino al minore
generalmente tutti disonestissimamente peccare in lussuria, e non
solo nella naturale ma ancora nella sogdomitica, senza freno alcuno di rimordimento o di vergogna, in tanto che la potenza delle
meretrici e de' garzoni in impetrare qualunque gran cosa non
v'era di picciol potere. Oltre a questo, universalmente gulosi,
bevitori, ebriachi e più al ventre serventi a guisa d'animali bruti,
appresso alla lussuria, che a altro gli connobbe apertamente; e
più avanti guardando, in tanto tutti avari e cupidi di denari gli
vide, che parimente l'uman sangue, anzi il cristiano, e le divine
cose, chenti che elle si fossero o a sacrificii o a benefici apparte-
nenti, a denari e vendevano e comperavano, maggior mercatantia
faccendone e più sensali avendone che a Parigi di drappi o d'alcuna altra cosa non erano, avendo alla manifesta simonia 'pro-
cureria' posto nome e alla gulosità 'substentazioni,' quasi Idio,
lasciamo stare il significato di vocaboli, ma la 'ntenzione de' pes-
simi animi non conoscesse e a guisa degli uomini a' nomi delle
cose si debba lasciare ingannare" (I, 2, 19-21).

11. Mary Douglas, like Freud, holds that all jokes are subversive: "Whatever the joke, however remote its subject, the telling
of it is potentially subversive. Since its form consists of a victorious
tilting of uncontrol against control, it is an image of the levelling
of hierarchy, the triumph of intimacy over formality, of unofficial
values over official ones . . . , all jokes are expressive of the social
situation in which they occur" ("Jokes," in *Implicit Meanings—
Essays in Anthropology*, p. 98). It should be remembered that the
clergy not only considered itself superior to ordinary humans but

also had a separate judiciary system and was exempt from any but canon law. Most of Boccaccio's joking stories fall into two categories: religious, and female vs. male, another "juxtaposition of a control against that which is controlled" (Douglas, idem.).

De' Negri has pointed out that "making light of religious subjects was in accord with the ecclesiastical practice of reaching the sinner, not frightening him away, and inducing him not to consider himself outside the Church, or in conflict with its dogmatic tenets" (p. 169) and also that "the presentation of amusing examples within the framework of Christian dogma and ethics becomes possible. This edification through joy presupposes a solid faith; hence the humor never takes on a tone of destructive satire" (p. 170). One's interpretation of destructive satire depends to some extent on one's own beliefs, however, and the bitterness of tone in the *cornice* passages cited goes far beyond "making light of religious subjects." On the meaning of humor in the *Decameron* see Mazzotta's essay on the beffa, "Games of Laughter."

12. Lucien Goldmann, *Le dieu caché*, p. 17.

13. Rappaport, "Liturgies and Lies," *Beitrage zur Wissenssoziologie/Beitrage zur Religionssoziologie*, Vol. 10. Rappaport has written extensively on this subject. I have cited only the above study as it is one of the briefest and most accessible.

14. For a rather thorough and amusing, albeit not always kind, summary of the main lines of twentieth-century criticism on this story see Almansi, *The Writer as Liar*, pp. 25ff. Almansi divides the critics into those who dub Cepparello saint and those who see him as an artist. Almansi himself belongs to the latter school and suggests that Cepparello's false confession be read "as an analogue of the literary process." Cepparello would thus be "the negative print of the writer . . . master of all deceptions" and his auto-apotheosis reflects "the writer's ability to create the far larger fictitious universe of the *Decameron* which shines with the unabated radiance of lying" (p. 29).

15. "Era questo Ciappelletto di questa vita: egli, essendo notaio, avea grandissima vergogna quando uno de' suoi strumenti, come che pochi ne facesse, fosse altro che falso trovato; de' quali tanti avrebbe fatti di quanti fosse stato richesto, e quegli più volentieri in dono che alcuno altro grandemente salariato. Testimonianze false con sommo diletto diceva, richesto e non richesto; e dandosi a quei tempi in Francia a' saramenti grandissima fede, non curandosi fargli falsi, tante quistioni malvagiamente vincea a quante

a giurare di dire il vero sopra la sua fede era chiamato. Aveva oltre modo piacere, e forte vi studiava, in commettere tra amici e parenti e qualunque altra persona mali e inimicizie e scandali, de' quali quanto maggiori mali vedeva seguire tanto più d'allegrezza prendea. Invitato a uno omicidio o a qualunque altra rea cosa, senza negarlo mai, volonterosamente v'andava, e più volte a fedire e a uccidere uomini con le proprie mani si ritrovò volentieri. Bestemmiatore di Dio e de' Santi era grandissimo, e per ogni piccola cosa, sì come colui che più che alcuno altro era iracundo. A chiesa non usava giammai, e i sacramenti di quella tutti come vil cosa con abominevoli parole scherniva; e così in contrario le taverne e gli altri disonesti luoghi visitava volentieri e usavagli. Delle femine era così vago come sono i cani de' bastoni; del contrario più che alcuno altro tristo uomo si dilettava. Imbolato avrebbe e rubato con quella coscienza che un santo uomo offerrebbe. Gulosissimo e bevitor grande, tanto che alcuna volta sconciamente gli facea noia. Giucatore e mettitore di malvagi dadi era solenne. Perché mi distendo io in tante parole? egli era il piggiore uomo forse che mai nascesse" (I, 1, 10-15).

De' Negri calls the description "a joke, and above all a stylistic joke." He points out that Ser Cepparello "is . . . typical of exemplaristic *compendia* of every vice and abomination" and that he is "a caricature in the most literal meaning of the word, which implies the acceptance of a certain form in order to carry it to absurdity by overloading it with its very own elements" (p. 177). He interprets the story as an example of poking fun "at the literary flowering of the overcharged legends of the saints and the *exempla* of his own times" (p. 178). In this he is close to the position taken by Almansi, and his whole argument is very coherent. (Part IV of the article is especially interesting: De' Negri argues convincingly that Boccaccio has created a "legenda aurea" for love—as opposed to piety—and therefore emphasized the unreal, impractical, and legendary character of his creations. The critic may be right: my own argument deals with the *purpose* of Boccaccio's legendary creation.)

16. Again, the *Decameron* is using lies and laughter to underline a problem that is very much a part of social reality. Like many other "sins" that were officially denounced, usury (which Boccaccio is known to have detested), was practiced by laymen and clergy alike. There were even lengthy statements of the prescribed punishments for usurious clergy, the lightness of which is sur-

prising. See Richard Trexler, *Synodal Law in Florence and Fiesole, 1306-1518*, pp. 52-53, 105-113, 137-138.

17. On the various audiences in the *Decameron* see Nino Borsellino, *"Decameron* come teatro"; M. J. Marcus, *An Allegory of Form*, pp. 5, 21ff.; Claude Perrus, "Remarques sur les rapports entre écrivain et public dans le *Décaméron* de Boccace," pp. 294-299, and Antonio Staüble, "La brigata del 'Decameron' come pubblico teatrale."

18. "Così adunque visse e morì Ser Cepparello da Prato e santo divenne come avete udito. Il quale negar non voglio esser possibile lui esser beato nella presenza di Dio, per ciò che, come che la sua vita fosse scelerata e malvagia, egli poté in su lo stremo aver sì fatta contrizione, che per avventura Iddio ebbe misericordia di lui e nel suo regno il ricevette: ma per ciò che questo n'è occulto secondo quello che ne può apparire ragiono, e dico costui più tosto dovere essere nelle mani del diavolo in perdizione che in Paradiso" (I, 1, 89).

19. (I, 1, 11). Ser Cepparello's social destructiveness is an aspect of the story that has not been discussed in the literature.

20. Come la salamandra—sempre vive nel fuoco
    così par che lo scandalo—te sia sollazzo e gioco;
    dell'aneme redente—par che te curi poco:
    ove t'acconci loco—saperailo al partire. (Lauda lviii)
As the salamander always lives in fire / so it seems that scandal is pleasure and solace to you / It seems that you care little about saved souls / you will find out where you are preparing a place for yourself upon your death (*Poeti del Duecento*, a cura di Gianfranco Contini, p. 140). On the concept, behavior and role of the Church during the period, see Richard Trexler, *Synodal Law*; also his *The Spiritual Power: Republican Florence under Interdict*, pp. 1-28.

21. ". . . primieramente alquanto su per le rugiadose erbette andarono, e poi in su la mezza terza una chiesetta lor vicina visitata, in quella il divino oficio ascoltarono. E a case tornatisine, poi che con letizia e con festa ebber mangiato, cantarono . . ." (VIII, Intro., 2).

22. The anti-clerical stories are I, 1, 2, 4, 6, 7; II, 2; III, 1, 3, 4, 8, 10; IV, 2; V, 8; VI, 3, 10; VII, 3, 5, 10; VIII, 2, 4; IX, 2, 10 and X, 2.

23. Real life behavior differed a great deal from expectations, just as it did in Boccaccio's stories. According to Richard Trexler,

the actual cultic power of priests at this time was very low, and they were regarded as protectors of the sacred rather than as being in communion with it. Nevertheless, the clergy was supposed to have habits different from those of secular men, and it was supposed to pursue a clerical ritual. The facts of the case are most clearly shown by the contemporary ordinances, such as one drawn up in 1306 prohibiting the presence of a priest's sons as sextants or altar boys in their father's church (*Synodal Law*, pp. 36, 49-51).

24. See Franco Fido, "Boccaccio's Ars Narrandi in the Sixth Day of the *Decameron*," in *Italian Literature—Roots and Branches*, ed. G. Rimanelli and K. J. Atchety, pp. 225-242. (An Italian version of the article appeared in *Le metamorfosi del centauro*, pp. 43-61). Fido discusses the whole sixth day as an example of "the dialectics between reality and words" or the interplay between life and literature. According to Fido, Boccaccio treats narration itself as a further exploration of a familiar reality. He points out that VI, 1, the tale of Madonna Oretta, is especially important for four reasons: (1) its central position in the book corresponds to the equally central position of its content in Boccaccio's poetics; (2) it shows that the ability to "speak well" is basic to nobility or pretensions to aristocracy; (3) the effect that the gentleman's poor narration has on Madonna Oretta is exactly the opposite of the effect Boccaccio hopes that his stories will have on lovesick ladies, and (4) "the story is at the same time the negative presentation of a poetics on the content level and the positive illustration of that same poetics on the level of style" (pp. 58-60). Giovanni Sinicropi holds a somewhat different point of view. He finds evidence in the *Decameron*, and especially in the tale of Ser Cepparello, of a crisis of language and a loss of faith in its semantic reliability connected with the rise of nominalism ("Il segno linguistico del Decameron," *Studi sul Boccaccio* 9 [1975-1976], 169-224). See also Branca, *Boccaccio Med.*; Almansi, *The Writer as Liar*, Chapters 1 and 2, and Stavros Deligiorgis, "Sixth Day," in *Narrative Intellection in the Decameron*, pp. 131-150.

25. The centrality of the tale of Madonna Oretta has been emphasized by various critics. See Baratto, *Realtà e Stile nel Decamerone*, pp. 74-76; Pamela Steward, "La novella di Madonna Oretta e le due parti del *Decameron*," in *Yearbook of Italian Studies*, 1973-1975, pp. 27-40; Franco Fido, "*L'ars narrandi*"; Almansi *The Writer as Liar*, pp. 20-23.

26. The bibliography on this story is mountainous. Almost every critic dealing with the *Decameron* has written on it, and the indications are too numerous to list here.

27. "Vezzose donne, quantunque io abbia per privilegio di poter di quel che più mi piace parlare, oggi io non intendo di volere da quella materia separarmi della quale voi tutte avete assai acconciamente parlato; ma seguitando le vostre pedate, intendo di mostrarvi . . ." (VI, 10, 3).

28. The name is not only due to the fact that Certaldo, as Boccaccio tells us, was situated in an onion-growing region. Marcus has pointed out that onions stood for duplicity in the herbalist lore of the times (*An Allegory of Form*, pp. 75f.).

29. ". . . oltre a questo, niuna scienza avendo, sì ottimo parlatore e pronto era, che chi conosciuto non l'avesse non solamente un gran rettorico l'avrebbe estimato, ma avrebbe detto esser Tulio medesimo o forse Quintiliano . . ." (VI, 10, 7).

30. The speech is also an example of careful psychological and rhetorical construction and its devices could profitably be studied by politicians' aides today.

31. "Per la qual cosa messom'io in cammino, di Vinegia partendomi e andandomene per lo Borgo de' Greci e di quindi per lo reame del Garbo cavalcando e per Baldacca, pervenni in Parione, donde, non senza sete, dopo alquanto pervenni in Sardigna. Ma perché vi vo io tutti i paesi cerchi da me divisando? Io capitai, passato il Braccio de San Giorgio, in Truffia e in Buffia, paesi molto abitati e con gran popoli; e di quindi pervenni in terra di Menzogna, dove molti de' nostri frati e d'altre religioni trovai assai, li quali tutti il disagio andavan per l'amor di Dio schifando, poco dell'altrui fatiche curandosi dove la loro utilità vedessero seguitare, nulla altra moneta spendendo che senza conio per quei paesi: e quindi passai in terra d'Abruzzi, dove gli uomini e le femine vanno in zoccoli su pe' monti rivestendo i porci delle lor busecchie medesime; e poco più là trovai gente che portano il pan nelle mazze e 'l vin nelle sacca: da' quali alle montagne de' Bachi pervenni, dove tutte l'acque corono alla 'ngiù. E in brieve tanto andai adentro, che io pervenni mei infino in India Pastinaca, là dove io vi giuro per l'abito che io porto addosso che io vidi volare i pennati, cosa incredibile a chi non gli avesse veduti; ma di ciò non mi lasci mentire Maso del Saggio, il quale gran mercatante io trovai là, che schiacciava noci e vendeva gusci a ritaglio. Ma non potendo quello che io andava cercando trovare, per ciò

che da indi in là si va per acqua, indietro tornandomene, arrivai in quelle sante terre dove l'anno di state vi vale il pan freddo quatro denari e il caldo v'è per niente. E quivi trovai il venerabile padre messer Nonmiblasmete Sevoipiace, degnissimo patriarca de Ierusalem. Il quale, per reverenzia dell'abito che io ho sempre portato del baron messer santo Antonio, volle che io vedessi tutte le sante reliquie le quali egli appresso di sé aveva; e furon tante che, se io ve le volessi tutte contare, io non ne verrei a capo in parecchie miglia, ma pure per non lasciarvi sconsolate, ve ne dirò alquante. Egli primieramente mi mostrò il dito dello Spirito Santo così intero e saldo come fu mai, e il ciuffetto del serafino che apparve a san Francesco, e una dell'unghie de' gherubini, e una delle coste del Verbum-caro-fatti-alle-finestre e de' vestimenti della santa Fé catolica, e alquanti de' raggi della stella che apparve a' tre Magi in Oriente, e una ampolla del sudore di san Michele quando combatté col diavole, e la mascella della Morte di san Lazzero e altre. E per ciò che io liberamente gli feci copia delle piagge di Monte Morello in volgare e d'alquanti capitoli del Caprezio, li quali egli lungamente era andati cercando, mi fece egli partefice delle sue sante reliquie: e donommi uno de' denti della Santa Croce e in una ampoletta alquanto del suono delle campane del tempio di Salomone e la penna dell'agnol Gabriello, della quale già detto v'ho, e l'un de' zoccoli di san Gherardo da Villamagna (il quale io, non ha molto, a Firenze donai a Gherardo di Bonsi, il quale in lui ha grandissima divozione) e diedemi de' carboni co' quali fu il beatissimo martire san Lorenzo arrostito; le quali cose io tutte di qua con meco divotamente le recai, e holle tutte" (VI, 10, 38-47). McWilliam's translation brilliantly renders the spirit and meaning of the original.

32. The speech has been read in different ways. Marcus sees it as an example of "words no longer pointing to extralinguistic signficance, but elements in a system which is self referential . . . emptying the language of all conventional content and disabusing his public of any linguistic preconceptions it may bring to his discourse" (p. 69). Luigi Russo had given a similar reading, calling the speech senseless and a mere heaping up of words upon words (see his edition of the *Decameron*, p. 440).

33. "This Friar Cipolla was a little man with red hair and a merry face, and he was the most sociable fellow in the world . . . a lively and excellent speaker . . ." (p. 506). "Era questo frate Cipolla di persona piccola, di pelo rosso e lieto nel viso e il miglior

brigante del mondo . . . sì ottimo parlatore e pronto era . . ."
(VI, 10, 7).

34. Italy, then as now, was an overpopulated country with limited resources. The quality of "furbizia" or cunning was, and still is, considered a virtue rather than a fault. Practical jokes are also an admired tradition in Florence.

35. See Huizinga's pages on the general subject of the "crystallizing into images" of religion in *The Waning of the Middle Ages*, Chapters XII-XV.

36. Furthermore, "by corporealizing the incorporeal, the friar usurps a divine prerogative and calls down upon himself the inexorable charge of idolatry" (Marcus, *An Allegory of Form*, p. 75).

37. "Verbum-caro-fatti-alla-finestra" (VI, 10, 45).

CHAPTER III

1. Šklovsky upholds the Thucydides theory (pp. 195-247, and note 17), while Branca gives rather convincing evidence in favor of Paolo Diacono, (*Boccaccio Med.*, pp. 301-307). Jurgen Grimm ascribes Boccaccio's richness of detail to the fact that he actually witnessed the plague in Florence, but also points out the literary quality of his description, which is similar to that of Thucydides and could also have come down to Boccaccio via Virgil and Ovid (*Die literarische Darstellung der Pest in der Antike und in der Romania*, pp. 11-126). On the realism of the plague description see the documents edited by Brucker, *Renaissance Florence*, pp. 46ff., and William Bowsky, *The Black Death: A Turning Point in History?*, pp. 12ff. Brucker's essay "Florence and the Black Death" in *Boccaccio: Secoli di vita*, pp. 21-30, argues that the chaos was actually less and the social morality greater than Boccaccio's description implies.

2. See, for example, Singleton: "the perfect and calm moment of art" (On Meaning in the *Decameron*," p. 121) and Almansi: "The other world, the world of the story-tellers themselves, is in flight from the historical world, and content to relate the vicissitudes of the fictional world, while at the same time denying the evidence of both by virtue of its incorrupt life-style" (*The Writer as Liar*, p. 11). Marcus is an exception. She quotes the ending of the description of the plague, citing it as an example of "the most obtrusive of rhetorical devices" and claiming that Boccaccio wrote

it deliberately to call attention away from content and toward pure form: "it is a statement about the nature of his fictions and their relationship to history. By introducing his frame story with rhetoric, the writer is asserting its status as pure artifice, and the rhetorical ligature which connects the frame story with the preceding history betrays the radical discontinuity between these two narrative orders. The mediating passage thus serves less as a transition from history to fiction than as a commentary on their irreconcilability, and accordingly, the entire introduction to the *Decameron* may be read as a meditation on that schism" (*An Allegory of Form*, p. 7). This extremely modern interpretation of the meaning of rhetoric does not take into account the very different aims of the art as interpreted by Cicero and Quintilian, who served as models for both medieval and renaissance authors. An excellent counter-argument on the subject of language and history may be found in Eugene Vance, "Mervelous Signals: Poetics, Sign Theory, and Politics in Chaucer's *Troilus*," *New Literary History* 10 (Winter 1979), esp. pp. 294-299.

3. See Eco: "stylistic norms are thus an instance of overcoding" (*Semiotics*, p. 263). Overcoding is the use of an established code, A, to set up a new code, B, which can be used to send messages: "It may be that, given a code assigning meaning to certain minimal expressions, overcoding will assign additional meanings to more macroscopic strings of those expressions. Rhetorical or iconological rules are of this sort. . . . All of the courtesy formulas come from an overcoded everyday language: the expression [*s'il vous plaît*] (. . .) is understood in terms of its real signification on the basis of an accepted and traditional overcoding. Obviously the operations of overcoding, when completely accepted, produce what has been called (. . .) a subcode: in this sense overcoding is an innovatory activity that increasingly loses its provocative power, thereby producing social acceptance" (p. 134).

4. *De Genealogiis Deorum Gentilium*, Bk. XIV in Giovanni Boccaccio, *Opere in Versi . . . Prose Latine . . .*, a cura di Pier Giorgio Ricci, p. 963. Vittore Branca holds that the ideal of the poet as hero and of poetry as *anima mundi* in Boccaccio is directly modeled on his study of Dante and on his personal friendship with Petrarch. See "The Myth of the Hero in Boccaccio," in *Concepts of the Hero in the Middle Ages and the Renaissance*, ed. M. T. Burns and C. J. Reagan, pp. 287-291.

5. "Taceant ergo blateratores inscii et omutescant superbi, si

possunt, cum ne dum insignes viros, lacte Musarum educatos et in laribus phylosophie versatos atque sacris duratos studiis, profundissimos in suis poematibus sensus apposuisse semper credendum sit, sed etiam nullam esse usquam tam delirantem aniculam, circa foculum domestici laris una cum vigilantibus ybernis noctibus fabellas orci, seu fatarum, vel lammiarum, et huiusmodi, ex quibus sepissime inventa conficiunt, fingentem atque recitantem, que sub pretextu relatorum non sentiat aliquem iuxta vires sui modici intellectus sensum minime quandoque ridendum, per quem velit aut terrorem incutere parvulis, aut oblectare puellas, aut senes ludere, aut saltem Fortune vires ostendere" (XIV, 10; p. 970, translation mine).

6. ". . . sed ut que apposita viluissent labore ingeniorum quesita et diversimode intellecta comperta tandem faciant cariora" (p. 980 translation mine).

7. On the idea of cultural codes see U. Eco, "Looking for a Logic of Culture," in T. Sebeok, ed., *The Tell Tale Sign*; J. M. Lotman and B. A. Uspensky, *Tipologia della cultura*, and J. M. Lotman, *La struttura del testo poetico*. The problems inherent in the use of a term such as *code* in a study like this one have been clarified by Teresa de Lauretis: "The notion of code, borrowed by literary criticism from linguistics and other areas of communications research, is most often used either in the (linguistic) sense of set of internal rules organizing the elements within one system (i.e., Saussure's *langue*), or in a generalized way to indicate a supposedly homogeneous subset of elements in a complex system. The latter usage applies, for example, to the several codes or 'languages' that coexist in the theatre or in cinema; and it is also in this sense that Barthes identifies the five codes of Balzac's novella. In both usages, the term 'code' refers to a set of formal rules or elements of content internal to the work, and thus emphasizes the signifying aspect of the object studied over its communicative purpose; it focuses the attention on the object in isolation rather than on the process of signification-communication in which the object interacts with the reader/viewer and properly becomes a text. If, on the other hand, a code is defined by Eco as a conventionally (i.e., socially) established correlation between signs and contents, between the elements of a signifying system that make up a message and the meaning attributed to them by the receiver(s) of the message, then messages and codes act upon one another and both functives of the correlation (code) become

passible of change; thus a text can contribute to reshaping cultural conventions and consequently our view of the world, of nature, history, even our perception of the physical universe" ("Semiotic Models, *Invisible Cities*," *Yale Italian Studies* 2 [Winter 1978], p. 27). Eco distinguishes between codes and what he calls s-codes (from "code as system"). The latter may be (a) "a set of signals ruled by internal combinatory laws," (b) "a set of *notions . . .* which can become . . . a set of possible communicative contents," (c) "a set of possible *behavioral responses* on the part of the destination," (d) "a *rule* coupling some items from the (a) system with some from the (b) or the (c) system." Only the last "complex form of rule may properly be called a *code*" (Eco, *Semiotics*, pp. 36-37). I shall use the term *system* for the kinds of sets of rules Barthes identified as codes in *S/Z* and the term *code* in accordance with Eco's definition as given above and elucidated in the quotation from De Lauretis, which underlines the communicative aspect and hence the cultural and social importance of the concept. See also Lotman and Uspensky: "The very concept of sign and of sign system is inextricably linked with the problems of meaning. In human culture the sign fulfills the function of mediator. The aim of semic activity is the transmission of a given content" (*Tipologia della Cultura*, p. 44).

I shall also use Eco's concept of the *sign-function*: "When a code apportions the elements of a conveying system to the elements of a conveyed system, the former becomes the expression of the latter and the latter becomes the content of the former. A sign function arises when an expression is correlated to a content, both the correlated elements being the functives of such a correlation" (*A Theory of Semiotics*, p. 48). As De Lauretis has pointed out in an admirably lucid presentation of Eco's semiotic theories, "by replacing the traditional notion of sign (too often identified with the linguistic sign, or a single unit of a given system) with the notion of SIGN-FUNCTION, which includes various types of significant units such as strings of signs, texts and even macrotexts, Eco develops a much more flexible tool suitable for dealings with complex and interrelated cultural phenomena. . . . a sign-function 'is always an element of an *expression plane* conventionally correlated to one (or several) elements of a content plane' [*Semiotics*, p. 48]. . . . Of course, the correlation, or code, is a socially established one" ("Semiotics Unlimited," *PTL: A Journal for Descriptive Poetics and Theory of Literature* 2 [1977], 370).

8. "Umana cosa è aver compassione degli afflitti . . ." (Proemio, 2). As so often, I am indebted to Vittore Branca's invaluable notes for the information on the use of aphorism in medieval rhetoric (Branca, p. 976). On the whole problem of Boccaccio's stylistic devices see "Strutture della prosa: Scuola di rettorica e ritorni di fantasia," in Branca, *Boccaccio Med.*; "Il diletto narrativo e stilistico," in Baratto, *Realtà e Stile*; M. Cottino-Jones's detailed study, *An Anatomy of Boccccio's Style*; and Fido's essay "L'*ars narrandi* di Boccaccio nella sesta giornata," *Le metamorfosi del centauro*, pp. 43-61.

9. ". . . essendo Egli infinito, diede per legge incommutabile a tutte le cose mondane aver fine . . ." (Proemio, 5, translation mine).

10. Branca has pointed out the similarity of literary structure between the *Proemio* and the opening sonnet of Petrarch's *Canzoniere*. See Branca, *Decameron*, pp. 977, 980, and "Implicazioni strutturali e espressive fra Petrarca e Boccaccio," in *Atti del Convegno Internazionale su Francesco Petrarca dell'Accademia del Lincei*.

11. Branca, *Decameron*, p. 979. Courtly love is important in the *Decameron*, as Billanovich pointed out (*Restauri Boccacceschi*). See also Louise George Clubb, "Boccaccio and the Boundaries of Love," *Italica* 37 (1960), 188-196.

12. This word is untranslatable: it usually does not mean "poetry" in Italian but stands for the quality of being literature as opposed to other forms of writing.

13. ". . . cento novelle, o favole o parabole o istorie che dire le vogliamo . . ." (Proemio, 13).

14. "COMINCIA IL LIBRO CHIAMATO DECAMERON" (p. 1).

15. On the complexities involved see Eco, *Semiotics*, pp. 125-129. Given the fact that "book" could also refer to the "book of nature" or "the book of experience" at this time (see E. R. Curtius, *European Literature and the Latin Middle Ages*, pp. 316, 319ff.), in this case "the same sememe may derive two of its connotations from two opposed positions in a given semantic axis" (*Semiotics*, p. 128), and the opposition may seem stronger to a twentieth-century reader than it would have to Boccaccio, in view of his conviction of the hidden truth in all *poesia*.

16. The apparent frame is actually a double one, as will be shown in Chapters IV and V.

17. Almansi would disagree: "Suppose the *cornice* (meaning the inner frame) actually serves the purpose of the standard picture

frame, i.e. a reminder that what is inside is an artistic object? What if one were to see the *cornice* of *The Decameron* as declaring that everything within it is a stylized narrative creation, a sum of narrative items which the *cornice* thus automatically sets apart from the items of the everyday world which the reader lives in and knows about?" (p. 13). I believe that the former part of the statement should be applied to the *Preface*, not the *cornice* and that its aim is rather to underline the importance of the narrative creation for the everyday world (the "vécu") which Almansi believes it excludes.

18. "Le cento novelle antiche o libro di novelle e di bel parlar gentile detto anche Novellino." This, as Giovanni Sinicropi points out, is a code that testifies to the importance of the word not only as indicator of *savoir faire*, intelligence and spiritual aristocracy but as a real "weapon" or "act" in life ("Il segno linguistico del *Decameron*," pp. 187-188). The remark is made in passing in a semiotic discussion of the implications for the functioning of the linguistic sign in the *Decameron* of Ockham's relationships between *vox* (signifier), *conceptus* (signified), and *res* (referent), the latter two having an interdependent relationship while the relationship of the first term with the other two is determining. Sinicropi points out that fifty-six of the hundred tales are based on aberrant functions of the sign, in connection with either the *signified*—(twenty stories on witty replies)—or the *referent* (thirty-six stories on practical jokes or *beffe*)—(p. 187) and concludes that the crisis of the structures of the sign in Boccaccio reflects that in Ockham.

19. "Comincia la prima giornata del *Decameron*, nella quale, dopo la dimostrazione fatta dall'autore per che cagione avvenisse di doversi quelle persone che appresso si mostrano, ragunare a ragionare insieme . . ." (I, Intro., 1).

20. ". . . la presente opera al vostro iudicio avrà grave e noioso principio, sì come è la dolorosa ricordazione della pestifera mortalità trapassata . . ." (I, Intro., 2; translation mine).

21. I am following Branca's paragraphing here; there is unfortunately a lacuna in the Hamilton codex at this point. See Charles Singleton, *Decameron, Edizione diplomatico-interpretativa dell'autografo Hamilton 90*.

22. "E si come la estremità della allegrezza il dolore occupa . . ." (Intro., 5). Branca points out that the use of this biblical

proverb was frequent in the literature of the time, citing Petrarch and the chronicler and historian Villani (p. 981).

23. "Dico adunque che già erano gli anni della fruttifera incarnazione del Figliuolo di Dio al numero pervenuti di milletrecentoquarantotto, quando nella egregia città di Fiorenza, oltre a ogn'altra italica bellissima, pervenne la mortifera pestilenza . . ." (I, Intro., 8). The use of Fiorenza rather than Boccaccio's more usual Firenze underscores the solemnity (Branca, *Decameron*, p. 982). Mazzotta has pointed out that "While Boccaccio attempts to situate the plague in historical space and time, he uses what in mediaeval rhetoric is a conventional *topos* of exordium. The vernal equinox, occurring on the feast of the Annunciation, 25 March, is the emblem of the beginning of the world, the fall of man and his redemption. The date stands as the exact center of the historic process and is a typological recapitulation of the great events of salvation history. Conventionally, mediaeval works of fiction begin with this typological *ab initio*. Most prominently, the *Divine Comedy* and the *Canterbury Tales*, with significant differences, employ this rhetorical device as a deliberate sign that the book is a synopsis of the pilgrimage of human history and a way of creatively participating in the *renovatio mundi*" ("Marginality," p. 66).

24. ". . . la quale, per operazion de'corpi superiori o per le nostre iniquie opere da giusta ira di Dio a nostra correzione mandata sopra i mortal . . ." (I, Intro., 8). McWilliam's translation adds a possibly interpretative "Some say that . . . others that" to the passage, so I have used my own translation here. Many critics read the "or" clause as a presumed antidote to superstition.

25. See Brucker, *Florentine Politics*, pp. 238ff. See also the chapter "Storicità e invenzione" in Baratto, esp. pp. 29-33 and 66-67, which discuss Boccaccio's Florentinism and finally define him as a "European-municipal" writer.

26. Branca, *Decameron*, p. 990.

27. These rules were well known at the time and had been codified and disseminated for the "vulgar tongue" by Dante's *De vulgari eloquentia*.

28. This is according to the precepts of classical and medieval rhetoric. For bibliography and possible sources of the names see Branca, *Decameron*, pp. 992-993.

29. Victoria Kirkham has done some interesting studies on the numerology in Boccaccio's works. See her "Reckoning with Boc-

caccio's *questioni d'amore*," *MLN* 89 (1974), 47-59; "Numerology and Allegory in Boccaccio's 'Caccia di Diana,' " *Traditio* 34 (1978), 303-329 and " 'Chiuso parlare' in Boccaccio's *Teseida*," forthcoming in *Studies in the Italian Trecento*, Festschrift for C. S. Singleton. J. Levarie Smarr has presented a closely reasoned and convincing study of the patterns of symmetry in the *Decameron*, "Symmetry and Balance in the *Decameron*," *Medievalia* 2 (1976), 159-187. See also her study on astrology in the *Teseida*, forthcoming in *Traditio*, 39. The article by Pamela D. Steward, "La novella di Madonna Oretta e le due parti del *Decameron*," argues a two-part division of the hundred stories into parallel groups of five (*Yearbook of Italian Studies*, 1973-1975, pp. 27-40). Her argument draws on F. Neri's "Il disegno ideale del *Decameron*."

30. See Christopher Butler, *Number Symbolism*, Chapters I-III; J. E. Cirlot, *A Dictionary of Symbols*, tr. Jack Sage; V. H. Hopper, *Medieval Number Symbolism*; and Curtius, pp. 500-509. See also Branca, *Decameron*, p. 992.

31. See Kirkham's articles cited in note 29.

32. It is less likely that the 18 is the product of 2×9, for while 9 is a highly symbolic and positively charged number (3×3), 2 is regarded as ominous in esoteric thought.

33. Boccaccio most certainly knew of this type of number play, which was extensively used by St. Augustine. See Butler, pp. 24-28.

34. Butler, pp. 34, 37. Five is therefore one of the "marriage numbers."

35. Ibid., p. 7. The use of justice as a symbol underlines certain ambiguities in the Fourth Day.

36. "Comincia il libro chiamato *Decameron* cognominato Prencipe Galeotto nel quale si contengono cento novelle in diece dì dette da sette donne e da tre giovani uomini" (p. 1).

37. ". . . savia ciascuna e di sangue nobile e bella di forma e ornata di costumi e di leggiadra onestà" (I, Intro., 49; translation mine). On the aristocratic or high bourgeois nature of the group see Getto, Baratto, and Padoan as well as Branca.

38. "Il metalinguagio delle descrizioni tipologiche della cultura," in Lotman and Uspensky, pp. 155-157, translation mine. See also p. 145. I have used the Italian editions of their work rather than the later English ones because the Italian versions are more extensive and probably better. Some of the ideas referred to here are not in the English editions.

39. "Ma per ciò che le cose che sono senza modo non possono lungamente durare . . ." (I, Intro., 95).

40. "The Gardens in the *Decameron* Cornice," *PMLA* 66 (1951), 505-523.

41. "The Structural Isomorphism of Art," in *A Poetics of Composition*, trans. V. Zavarin and S. Wittig, pp. 162-163.

42. An attempt has been made to show that the frame characters represent the virtues necessary to upright living in the world. See Joan M. Ferrante, "The Frame Characters of the *Decameron*: A Progression of Virtues." Battaglia argues that the protagonists had fled from a society in dissolution to an ideal and idyllic space and that their lack of individuality is due to the author's desire not to disturb the peace of their deliberate self-exile from real life. See also Franco Fido: "The members of the group do not change sensibly from the beginning to the end of the book, as do Dante and Ameto. This incapacity to change is a correlation of their stylized perfection, to their being, to all intents and purposes, outside history. The three young men's and seven girls' chaste sojourn in the country rather represents an ideal goal, a theorem whose demonstration is constituted by the hundred tales" ("Il sorriso di Messer Torello," in *Le metamorfosi del centauro*, p. 16).

43. The other two translations are my own; "formosa e di piacevole aspetto molto" (II, Intro., 4); "occhi vaghi e scintillanti non altramenti che matutina stella (II, Concl., 3); "li cui capelli eran crespi, lunghi e d'oro e sopra li candidi e dilicati omeri ricadenti e il viso ritondetto con un color vero di bianchi gigli e di vermiglie rose mescolati tutto splendido, con due occhi in testa che parean d'un falcon pellegrino e con una boccuccia piccolina li cui labbri parevan due rubinetti . . ." (IV, Concl., 4). Branca pointed out the similarities to Boccaccio's previous ladies (*Decameron*, p. 1260).

44. "Con un vestimento indosso tanto sottile, che quasi niente delle candide carni nascondea. . . . lodando i capelli, li quali d'oro estimava, la fronte, il naso e la bocca, la gola e le braccia e sommamente il petto, poco ancora rilevato . . ." (V, 1, 7 and 9; translation mine).

45. ". . . grassa e grossa e piccola e mal fatta, con un paio di poppe che parean due ceston da lettame e con un viso che parea de' Baronci, tutta sudata, unta e affumicata . . ." (VI, 10, 21; translation mine).

46. "Le vivande dilicatamente fatte vennero" (I, Intro., 105); "con festa e con piacer cenarono" (II, Concl., 11); "con grandis-

simo diletto cenarono" (III, Concl., 8); "lietamente si misero a mangiare" (V, Intro., 4); "riposatamente e con letizia cenarono" (VII, Concl., 6).

47. "Estimava io che lo 'mpetuoso vento e ardente della 'nvidia non dovesse percuotere se non l'alte torri o le più levate cime degli alberi"; "le presenti novellette . . . le quali non solamente in fiorentin volgare e in prosa scritte per me sono e senza titolo, ma ancora in istilo umilissimo e rimesso quanto il più si possono."

48. Page 412. On this whole problem, see Curtius, pp. 407-413. Branca points out that Boccaccio had made similar traditional statements about his "humble" work in the *Filostrato*, *Fiammetta*, and the *Trattatello in lode di Dante* (p. 1198).

49. "Aiutaronmi elle bene e mostraronmi comporre que' mille; e forse a queste cose scrivere, quantunque sieno umilissime, si sono elle venute parecchie volte a starsi meco, in servigio forse e in onore della simiglianza che le donne hanno a esse; per che, queste cose tessendo, né dal monte Parnaso né dalle Muse non mi allontano quanto molti per avventura s'avisano" (IV, Intro., 36; translation mine).

50. "Ma che direm noi a coloro che della mia fame hanno tanta compassione che mi consigliano che io procuri del pane? Certo io non so, se non che, volendo meco pensare quale sarebbe la loro risposta se io per bisogno loro ne dimandassi, m'aviso che direbbono: 'Va cercane tralle favole,' E già più ne trovarono tralle loro favole i poeti, che molti ricchi tra' loro tesori, e assai già, dietro alle loro favole andando, fecero la loro età fiorire, dove in contrario molti nel cercar d'aver più pane, che bisogno non era loro, perirono acerbi. Che più? Caccinmi via questi cotali qualora io ne domando loro, non che la Dio mercé ancora non mi bisogna; e, quando pur sopravenisse il bisogno, io so, secondo l'Appostolo, abbondare e necessità sofferire; e per ciò a niun caglia più di me che a me" (IV, Intro., 37-38; translation mine).

51. E ciò fa certo che' l primo superbo,
     che fu la somma d'ogni creatura,
     per non apsettar lume, cadde acerbo. (*Par.* XIX, 46-48)

52. "Quegli che queste cose così non essere state dicono, avrei molto caro che essi recassero gli originali: li quali se a quel che io scrivo discordanti fossero, giusta direi la lor reprensione e d'amendar me stesso m'ingegnerei; ma infino che altro che parole non apparisce, io gli lascerò con la loro opinione, seguitando la

mia, di loro dicendo quello che essi di me dicono" (IV, Intro., 39).

53. *De Vulgari Eloquenzia*, II, iii.

54. "Nobilissime giovani" (Concl., 1).

55. ". . . io mi credo aiutantemi la divina grazia, sì come io avviso, per li vostri pietosi prieghi non già per li miei meriti, quello compiutamente aver fornito che io nel principio della presente opera promisi di dover fare: per la qual cosa Idio primieramente e appresso voi ringraziando, è da dare alla penna e alla man faticata riposo." ". . . tempo è da por fine alle parole, Colui umilmente ringraziando che dopo sì lunga fatica col suo aiuto n'ha al disiderato fine condotto. E voi, piacevoli donne, con la sua grazia in pace vi rimanete, di me ricordandovi, se a alcuna forse alcuna cosa giova l'averle lette" (Concl., 1 and 29).

56. "Primieramente se alcuna cosa in alcuna n'è, [the *ne* refers to the *licenzia* in Concl. 3] la qualità delle novelle l'hanno richesta, le quali se con ragionevole occhio da intendente persona fian riguardate, assai aperto sarà conosciuto, se io quelle della lor forma trar' non avessi voluto, altramenti raccontar non poterlo" (Concl., 4).

57. ". . . la chiesa, delle cui cose e con animi e con vocaboli onestissimi si convien dire, quantunque nelle sue storie d'altramenti fatte che le scritte da me si truovino assai" (Concl., 7). Bakhtin cites the same passage as an example of Boccaccio's posing of the problem of "frankness," which is envisaged in a special sense. "Thought and speech had to be placed under such conditions that the world could expose its other side; the side that was hidden, that nobody talked about . . ." (*Rabelais and His World*, trans. H. Iwolsky, pp. 271-272). Bakhtin's understanding of Boccaccio and his world is placed in doubt by the later comment, "Another solution of the same problem [the plague as a condensed image of death] is offered by Boccaccio in his hero's madness" (p. 273). Presumably he means Ariosto's hero's madness.

58. ". . . ma ne' giardini, in luogo di sollazzo, tra persone giovani benché mature e non pieghevoli per novelle, in tempo nel quale andar con le brache in capo per iscampo di sé era alli più onesti non disdicevole, dette sono."

59. "Niuna corrotta mente intese mai sanamente parola: e così come le oneste a quella non giovano, così quelle che tanto oneste non sono la ben disposta non posson contaminare, se non come il loto i solari raggi o le terrene brutture le bellezze del cielo"

(Concl., 11). "Fere lo sol lo fango tutto'l giorno:/ vile riman, né'l sol perde calore," 11. 31-32 (*Poeti del Duccento*, VII, ed. G. Contini, p. 462).

60.   il padre
mio e delli altri miei miglior che mai
rime d'amore usar dolci e leggiadre.
(Purg. XXVI, 97-99)

61. Comincia il libro chiamato Decameron, cognominato Prencipe Galeotto, nel quale si contengono cento novelle in dieci dì dette da sette donne e da tre giovani uomini.

Qui finisce la decima
E ultima giornata del libro
Chiamato Decameron cognominato
Prencipe Galleotto
(Translation mine)

62. Personal communication from Professor Ruggero Stefanini in answer to my question. I also owe him the information on the general medieval opposition between name and nickname.

63. Although, as D. Howard pointed out, the word Galleotto may not demonstrably have undergone "semantic degeneration" to the meaning of "go-between" or "pander" and may have meant only "matchmaker" or "messenger between lovers" (review of *Boccaccio's Two Venuses*, *Renaissance Quarterly*, 31, 4 [Winter 1978], 606), its sense in Dante's *Inferno* is clear. From De Sanctis on, critics have been using the expression as evidence for the book's frivolity, calling it "a real go-between for pleasure and love" (*Storia della letteratura italiana*, p. 310), though recently some have claimed that the subtitle is either self-deprecating (Mazzotta, "Marginality," p. 68) or "a device to expose the seductions of literature" which will warn against some of the "uses and abuses of literary creation" (Marcus, *An Allegory of Form*, pp. 2, 110). I disagree. Hollander sums up many of the arguments and gives considerable bibliographical information on the problem (pp. 102-107 and 225-228). He belongs to the pander school of thought. Padoan believes that the nickname is meant to underline the book's function as *courtly* love messenger (p. 124).

64. "E chi utilità e frutto ne vorrà, elle nol negheranno, né sarà mai che altro che utile e oneste sian dette o tenute, se a que' tempi o a quelle persone si leggeranno per cui e pe' quali state son raccontate" (Concl., 14).

65. See Branca, *Decameron*, note 1, p. 976.

CHAPTER IV

1. "The aesthetic use of a language deserves attention on a number of different levels: (i) an aesthetic text involves a very peculiar labor, i.e. a particular *manipulation of the expression* (. . .); (ii) this manipulation of the expression releases (and is released by) a *reassessment of the content* (. . .); (iii) this double operation, producing an idiosyncratic and highly original instance of sign function (. . .), is to some degree reflected in precisely those codes on which the aesthetic sign-function is based, thus releasing a process of *code changing;* (iv) the entire operation, even though focused on codes, frequently produces a new type of *awareness about the world* (. . .); (v) insofar as the aesthetic labor aims to be detected and scrutinized repeatedly by the addressee, who thereby engages in a complex labor of interpretation, the aesthetic sender must also focus his attention on the addressees' possible reactions, so that the aesthetic text represents a network of diverse *communicational acts* eliciting highly original responses (. . .)" (p. 261). As Teresa de Lauretis pointed out, messages and codes act upon one another and both can undergo changes. In this sense a text can "contribute to reshaping cultural conventions and consequently our view of the world, of nature, history, even our perceptions of the physical universe" ("Semiotic Models: *Invisible Cities,*" p. 27).

2. There are also, however, aspects of the *cornice* that are not in the least innovative, but modeled on the "courts of love." The idea of a group of ladies and men seated on the grass in discussion is of course not new, and had been used by Boccaccio himself in the well-known "questions of love" episode of the *Filocolo.* The originality here lies in the continued coherence and architectonic rather than episodic nature of the *cornice* and in the use of the court-of-love model together with the *novella* form. Mazzotta characterized the latter as one whose "mode of being is one of marginality in relationship to existing literary traditions, cultural myths and social structures, to that which, in one word, we call history" ("Marginality," p. 64). Although I strongly disagree with all but the first phrase, it is noteworthy that the *novella* form did not have a recognized literary position.

3. Although the greater part of the Introduction to Day IV is formally addressed to the ladies for whom Boccaccio purports to be writing, the story of Filippo Balducci and the women/geese is

addressed directly to Boccaccio's critics (and hence to his readers): "and speaking to my assailants I say . . ." (IV, Intro., 11, translation mine. McWilliam has translated "For the benefit of my assailants, then, I say . . . ," p. 326).

4. The pun on the idea of telling an untruth is intentional and I also have in mind the obsolete meaning of "talk, discourse" listed by the *Oxford Dictionary of English Etymology*. The meanings of "to talk," which include "to make known, declare, inform," as well as "to mention in order, narrate," should also be remembered.

5. "E nel vero, se io potuto avessi onestamente per altra parte menarvi a quello che io desidero che per così aspro sentiero come fia questo, io l'avrei volentier fatto . . ." (I, Intro., 7).

6. Gabriel Pérouse sees the social nature of storytelling as the essence of the genre of the *novella*: "It seems that the origin and the very substance of the genre can be found in the presentation of the storytellers and the circumstances of their meeting, in the story (if one dares to say so) of their exchanges. . . . the *novella* [there is a play on the French *nouvelle*—news—involved] is an oral phenomenon, which comes from a group, a 'society' " (*Nouvelles Françaises du XVIe Siècle* [Geneva, 1977], pp. 24-25). The quotation fits the *Decameron*, but not its predecessor the *Novellino*.

7. Guillaume de Lorris and Jean de Meun, *The Romance of the Rose*, trans. H. W. Robbins (New York, 1962), p. 405.

> Car el sot des qu'el le portait,
> Don au porter se confortait,
> Qu'il iert l'espere merveillable
> Qui ne peut estre terminable,
> Qui par touz leus son centre lance,
> Ne leu n'a la circonference;
> Qu'il iert li merveilleus triangles
> Don l'unité fait les treis angles,
> Ne li trei tout entierement
> Ne font que l'un tant seulement;
> C'est li cercles trianguliers,
> C'est li triangles circuliers
> Qui en la vierge s'ostela.

Le Roman de la Rose, ed. E. Langlois (Paris, 1922), vol. 4, 11. 19127-19139.

8. ". . . quasi in cerchio a seder postesi . . ."; ". . . tutti sopra

la verde erba si puosero in cerchio a sedere . . ." (I, Intro., 52 and 110, translation mine).

9. ". . . on the basis of an established rule, a new rule was proposed which governed a rarer application of the previous rule." "A basic code establishes that a certain grammatical disposition is understandable and acceptable (how and why) and a further rule (which, far from denying the previous one, uses it as a starting point) establishes that the disposition in question has to be used under given circumstances and with a certain stylistical connotation (for example 'epic style' or 'poetic dignity'). Overcoding works even at the level of grammatical rules . . ." (Eco, *Semiotics*, p. 133). On the theological content of numbers see "The Early Medieval Period: Biblical Exegesis and World Schemes," in Butler, *Number Symbolism*, pp. 22-46.

10. Originally I saw the s-code based on five as *subverting* that based on ten and one hundred. I am indebted to Janet Levarie Smarr for pointing out that there is no real evidence for believing in a subversion.

11. "Forms of Accommodation in the *Decameron*." Janet Smarr's work further bears out this point (see her "Symmetry and Balance in the *Decameron*").

12. James Wimsatt has pointed out to me that since Christian marriage is a sacrament and an image of God's marriage with His Church, an opposition between man-in-the-world and the-universe-as-a-reflection-of-God is not necessarily involved here (private correspondence). I believe that other evidence in the *Decameron* tends to bear out my point when this is regarded as part of a cumulative pattern.

13. "Comincia il libro chiamato *Decameron* cognominato Prencipe Galeotto nel quale si contengono cento novelle in diece dì dette da sette donne e da tre giovani uomini" (p. 1).

14. ". . . il venerdì, avendo riguardo che in esso Colui che per la nostra vita morì sostenne passione, è degno di reverenza, per che giusta cosa e molto onesta reputerei che, a onor di Dio, più tosto a orazioni che a novelle vacassimo. E il sabato . . . soglion similmente assai, a reverenza della Vergine madre del Figliuolo di Dio, digiunare, e da indi in avanti per onor della sopravegnente domenica da ciascuna opera riposarsi" (II, Concl., 5).

15. The number three not only immediately signaled Trinity to the medieval reader but traditionally had connotations of spirit and intellect as well. It also was the number of the whole in the

Pythagorean system, as it has a beginning, a middle, and an end (see Walter Burkert, "Pythagorean Number Theory," in *Lore and Science in Ancient Pythagoreanism*, trans. E. L. Miner, Jr., p. 467). Boccaccio very probably knew the Pythagorean system in view of the extensive interest in numerology during his time and especially as Pythagorean numerology was used as a basis for certain widely discussed Gnostic heresies combatted by the Church fathers (Butler, *Number Symbolism*, p. 36). Supporting evidence for the theory that the three was assigned to the men as a more perfect number can be found in Elissa's remark: "It is certainly true that man is the head of woman" (p. 82; "Veramente gli uomini sono delle femmine capo," I, Intro., 76). The origin of the image is biblical. Branca (p. 996) and Mazzotta refer it to the Pauline doctrine of the mystical body of the Church: "wives be subject to your husbands as to the Lord for the husband is the head of the wife even as Christ is the head of the Church" (Eph. 5, 23). Mazzotta adds that this doctrine is "uniformly used as the rationale of the body politic in the political theology of the Middle Ages." He regards the statement as ironic ("Marginality," pp. 67-68).

16. The temptations of numerology are many. The *seven* women, representative of the class of beings who inspired Boccaccio to write, also present interesting numerological possibilities beyond those discussed in the preceding chapters. Seven is made up of three and four. Four usually stood for the elements and it could also be argued that the three, via its connotations of spirit and intellect, represents form. Ciriaco Moròn-Arroyo has suggested to me that Boccaccio may have had in mind the Aristotelian idea that the male contributed form and the female matter to the process of generation (in *The Generation of Animals*). If the seven is indeed meant to represent form and matter, it may on another level stand for humanity (being composed of soul and matter), which could then be read indirectly as the real inspiration of Boccaccio's work, filtered through the images of women/Muses. On yet another level the "structure" of the ten protagonists could be read as a 3 plus 4 plus 3, perhaps representing humanity and creativity, or the human and the divine as the elements that make up the life of the world.

Further possibilities are not lacking. The number four generally has female connotations, while the number three has male connotations. There are interesting examples in Hippocratic medicine and in general anthropological observations. Burkert cites a whole numerological system in Hippocratic medicine, beginning with the belief that the male embryo stirs in the womb after three months and the female only after four (p. 475). He also cites the anthropologist Emil Fettweiss: "In certain Negro peoples the King of the gods is invoked thrice; the queen four times; the amulet worn by a man has three knots, that of a woman four. The birth of a boy is celebrated after three days, that of a girl after four; a dead son is mourned for thirty-three days, a daughter forty-four. Fettweiss found similar beliefs among Alaskan Eskimos ("Über das Verhältnis des mathematischen Denkens zum mystischen Denken auf niederen Kulturstufen," *Archeion* 14 [1932], pp. 207-220 and "Berührungspunkte der pythagoräischen Zahlenlehre mit dem Totemismus," *Zeitschrift fur Philosophischen Forschungen* 5 [1950-1951], p. 190. Both sources are cited in Burkert, p. 469).

In view of the generally male connotations of the number three and the female ones of the number four and of Aristotle's theory, Boccaccio's seven ladies in the *Decameron* may well metaphorically bear the seed of his three men within them. Another interpretative possibility lies in the fact that three is the number of Venus, while seven is the number of Diana, or chastity. (I am indebted to Janet L. Smarr for pointing this possibility out to me.)

The ages of the protagonists also leave room for interpretative play. None of the women are older than 28, the sum of the numbers from 1 to 7. None is younger than 18 (8 − 1 is also 7), and that number could be read either as 2×9 (9 − 2 is 7) or as the product of the "perfect" number 6 (1 + 2 + 3 = 6)—which is even and thus feminine—and the potent masculine number 3. The ages of the women thus repeat the possible play on generation inherent in the number of the feminine protagonists. Furthermore, the addition of 5 (the square root of the only number given in connection with the ages of the men) to 18 or its subtraction from 28 both give 23, the first male number and the first female number paired.

The number three also seems to be functioning in the choice of the days when one of the men is king. This office goes to Filostrato on the fourth day, to Dioneo on the seventh and to Panfilo on the tenth. The series could be read as $3 \times 1 + 1$; $3 \times 2 + 1$, and $3 \times 3 + 1$. The possibilities seem almost infinite and Boccaccio seems to have enjoyed them thoroughly. Numerology may also serve as a clue to the reason for Boccaccio's choice of the Introduction to the *fourth* day for his defense of his work. Four not only represented the elements and thus material things and the realm of the earth, it also represented justice in the Pythagorean system, being composed of the first instance of equal times equal (Burkert, p. 467, and Butler: "Justice was the number four on the ground that justice essentially involved a reciprocal relationship between persons," p. 7).

The possible semantic content of the numbers Boccaccio uses is multiple, but there can be no doubt that he set up a numerological system. As Eco put it (in the somewhat different context of abstract painting and atonal musical composition), "nobody can deny that there is an expression system, even though the content plane remains, as it were, open to all comers" (p. 243). However, it is possible to narrow the field somewhat. The system is secular, the implied comparison with Dante's text almost surely deliberate and the content undoubtedly plays on the male/female opposition. The system is also rather rigid and operates in the best tradition of the numerical play of the times, one of whose best-known exponents was St. Augustine.

17. A. D. Sellstrom, in a spirit of pure mockery, pointed out that "55 added to itself is 110, that is 10 × 10 plus 10, while 55 squared is 3025" (3 and 0 and 2 + 5). Boccaccio may well have done these sums; if not, he would probably have been delighted at the results.

18. Nino Borsellino pointed out that it became a habit in Renaissance literature—and especially in theater—after the *Decameron* ("*Decameron* come teatro," pp. 39-40). I am indebted to Franco Fido for reminding me that the addressing of the stories to the ladies may not be only a technique to remind the reader of the outermost frame of the work. Borsellino emphasizes the newness and the social aspects of what he calls "this social promotion of woman to the status of participating public at an event rather than mere object of erotic devotion [which] implies a close bond of literary solidarity with the author" (pp. 38-39).

19. I am indebted to Ruggero Stefanini for reminding me of this possibility.

20. This sort of statement is made seven times by one protagonist or another: I, 2 and 4; IV, 1 (!); V, 10; IX, 3, 5 and X, 9. There are four statements within the same frame (also by protagonists) referring to various tales as "useful": II, 2, 3; VII, 1, 2.

21. See Bateson, " A Theory of Play and Fantasy," pp. 177-193.

Bateson points out, however, that "play is a phenomenon in which the actions of 'play' are related to or denote other actions of 'not play' " (p. 181). The metacommunicative message "this is play" thus immediately generates ambiguities. Further ambiguities are generated by the fact that the message "this is play" creates a paradox similar to the Epimenides paradox

| All statements within this frame are untrue. |
| I love you. |
| I hate you. |

(Reproduced from Bateson, p. 184)

as the frame itself is involved in the evaluation of the message.

Psychological frames, defined as a class or set of messages, have a peculiar quality: they are "exclusive, i.e. by including certain messages (or meaningful actions) within a frame, certain other messages are excluded." But psychological frames are also "inclusive, i.e. by excluding certain messages certain others are included." They thus help us to organize our experience and perceptions. (It is in this sense that all frames, from punctuation marks on up through extremely complicated situations, are metacommunicative—and all metacommunicative messages are frames). The results of Bateson's Cadmian sowing of the frame concept are complex and become even more so when he points out that the function of a frame is to delimit a logical type, but that whereas the rule for avoiding paradox insists that the items outside any enclosing line be of the same logical type as those within, a frame such as a picture frame is a line dividing items of one logical type from those of another, thus precipitating paradox (pp. 186-188). For a discussion of the implications of the metacommunicative message "this is play" in literature, see Barbara Babcock-Abrahams, "The Novel and the Carnival World," *MLN* 89 (December 1974), 914, 923ff.

22. Mazzotta, "Marginality," p. 69.

23. Goffman's definitions are seldom clear-cut: in *Frame Analysis: An Essay on the Organization of Experience* he writes that he is trying "to isolate some of the basic frameworks of understanding available in our society for making sense out of events and to analyze some of the special vulnerability to which these frames of reference are subject. . . . Definitions of a situation are built up in accordance with principles of organization which govern

events—at least social events—and our subjective involvement in them; frame is the word I use to refer to such of these basic elements as I am able to identify. My phrase 'frame analysis' is a slogan to refer to the examination in these terms of the organization of experience" (pp. 10-11). The concept can be transferred to the expectations raised by certain medieval styles and situations.

24. "Convenevole cosa è, carissime donne, che ciascheduna cosa la quale l'uomo fa, dallo ammirabile e santo nome di Colui, il quale di tutte fu facitore, le dea principio. Per che, dovendo io al vostro novellare, sì come primo, dare cominciamento, intendo da una delle sue maravigliose cose incominciare, acciò che, quella udita, la nostra speranza in Lui, sì come in cosa impermutabile, si fermi e sempre sia da noi il suo nome lodato" (I, 1, 2-3, translation mine).

25. "Dico adunque che già erano gli anni della fruttifera incarnazione del Figliuolo di Dio al numero pervenuti di milletrecentoquarantotto . . ." (I, Intro., 8).

26. "Manifesta cosa è che, sì come le cose temporali tutte sono transitorie e mortali, così in sé e fuor di sé esser piene di noia, d'angoscia e di fatica e a infiniti pericoli sogiacere; alle quali senza niuno fallo né potremmo noi, che viviamo mescolati in esse e che siamo parte d'esse, durare né ripararci, se spezial grazia di Dio forza e avvedimento non ci prestasse" (I, 1, 4).

27. "La quale a noi e in noi non è da credere che per alcun nostro merito discenda, ma dalla sua propria benignità mossa e da' prieghi di coloro impetrata che, sì come noi siamo, furon mortali, e bene i suoi piaceri mentre furono in vita seguendo ora con Lui eterni son divenuti e beati; alli quali noi medesimi, sì come a procuratori informati per esperienza della nostra fragilità, forse non audaci di porgere i prieghi nostri nel cospetto di tanto giudice, delle cose le quali a noi reputiamo oportune gli porgiamo. E ancor più in Lui, verso noi di pietosa liberalità pieno, discerniamo, che, non potendo l'acume dell'occhio mortale nel segreto della divina mente trapassare in alcun modo, avvien forse tal volta che, da oppinione ingannati, tale dinanzi alla sua maestà facciamo procuratore che da quella con eterno essilio è iscacciato: e nondimeno Esso, al quale niuna cosa è occulta, più alla purità del pregator riguardando che alla sua ignoranza o allo essilio del pregato, così come se quegli fosse nel suo cospetto beato, essaudisce coloro che 'l priegano" (I, 1, 4-5).

28. "Il che manifestamente potrà apparire nella novella la quale di raccontare intendo: manifestamente, dico, non il giudicio di Dio ma quel degli uomini seguitando" (I, 1, 6).

29. This whole structure is of the Chinese box type.

30. ". . . e chi sarebbe colui che no'l credesse, veggendo uno uomo in caso di morte dir così?" (I, 1, 74).

31. "Li due fratelli, li quali dubitavan forte non ser Ciappelletto gl'ingannasse, s'eran posti appresso a un tavolato, il quale la camera dove ser Ciappelletto giaceva dividea da un'altra, e ascoltando leggiermente udivano e intendevano ciò che ser Ciappelletto al frate diceva; e aveano alcuna volta sì gran voglia di ridere, udendo le cose le quali egli confessava d'aver fatte, che quasi scoppiavano: e fra sé talora dicevano 'Che uomo è costui, il quale né vecchiezza né infermità né paura di morte, alla qual si vede vicino, né ancora di Dio, dinanzi al giudicio del quale di qui a picciola ora s'aspetta di dovere essere, dalla sua malvagità l'hanno potuto rimuovere, né far che egli così non voglia morire come egli è vivuto?' " (I, 1, 78-79).

32. "Così adunque visse e morì Ser Cepparello da Prato e Santo divenne come avete udito" (I, 1, 89).

33. "E se così è, grandissima si può la benignità di Dio cognoscere verso noi, la quale non al nostro errore ma alla purità della fé riguardando, così faccendo noi nostro mezzano un suo nemico, amico credendolo, ci essaudisce, come se a uno veramente santo per mezzano della sua grazia ricorressimo" (I, 1, 90).

34. "e qui si tacque."

35. Branca noted this (p. 1014, note 7), as did Almansi, who wrote, "as a minor device, this little touch serves to distance the second liar in the narrative chain even further from reality" (*The Writer as Liar*, p. 47).

36. Dioneo could in fact be said to be a mediator between his group (the protagonists) and the world of the stories, for though he belongs to the former and has all its attributes, he is not only the least conventional and most human of the characters, but also the only one to join in the broad humor that many of the stories themselves share not with the protagonists but with their servants. This is brought out by the quarrel between Tindaro and Licisca (VI, Intro., 6-10), which Dioneo is chosen to settle. He further shows that he shares this world in two episodes: the series of bawdy songs he proposes instead of the regulation *canzone* at the end of the fifth day, and his comment upon being chosen

King that if he were a real king he would exercise his *droit de seigneur* (VI, Concl., 3).

37. "The Structural Isomorphism of Art," in *A Poetics of Composition*, pp. 162-163.

38. Lotman and Uspensky, *Semiotica e Cultura*, pp. 59-96. The quotation is on p. 64.

39. *Tipologia della Cultura*, pp. 49ff. Sinicropi's article on the *Decameron* and the nominalist crisis of language assumes added interest in the light of this model.

40. The stories are also the "learning content" of the liminal ritual which the *cornice* protagonists are undergoing. These facts do not imply that the one is less important than the other in the general economy of the work: it is the *cornice* that clarifies the aim of the stories and molds them into a coherent, meaningful whole.

41. See "Il metalinguaggio delle descrizioni della cultura," in *Tipologia della Cultura*, pp. 145-181.

42. "Sul meccanismo semiotico della cultura," p. 62.

43. "Marginality," pp. 64-65.

44. On these two tendencies in the *Decameron* see Padoan, "Mondo aristocratico e mondo comunale."

45. "Insofar as the aesthetic text has a self-focusing quality, so that its structural arrangement becomes one of the contents that it conveys (and maybe even the most important one), the way in which the rules are rearranged on one level will represent the way in which they are rearranged on another. Furthermore, it is the ambiguous arrangement on one level that provokes a reassessment on another: in / a rose is a rose is a rose is a rose / the puzzling redundancy of the lexical level stands for a semantic complication on the definitional one. Thus the deviational matrix not only represents a structural rearrangement: it entails a rearrangement of the codes themselves. It thus represents the proposal of a *new coding possibility*" (Eco, *Semiotics*, pp. 271-272).

46. "Thus art seems to be a way of interconnecting messages in order to produce a text in which: (a) *many* messages, on different levels and planes of the discourse, are *ambiguously* organized; (b) these ambiguities are not realized at random but follow a *precise design*; (c) both the normal and the ambiguous devices within a given message exert a *contextual pressure* on both the normal and ambiguous devices within all the others; (d) the way in which the norms of a given system are offended by one message

is the same as that in which the norms of other systems are offended by the various messages they permit.

At every level (for every message) the solutions are articulated according to a homologous system of solutions, and every deviation springs from a *general deviational matrix*. Therefore, in a work of art a *super-system of homologous structural relationships* is established rather as if all levels were definable on the basis of a single *structural model* which determined all of them . . ." Eco, *Semiotics*, p. 271).

"The aesthetic idiolect has not to be considered a code ruling one and only one message (which, however, should not be viewed as a theoretical contradiction); it is rather a code ruling the various different messages which compose that complex network of messages called 'aesthetic text.' Nevertheless it is (or it may in principle be) a code ruling one and only one text, a code destined to produce a unique discourse. This (and nothing else) explains the creative and individual character of a work of art. Ruled by the idiolectal aesthetic code and connecting various messages which are to be taken as radical instances of a rearranged underlying system, the work of art is a system of systems . . ." (*ibid.*, p. 310).

47. For other and different semiotic approaches to Boccaccio's work, usually dealing with individual stories, see Tzvetan Todorov, *Grammaire du Décaméron*, amply discussed by Renato Barilli in "Semiologia e retorica nella lettura del *Decameron*," *Il Verri* 35-36 (1970), 27-48; Aldo Rossi, "La combinatoria decameroniana: Andreuccio," in *Strumenti critici* 7 (1973), 3-52; James T. Wheelock, "The Rhetoric Polarity in *Decameron* III, 3," *Lingua e stile* IX (1974), 257-274; Giovanni Sinicropi, "Il segno linguistico nel *Decameron*"; M. Picone, "Codici e strutture narrative." The best essays are those by Cesare Segre, now in *Le strutture e il tempo: Narrazione, poesia, modelli* (Turin, 1974).

CHAPTER V

1. A shorter version of this chapter appeared in the *Humanities Association Review* (26 [Fall 1975], 327-345) as "Boccaccio as Illusionist: The Play of Frames in the *Decameron*."

2. On this see Marvin Becker, who pointed out a "daring secular trend at work" during the 1330s and traced the reaction to the freer thought of that period provoked by the financial disasters of the 1340s (before the plague). He has shown how what he calls

"the gentle paideia" was already disappearing well before 1348 (*Florence in Transition*, pp. 53ff.).

3. "Comincia la prima giornata del Decameron, nella quale, dopo la dimostrazione fatta dall'autore per che cagione avvenisse di doversi quelle persone, che appresso si mostrano, ragunare a ragionare insieme, sotto il reggimento di Pampinea si ragiona di quello che più aggrada a ciascheduno."

4. The book is in part the basis for this chapter.

5. "I refer [by the expression 'key'] to the set of conventions by which a given activity, one already meaningful in terms of some primary framework, is transformed into something patterned on this activity but seen by the participants to be something quite else. The process of transcription can be called keying. A rough musical analogy is intended" (Goffman, *Frame Analysis*, pp. 43-44).

6. ". . . intendo di raccontare cento novelle, o favole o parabole o istorie che dire le vogliamo, raccontate in diece giorni da una onesta brigata di sette donne e di tre giovani nel pistelenzioso tempo della passata mortalità fatta, e alcune canzonette dalle predette donne cantate al lor diletto. Nelle quali novelle piacevoli e aspri casi d'amore e altri fortunati avvenimenti si vederanno così ne' moderni tempi avvenuti come negli antichi; delle quali le già dette donne, che queste leggeranno, parimente diletto delle sollazzevoli cose in quelle mostrate e utile consiglio potranno pigliare, in quanto potranno cognoscere quello che sia da fuggire a che sia similmente da seguitare: le quali cose senza passamento di noia non credo che possano intervenire" (Proemio, 13-14, translation mine so as to keep to the original verb tenses and render the passage as literally as possible).

7. Boris Uspensky, *A Poetics of Composition*, p. 67. See also Goffman's chapter on "The Theatrical Frame."

8. There is of course the possibility that the passage merely fits into a tradition of rhetorical paradox, but this is unlikely. On paradox, see Rosalie Colie, *Paradoxia Epidemica: The Renaissance Tradition of Paradox*.

9. "Il che se avviene, che voglia Idio che così sia, a Amore ne rendano grazie, il quale liberandomi da' suoi legami m'ha conceduto il potere attendere a' lor piaceri" (Proemio 15, translation mine).

10. See Branca, *Decameron*, note 9, p. 979.

11. Much has been written on these pages. See especially

A. Scaglione in *Nature and Love in the Late Middle Ages*, S. Battaglia in *La Coscienza Letteraria del Medioevo*, and G. Padoan, "Sulla genesi del *Decameron*."

12. "Sono adunque, discrete donne, stati alcuni che, queste novellette leggendo, hanno detto che voi mi piacete troppo e che onesta cosa non è che io tanto diletto prenda di piacervi e di consolarvi e, alcuni han detto peggio, di commendarvi, come io fo" (IV, Intro., 5).

13. "Adunque da cotanti e da così fatti soffiamenti, da così atroci denti, da così aguti, valorose donne, mentre io ne' vostri servigi milito, sono sospinto, molestato e infino nel vivo trafitto. Le quali cose io con piacevole animo, sallo Idio, ascolto e intendo: e quantunque a voi in ciò tutta appartenga la mia difesa, non-dimeno io non intendo di risparmiar le mie forze, anzi, senza rispondere quanto si converrebbe, con alcuna leggiera risposta tormegli dagli orecchi, e questo far senza indugio. Per ciò che, se già, non essendo io ancora al terzo della mia fatica venuto, essi son molti e molto presumono, io avviso che avanti che io pervenissi alla fine essi potrebbono in guisa esser multiplicati, non avendo prima avuta alcuna repulsa, che con ogni piccola lor fatica mi metterebbono in fondo; né a ciò, quantunque elle sien grandi, resistere varrebbero le forze vostre" (IV, Intro., 8-10).

14. "Ma avanti che io venga a far la risposta a alcuno, mi piace in favor di me raccontare, non una novella intera, acciò che non paia che io voglia le mie novelle con quelle di così laudevole compagnia, quale fu quella che dimostrata v'ho, mescolare, ma parte d'una, acciò che il suo difetto stesso sé mostri non esser di quelle . . ." (IV, Intro., 11).

15. See Branca, *Decameron*, note 13, p. 1199 and Chap. 1, note 53.

16. "Ma avere infino a qui detto della presente novella voglio che mi basti e a coloro rivolgermi alli quali l'ho raccontata . . ." (IV, Intro., 30).

17. "Le quali cose io apertissimamente confesso, cioè che voi mi piacete e che io m'ingegno di piacere a voi: e domandogli se di questo essi si maravigliano, riguardando, lasciamo stare gli aver conosciuti gli amorosi basciari e i piacevoli abbracciari e i congiugnimenti dilettevoli che di voi, dolcissime donne, sovente si prendono, ma solamente a aver veduto e veder continuamente gli ornati costumi e la vaga bellezza e l'ornata leggiadria e oltre a ciò la vostra donnesca onestà; quando colui che nudrito, al-

levato, accresciuto sopra un monte salvatico e solitario, infra li termini d'una piccola cella, senza altra compagnia che del padre, come vi vide, sole da lui disiderate foste, sole adomandate, sole con l'affezion seguitate" (IV, Intro., 31).

18. "E se non fosse che uscir sarebbe del modo usato del ragionare, io producerei le istorie in mezzo" (IV, Intro., 34).

19. On connotative systems see R. Barthes, *Writing Degree Zero and Elements of Semiology*, pp. 89ff.

20. For this term see R. Jakobson, "Two Aspects of Language and Two Types of Aphasic Disturbances."

21. On this see J. Kristeva, *Le Texte du Roman*.

22. He is still addressing himself to the ladies, in the vocative.

23. On the Epimenides paradox see Chapter IV, note 21.

24. "Per ciò che io non veggo che di me altro possa avvenire che quello che della minuta polvere avviene, la quale, spirante turbo, o egli di terra non la muove, o se la muove la porta in alto e spesse volte sopra le teste degli uomini, sopra le corone dei re e degl'imperadori, e talvolta sopra gli alti palagi e sopra le eccelse torri la lascia; delle quali se ella cade, più giù andar non può che il luogo onde levata fu" (IV, Intro., 40).

25. "Ma da ritornare è, per ciò che assai vagate siamo, o belle donne, là onde ci dipartimmo e l'ordine cominciato seguire" (IV, Intro., 43, translation mine).

26. "Saranno per avventura alcune di voi che diranno che io abbia nello scriver queste novelle troppa licenzia usata, sì come in fare alcuna volta dire alle donne e molto spesso ascoltare cose non assai convenienti né a dire né a ascoltare a oneste donne. La qual cosa io nego . . ." (Concl., 3).

27. "E se forse pure alcuna particella è in quella, alcuna paroletta più liberale che forse a spigolistra donna non si conviene, le quali più le parole pesan che' fatti e più d'apparer s'ingegnan che d'esser buone, dico che più non si dee a me esser disdetto d'averle scritte che generalmente si disdica agli uomini e alle donne di dir tutto dì 'foro' e 'caviglia' e 'mortaio' e 'pestello' e 'salsiccia' e 'mortadello,' e tutto pien di simiglianti cose. Sanza che alla mia penna non dee essere meno d'auttorità conceduta che sia al pennello del dipintore, il quale senza alcuna riprensione, o almen giusta, lasciamo stare che egli faccia a san Michele ferire il serpente con la spada o con la lancia e a san Giorgio il dragone dove gli piace, ma egli fa Cristo maschio e Eva femina, e a Lui medesimo, che volle per la salute della umana generazione sopra

la croce morire, quando con un chiovo e quando con due i piè gli conficca in quella" (Concl., 5-6).

28. "Ma se pur prosuppor si volesse che io fossi stato di quelle e lo 'nventore e lo scrittore, che non fui, dico che io non mi vergognerei che tutte belle non fossero . . ." (Concl., 17, translation mine).

29. See Branca, *Decameron*, note 6, p. 1566.

30. ". . . sono buone persone e fuggono il disagio per l'amor di Dio e macinano a raccolta e nol ridicono . . ." (Concl., 26).

31. ". . . li quali tutti il disagio andavan per l'amor di Dio schifando . . ." (VI, 10, 39).

32. "Il prete rispose: '. . . perchè noi maciniamo a raccolta' . . ." (VIII, 2, 23).

33. See Uspensky, *A Poetics of Composition*, p. 137.

34. See Chapter III, note 1.

35. "A me medesimo increce andarmi tanto tra tante miserie ravolgendo: per che, volendo omai lasciare star quella parte di quelle che io acconciamente posso schifare, dico che, stando in questi termini la nostra città, d'abitatori quasi vota, addivenne, sì come io poi da persona degna di fede sentii, che nella venerabile chiesa di Santa Maria Novella, un martedì mattina, non essendovi quasi alcuna altra persona, uditi li divini ufici in abito lugubre quale a sì fatta stagione si richiedea, si ritrovarono sette giovani donne . . ." (I, Intro., 49).

36. "Queste parole sommamente piacquero, e a una voce lei prima del primo giorno elessero; e Filomena, corsa prestamente a uno alloro (per ciò che assai volte aveva udito ragionare di quanto onore le frondi di quello eran degne e quanto degno d'onore facevano chi n'era meritamente incoronato), di quello alcuni rami colti, ne le fece una ghirlanda onorevole e apparente; la quale, messale sopra la testa, fu poi mentre durò la lor compagnia manifesto segno a ciascuno altro della real signoria e maggioranza" (I, Intro., 97).

37. "Già era il sole inclinato al vespro e in gran parte il caldo diminuito, quando le novelle delle giovani donne e de' tre giovani si trovarono esser finite" (I, Concl., 1).

"Questa novella diè tanto che ridere a tutta la compagnia . . ." (II, Concl., 1).

"Mille fiate o più aveva la novella di Dioneo a rider mosse le oneste donne . . ." (III, Concl., 1).

"Se le prime novelle li petti delle vaghe donne avevano con-tristate . . ." (IV, Concl., 1).

"Essendo adunque la novella di Dioneo finita . . ." (V, Concl., 1).

"Questa novella porse igualmente a tutta la brigata grandissimo piacere e sollazzo . . ." (VI, Concl., 1).

"La novella di Dioneo era finita . . ." (X, Concl., 1).

38. "Zefiro era levato per lo sole che al ponente s'avvicinava, quando il re finita la sua novella . . ." (VII, Concl., 1).

"Come Dioneo ebbe la sua novella finita, così Lauretta . . ." (VIII, Concl., 1).

"Quanto di questa novella si ridesse . . . colei sel pensi che ancora ne riderà" (IX, Concl., 1).

39. ". . . mi vuol dare a vedere che la notte prima che Sicofante giacque con lei messer Mazza entrasse in Monte Nero per forza e con ispargimento di sangue; e io dico che non è vero, anzi v'entrò paceficamente e con gran piacer di quei d'entro . . ." (VI, Intro., 8, translation mine).

40. "—Donne, io conosco ciò che io ho imposto non meno che facciate voi, e da imporlo non mi poté istorre quello che voi mi volete mostrare, pensando che il tempo è tale che, guardandosi e gli uomini e le donne d'operar disonestamente, ogni ragionare è conceduto. Or non sapete voi che, per la perversità di questa stagione, li giudici hanno lasciati i tribunali? le leggi, così le divine come le umane, tacciono? e ampia licenzia per conservar la vita è conceduta a ciascuno? Per che, se alquanto s'allarga la vostra onestà nel favellare, non per dover con l'opere mai alcuna cosa sconcia seguire ma per dar diletto a voi e a altrui, non veggio con che argomento da concedere vi possa nello avvenire riprendere alcuno. Oltre a questo la nostra brigata, dal primo dì infino a questa ora stata onestissima . . ." (VI, Concl., 8-10).

41. ". . . Pampinea ridendo disse: —Oggi vi pure abbiam noi ingannati.—

—E come? —disse Dioneo—cominciate voi prima a far de' fatti che a dir delle parole?—" (VI, Concl., 33-34, translation mine).

42. See Branca, note 4, p. 1431.

43. The exceptions are II, 5 and 8; III, 4, 5, 6, 7, 9; IV, 1; V, 5; VI, 6.

44. "Finisce la—giornata, comincia la—."

45. "—Graziosissime donne, niuno atto della fortuna, secondo il mio giudicio, si può veder maggiore che vedere uno d'infima

miseria a stato reale elevare, come la novella di Pampinea n'ha mostrato essere al suo Alessandro adivenuto. E per ciò che a qualunque della proposta materia da quinci innanzi novellerà converrà che infra questi termini dica, non mi vergognerò io di dire una novella, la quale, ancora che miserie maggiori in sé contenga, non per ciò abbia così splendida riuscita. Ben so che, pure a quella avendo riguardo, con minor diligenzia fia la mia udita: ma altro non potendo sarò scusata" (II, 4, 3-4).

46. ". . . mi tirano a dovervi contare una novelletta di loro: la quale, ancora che in sé abbia assai di quello che creder non si dee, nondimeno sarà in parte piacevole a ascoltare" (VII, 10, 7).

47. "—Poco prezzo mi parrebbe la vita mia a dover dare per la metà diletto di quello che con Guiscardo ebbe Ghismunda, né se ne dee di voi maravigliare alcuna, con ciò sia cosa che io, vivendo, ogni ora mille morti sento, né per tutte quelle una sola particella di diletto m'è data. Ma lasciando al presente li miei fatti ne' lor termini stare . . ." (IV, 2, 2-3).

48. "Avvenne che in questi tempi, che costui non ispendendo il suo multiplicava, arrivò a Genova un valente uomo di corte e costumato e ben parlante, il qual fu chiamato Guiglielmo Borsiere, non miga simile a quegli li quali sono oggi, li quali, non senza gran vergogna de' corrotti e vituperevoli costumi di coloro li quali al presente vogliono essere gentili uomini e signor chiamati e reputati, son più tosto da dire asini nella bruttura di tutta la cattività de' vilissimi uomini allevati che nelle corti. E là dove a que' tempi soleva essere il lor mestiere e consumarsi la lor fatica in trattar paci, dove guerre o sdegni tra gentili uomini fosser nati, o trattar matrimonii, parentadi e amistà, e con belli motti e leggiadri ricreare gli animi degli affaticati e sollazzar le corti e con agre riprensioni, sì come padri, mordere i difetti de' cattivi, e questo con premii assai leggieri; oggi dì rapportar male dall'uno all'altro, in seminar zizzania, in dir cattività e tristizie, e, che è peggio, in farle nella presenza degli uomini, in rimproverare i mali, le vergogne e le tristezze vere e non vere l'uno all'altro e con false lusinghe gli uomini gentili alle cose vili e scellerate ritrarre s'ingegnano il lor tempo di consumare. E colui è più caro avuto e più da' miseri e scostumati signori onorato e con premii grandissimi essaltato, che più abominevoli parole dice o fa atti: gran vergogna e biasimevole del mondo presente, e argomento assai evidente che le virtù, di qua giù dipartitesi, hanno nella feccia de' vizii i miseri viventi abbandonati.

Ma tornando a ciò che io cominciato avea, da che giusto sdegno un poco m'ha trasviata più che io non credetti . . ." (I, 8, 7-11).

49. "E per ciò si disse: 'Bocca basciata non perde ventura, anzi rinnuova come fa la luna' " (II, 7, 122, translation mine). "Poi l'una all'altra per la città ridicendolo, vi ridussono in volgar motto che il più piacevol servigio che a Dio si facesse era rimettere il. diavolo in inferno: il qual motto, passato di qua da mare, ancora dura" (III, 10, 35).

50. ". . . ardirò oltre alle dette dirvene una novella: la quale, se io dalla verità del fatto mi fossi scostare voluta o volessi, avrei ben saputo e saprei sotto altri nomi comporla e raccontarla; ma per ciò che il partirsi dalla verità delle cose state nel novellare è gran diminuire di diletto negl'intendenti, in propria forma, dalla ragion di sopra detta aiutata, la vi dirò" (IX, 5, 5).

51. ". . . ma chi sa che cagione moveva que' sospiri? Forse v'eran di quelle che non meno per vaghezza di così spesse nozze che per pietà di colei sospiravano. Ma lasciando questo stare al presente . . ." (II, 8, 2).

52. The bibliography on this story is also mountainous and easily accessible so I will not cite it here.

53. This would have very interesting implications for all the stories of the puzzling tenth day, which for reasons of overall coherence and space in this study, cannot be discussed here.

54. "Matta bestialità" (X, 10, 3).

55. "Che si potrà dir qui? se non che anche nelle povere case piovono dal cielo de' divini spiriti, come nelle reali di quegli che sarien più degni di guardar porci che d'avere sopra uomini signoria. Chi avrebbe, altri che Griselda, potuto col viso non solamente asciutto ma lieto sofferir le rigide e mai più non udite pruove da Gualtier fatte? Al quale non sarebbe forse stato male investito d'essersi abbattuto a una che quando, fuor di casa, l'avesse fuori in camiscia cacciata, s'avesse sì a un altro fatto scuotere il pilliccione che riuscito ne fosse una bella roba" (X, 10, 68-69).

CONCLUSION

1. Teresa de Lauretis, "Semiotic Models, *Invisible Cities*," p. 15.

2. Review of Robert Hollander, *Boccaccio's Two Venuses*, *Italica* 56 (Spring, 1979), 52.

3. Marvin Becker, *Florence in Transition*, p. 3.

4. See Branca, *Decameron*, p. 990, note 8.

~ BIBLIOGRAPHY ~

Almansi, Guido. *The Writer as Liar: Narrative Technique in the De-cameron*. London and Boston: Routledge & Kegan Paul, 1975.

Auerbach, Erich. *Mimesis: The Representation of Reality in Western Literature*. Translated by Willard Trask. Princeton: Princeton University Press, 1953. (Harper Torchbook, 1971).

Babcock-Abrahams, Barbara. "The Novel and the Carnival World." *MLN* 89 (1975), 913-934.

Bakhtin, Michael. *Rabelais and His World*. Translated by H. Iwolsky. Cambridge, Mass.: M.I.T. Press, 1968.

Ballerini, Carlo. "Il recupero della letizia dalla tragedia della peste alla libera vita di Bruno e Buffalmaco." In *Atti del Congresso di Nimega sul Boccaccio*. Bologna: Patron, 1976.

Baratto, Mario. *Realtà e stile nel Decameron*. 2d ed. Vicenza: Neri Pozza, 1974.

Bárberi-Squarotti, Giorgio. "La 'cornice' del *Decameron* o il mito di Robinson." In *Da Dante al Novecento, Studi offerti a G. Getto*. Milan: Mursia, 1970.

Barilli, R. "Semiologia e retorica nella lettura del *Decameron*." *Il Verri* 35-36 (1970), 27-48.

Barthes, Roland. *Writing Degree Zero and Elements of Semiology*. Translated by A. Lavers and C. Smith. Boston: Beacon Press, 1970.

Bateson, Gregory. "Theory of Play and Fantasy." In *Steps to an Ecology of Mind*. New York: Ballantine Books, 1973.

Battaglia, Salvatore. *La coscienza letteraria del medioevo*. Naples: Liguori, 1965.

———. *Giovanni Boccaccio e la riforma della narrativa*. Naples: Liguori, 1969.

Becker, Marvin B. *Florence in Transition*. Baltimore: Johns Hopkins University Press, 1967.

Berger, H. "The Renaissance Imagination: Second World and Green World." *The Centennial Review* 9 (1965), 36-78.

Billanovich, Giuseppe. *Restauri Boccacceschi*. Rome: Edizioni di "Storia e Letteratura," 1945.

Boccaccio, Giovanni. *Decameron*. Edited by Natalino Sapegno. Milan: Ricciardi, 1952.

———. *Tutte le opere*. Vol. 4, *Decameron*. Edited by Vittore Branca. Milan: Mondadori, 1976.

———. *Opere*. Edited by Pier Giorgio Ricci. Milan-Naples: Ricciardi, 1965.

———. *The Decameron*. Translated by G. H. McWilliam. Aylesbury, England: Penguin, 1972.

Borsellino, Nino. "*Decameron* come teatro." In *Rozzi e intronati— esperienze e forme del teatro dal "Decameron" al "Candelaio."* Rome: Bulzoni, 1976.

Bosco, Umberto, ed. *Il Decamerone*. Rieti: Biblioteca Editrice, 1929.

Bowsky, W. M. *The Black Death: A Turning Point in History?* New York: Holt-Rinehart, 1971.

Branca, Vittore. *Linee di una storia della critica al Decameron*. Milan: Società Dante Alighieri, 1939.

———. "Profilo biografico." In *Tutte le Opere di Giovanni Boccaccio*. Vol. I. Milan: Mondadori, 1964.

———. *Boccaccio Medievale*. Florence: Sansoni, 1970.

———. "Implicazioni strutturali e espressive fra Petrarca e Boccaccio." In *Atti del Convegno Internazionale su Francesco Petrarca dell'Accademia dei Lincei*. Rome: Accademia dei Lincei, 1975.

———. "The Myth of the Hero in Boccaccio." In *Concepts of the Hero in the Middle Ages and the Renaissance*. Edited by M. T. Burns and C. J. Reagan. Albany: State University of New York Press, 1975.

———. *Boccaccio: The Man and His Works*. Translated by R. Monges and D. McAuliffe. New York: New York University Press, 1976.

———. Introduction to *Tutte le Opere di Giovanni Boccaccio*. Vol. IV. Milan: Mondadori, 1976.

———. *Giovanni Boccaccio—Profilo biografico*. Florence: Sansoni, 1977.

———. "Boccaccio e la tradizione letteraria." In *Il Boccaccio nelle culture e letterature nazionali*, edited by F. Mazzoni, pp. 473-496. Florence: Sansoni, 1978.

Brown, Marshall. "In the Valley of the Ladies." *Italian Quarterly* 18 (1975), 33-52.

Brucker, Gene. *Florentine Politics and Society, 1343-1378*. Princeton: Princeton University Press, 1962.

Brucker, Gene. *Renaissance Florence.* New York: Wiley, 1969.

———. "Florence and the Black Death." In *Boccaccio: Secoli di Vita.*

Burkert, Walter. "Pythagorean Number Theory." In *Lore and Science in Ancient Pythagoreanism.* Translated by E. L. Minar, Jr. Cambridge, Mass.: M.I.T. Press, 1972.

Butler, Christopher. *Number Symbolism.* London: Routledge & Kegan Paul, 1970.

Cerisola, Pier Luigi. "La questione della *cornice* del *Decameron. Aevum* 49 (1975), 137-156.

Cirlot, J. E. *A Dictionary of Symbols.* Translated by Jack Sage. New York: Philosophical Library, Inc., 1974.

Clubb, Louise George. "Boccaccio and the Boundaries of Love." *Italica* 37 (1960), 188-196.

Colie, Rosalie. *Paradoxia Epidemica: The Renaissance Tradition of Paradox.* Princeton: Princeton University Press, 1966.

Collingwood, A. Lee. *The Decameron: Its Sources and Analogues.* London: Nutt, 1909. Reprint, Havertown, Pa.: Richard West, 1973.

Contini, Gianfranco, ed. *Poeti del Duecento, La Letteratura Italiana— Storia e testi,* Vol. II. Milan and Naples: Ricciardi, 1962.

Cottino-Jones, Marga. *An Anatomy of Boccaccio's Style.* Naples: Cymba, 1968.

———. "Fabula vs. Figura: Another Interpretation of the Griselda Story." *Italica* 1 (1973), 38-52.

———. "The City/Country Conflict in the *Decameron." Studi sul Boccaccio* 8 (1974), 152.

———, and Tuttle, Edward F., eds. *Boccaccio: Secoli di vita. Atti del Congresso Internazionale: Boccaccio 1975.* Ravenna: Longo, 1977.

Curtius, E. R. *European Literature and the Latin Middle Ages.* New York and Evanston: Harper Torchbook, 1963.

de Lauretis, Teresa. "Semiotics Unlimited." *PTL: A Journal for Descriptive Poetics and Theory of Literature* 2 (1977), 370.

———. "Semiotic Models, *Invisible Cities." Yale Italian Studies* 2 (1978), 27.

De Lorris, Guillaume, and De Meun, Jean. *Le Roman de la Rose.* Edited by E. Langlois. Paris: Société des Anciens Textes Français, 1922.

———. *The Romance of the Rose.* Translated by H. W. Robbins. New York: E. P. Dutton, 1962.

De Michelis, Cesare. "Rassegna Boccacciana—Dieci Anni di Studi." *Lettere Italiane* 25 (1973), 88-129.

De' Negri, Enrico. "The Legendary Style of the *Decameron*." *The Romanic Review* 53 (1952), 166-189.

Deligiorgis, Stavros. *Narrative Intellection in the Decameron*. Iowa City: University of Iowa Press, 1975.

Dombroski, R. S., ed. *Critical Perspectives on the Decameron*. New York: Barnes and Noble, 1977.

Douglas, Mary. *Purity and Danger*. New York and Washington: Frederick A. Praeger, 1966.

———. *Natural Symbols, Explorations in Cosmology*. New York: Vintage Books, 1973.

———. "Jokes." In *Implicit Meanings—Essays in Anthropology*. London & Boston: Routledge & Kegan Paul, 1975.

Eco, Umberto. "Looking for a Logic of Culture." In *The Tell Tale Sign*. Edited by T. Sebeok. Lisse: De Ridder, 1975.

———. *A Theory of Semiotics*. Bloomington and London: Indiana University Press, 1976.

Esposito, Enzo. *Boccacciana: Bibliografia delle edizioni e degli scritti critici, con la collaborazione di Christopher Kleinhenz*. Ravenna: Longo, 1976.

Falassi, Alessandro. "Il Boccaccio e il folklore." In *Boccaccio: Secoli di Vita. Atti del Congresso Internazionale: Boccaccio, 1975*. Edited by Marga Cottino-Jones and Edward F. Tuttle. Ravenna: Longo, 1977.

Ferrante, Joan M. "The Frame Characters of the *Decameron*: A Progression of Virtues." *Romance Philology* 19 (1965), 212-226.

———. "Narrative Patterns in the *Decameron*." *Romance Philology* 3 (1978), 585-604.

Fettweiss, Emil. Über das Verhältnis des mathematischen Denkens zum mystischen Denken auf niederen Kulturstufen." *Archeion* 14 (1932), 207-220.

———. "Berührungspunkte der pythagoräischen Zahlenlehre mit dem Totemismus." *Zeitschrift fur Philosophischen Forschungen* 5 (1950-1951), 190.

Fido, Franco. "Il sorriso di Messer Torello." *Romance Philology* 23 (1969): 154-171.

———. "Boccaccio's Ars Narrandi in the Sixth Day of the *Decameron*." In *Itálian Literature—Roots and Branches*. Edited by G. Rimanelli and K. J. Atchety. London and New Haven: Yale University Press, 1976.

Fido, Franco. "Dante personaggio mancato del *Decameron*." In *Boccaccio: Secoli di Vita*.

––––––. *Le metamorfosi del centauro*. Rome: Bulzoni, 1977.

Geertz, Clifford. *The Interpretation of Cultures*. New York: Basic Books, 1973.

Getto, Giovanni. *Vita di forme e forme di vita nel Decameron*. Turin: Petrini, 1958.

Gibaldi, Joseph. "The *Decameron* Cornice and the Responses to the Disintegration of Civilization." *Kentucky Romance Quarterly* 24 (1977), 349-357.

Goffman, Erving. *Frame Analysis: An Essay on the Organization of Experience*. New York: Harper and Row, 1974.

Goldmann, Lucien. *Le dieu caché*. Paris: Editions Gallimard, 1955.

Greene, Thomas. "Forms of Accommodation in the *Decameron*." *Italica* 15 (1968), 297-312.

––––––. "Review of *Boccaccio's Two Venuses*." *Italica* 56 (Spring, 1979), 52.

Grimm, Jurgen. *Die Literarische Darstellung der Pest in der Antike und in der Romania*. München: Wilhelm Fink Verlag, 1965.

Guarino, Guido A. *De Claris Mulieribus, Concerning Famous Women*. Translated by Guido A. Guarino. New Brunswick: Rutgers University Press, 1963.

Hauser, Arnold. *The Social History of Art*. New York: Vintage Books, 1951.

Hollander, Robert. *Boccaccio's Two Venuses*. New York: Columbia University Press, 1977.

Hopper, V. H. *Medieval Number Symbolism*. New York: Columbia University Press, 1938.

Howard, Donald R. Review of *Boccaccio's Two Venuses*. *Renaissance Quarterly* 31 (1978), 604-608.

Huizinga, Johann. *The Waning of the Middle Ages*. Garden City, N.Y.: Doubleday, 1954.

Jakobson, Roman. "Two Aspects of Language and Two Types of Aphasic Disturbances." In R. Jakobson and M. Halle, *Fundamentals of Language*. The Hague: Mouton, 1956.

Kern, Edith. "The Gardens in the *Decameron* Cornice." *PMLA* 66 (1951), 505-523.

Kirkham, Victoria. "Reckoning with Boccaccio's *questioni d'amore*." *MLN* 89 (1974), 47-59.

––––––. "Numerology and Allegory in Boccaccio's '*Caccia di Diana*.' " *Traditio* 34 (1978), 303-329.

———. " 'Chiuso parlare' in Boccaccio's *Teseida.*" *Studies in the Italian Trecento*, forthcoming.

Kristeva, Julia. *Le Texte du Roman.* Paris-The Hague: Mouton, 1970.

Lepschy, Anna Laura. "Boccaccio Studies in English." In *Studi sul Boccaccio* 6 (1971), 211-229.

Lévi-Strauss, Claude. *Les structures élémentaires de la parenté.* Paris: Presses Universitaires de France, 1949.

Lotman, J. M. *La struttura del testo poetico.* Milan: Mursia, 1976.

Lotman, J. M., and Uspensky, B. A. *Tipologia della cultura.* Milan: Bompiani, 1975.

———. *Semiotica e cultura.* Milan and Naples: Ricciardi, 1975.

Luzi, Mario. "Il novellare del *Decameron.*" In *Atti del Congresso di Nimega sul Boccaccio.*

Marcus, Millicent. *An Allegory of Form: Literary Self-Consciousness in the Decameron.* Stanford French and Italian Studies, Vol. XVIII. Saratoga, Calif.: Anma Libri, 1979.

———. "Ser Ciappelletto: A Reader's Guide to the *Decameron.*" *The Humanities Association Review* 26 (1975), 275-288.

———. "An Allegory of Two Gardens: A Gloss on the Tale of Madonna Dianora, (*Decameron* X, 5)." *Forum Italicum*, 14 (Fall, 1980), 162-174.

Marino, Lucia. *The Decameron Cornice: Allusion, Allegory and Iconology.* Ravenna: Longo, 1979.

Mazzotta, Giuseppe. "The *Decameron*: The Marginality of Literature." *University of Toronto Quarterly* 42 (1972), 64-81.

———. "The *Decameron*: The Literal and the Allegorical." *Italian Quarterly* 18 (1975), 53-73.

———. "Games of Laughter in the *Decameron.*" *Romanic Review* 69 (1978), 115-131.

Meiss, Millard. *Painting in Florence and Siena after the Black Death: 1350-1375.* Princeton: Princeton University Press, 1971.

Musa, Mark, and Bondanella, Peter, eds. and trans. *Decameron.* New York: Norton, 1977.

Muscetta, Carlo. *Giovanni Boccaccio.* Bari: Laterza, 1970.

Neri, Ferdinando. "Il disegno ideale del *Decameron.*" In *Storia e poesia.* Turin: Chiantore, 1936.

Neuschäfer, Hans-Jörg. *Boccaccio und der Begin der Novelle: Strukturen der Kurzerzählung auf der Schwelle zwischen Mittelalter und Neuzeit.* Munich: Wilhelm Fink Verlag, 1969.

Padoan, Giorgio. "Mondo aristocratico e mondo comunale

nell'ideologia e nell'arte di Giovanni Boccaccio." *Studi sul Boccaccio* 2 (1964): 81-216.

———. "Sulla genesi del *Decameron*." In *Boccaccio: Secoli di Vita*.

Peacock, James. *Rites of Modernization*. Chicago and London: University of Chicago Press, 1968.

———. *Consciousness and Change: Symbolic Anthropology in Evolutionary Perspective*. New York: John Wiley & Sons, 1975.

Perella, Nicholas. *Midday in Italian Literature: Variations on an Archetypal Theme*. Princeton: Princeton University Press, 1979.

Pérouse, Gabriel. *Nouvelles Françaises du XVIe Siècle*. Geneva: Droz, 1977.

Perrus, Claude. "Remarques sur les rapports entre écrivain et public dans le *Décaméron* de Boccace." In *Littérature et idéologies, Colloque de Cluny II* (1975). *La Nouvelle Critique*, Special 39 bis (1976), 296.

Petronio, G. *Il Decamerone*. Bari, Laterza, 1935.

———. "Giovanni Boccaccio." *I classici italiani nella storia della critica*. Edited by W. Binni. Florence: La Nuova Italia, 1954 and 1960.

———. "I volti del *Decameron*." In *Boccaccio: Secoli di Vita*.

———. "La posizione del *Decameron*." *Rassegna della letteratura italiana* 2 (1957): 189-207.

Picone, Michelangelo. "Codici e strutture nel *Decameron*." *Strumenti critici* 34 (1977), 434-443.

Potter, Joy Hambuechen. "Boccaccio as Illusionist: The Play of Frames in the *Decameron*. *Humanities Association Review* 26 (1975), 327-345.

Prete, Antonio. "La cornice del *Decameron*." In *La distanza da Croce*. Milan: C.E.L.U.C., 1970.

Procacci, Giuliano. *History of the Italian People*. Translated by Anthony Paul. New York and London: Harper and Row, 1970.

Ramat, Raffaello. "Indicazioni per una lettura del *Decameron*." *Saggi sul Rinascimento*. Florence: La Nuova Italia, 1967.

Rappaport, Roy. "Liturgies and Lies." *Beitrage zur Wissenssoziologie/Beitrage zur Religionssoziologie, Internationales Jahrbuch für Wissens-und Religionssoziologie*, Vol. 10. Opladen: Westdeutscher Verlag, 1976.

Rebhorn, Wayne. *Courtly Performances: Masking and Festivity in Castiglione's Book of the Courtier*. Detroit: Wayne State University Press, 1978.

Rossi, Aldo. "Dante nella prospettiva del Boccaccio." *Studi Danteschi* 37 (1960), 138.

———. "La combinatoria decameroniana: Andreuccio." *Strumenti critici* 7 (1973), 3-52.

Russo, Luigi, ed. *Decameron*. Florence: Sansoni, 1939.

Salinari, Carlo. "Il Trecento." *Antologia della Letteratura Italiana*, Vol. 1. Edited by Maurizio Vitale. Milan: 1965.

———. "L'empirismo ideologico del Boccaccio." *La critica della letteratura italiana*. Naples: Liguori, 1973.

Sapegno, Natalino. "Il Boccaccio." *Il Trecento*. Milan: Vallardi, 1960.

———, ed. *Il Decameron*. Milan: Ricciardi, 1952.

Scaglione, Aldo. *Nature and Love in the Late Middle Ages*. Berkeley and Los Angeles: University of California Press, 1963.

———. "Giovanni Boccaccio, or the Narrative Vocation." In *Boccaccio: Secoli di Vita*.

Segre, Cesare. *Lingua, stile e società*. Milan: Feltrinelli, 1974.

———. *Le strutture e il tempo: Narrazione, poesia, modelli*. Turin; Einaudi, 1974.

Seung, T. K. "The Boccaccian Tour de Force." *Cultural Thematics*. New Haven and London: Yale University Press, 1976.

Shapiro, Harvey L., ed. "The Family." In *Man, Culture and Society*. New York: Oxford University Press, 1956.

Singleton, Charles. "On Meaning in the *Decameron*." *Italica* 21 (1944), 117-124.

———, ed. *Decameron, Edizione diplomatico-interpretativa dell'autografo Hamilton 90*. Baltimore and London: Johns Hopkins University Press, 1974.

Sinicropi, Giovanni. "Il segno linguistico nel *Decameron*." *Studi sul Boccaccio* 9 (1975-1976), 169-224.

Sklovsky, Victor. *Lettura del Decameron: Dal Romanzo d'avventura al romanzo di carattere*. Bologna: Il Mulino, 1969.

Slater, Marian Kreiselman. "Ecological Factors in the Origin of Incest." *American Anthropologist* 61 (1959), 1042-1059.

Smarr, J. Levarie. "Symmetry and Balance in the *Decameron*." *Medievalia* 2 (1976), 159-187.

Staüble, Antonio. "La brigata del *Decameron* come pubblico teatrale." *Studi sul Boccaccio* 9 (1975-1976), 103-118.

Steward, Pamela. "La novella di Madonna Oretta e le due parti del *Decameron*." In *Yearbook of Italian Studies*, 1973-1975, pp. 27-40.

Tateo, Francesco. "Il 'realismo' nella novella boccaccesca." *Retorica e poetica fra medioevo e rinascimento*. Bari: Adriatica Editrice, 1960.

Todorov, Tzvetan. *Grammaire du Décaméron*. The Hague and Paris: Mouton, 1969.

Trexler, Richard. *Synodal Law in Florence and Fiesole, 1306-1518*. Città del Vaticano: Biblioteca Apostolica Vaticana, 1971.

————. *The Spiritual Power: Republican Florence under Interdict*. Leiden: E. J. Brill, 1974.

Turner, Victor. "Betwixt and Between: Liminal Period." In *The Forest of Symbols*. Ithaca: Cornell University Press, 1967 and 1970.

————. *The Ritual Process*. Chicago: Aldine, 1969.

————. *Dramas, Fields and Metaphores*. Ithaca and London: Cornell University Press, 1974.

————. "Liminal to Liminoid in Play, Flow and Ritual: An Essay in Comparative Symbology." *Rice University Studies* 60 (1974), 53-92.

Uspensky, Boris. "The Structural Isomorphism of Art." In *A Poetics of Composition*. Translated by U. Zavarin and S. Wittig. Berkeley: University of California Press, 1973.

Vance, Eugene. "Mervelous Signals: Poetics, Sign Theory, and Politics in Chaucer's *Troilus*." *New Literary History* 10 (1979), pp. 294-337.

Van Gennep, Arnold. *The Rites of Passage*. Translated by M. Vizedom and G. Caffee. Chicago: The University of Chicago Press, 1972.

Wheelock, James T. "The Rhetoric Polarity in *Decameron* III, 3. *Lingua e stile* 9 (1974), 257-274.

White, Leslie. *The Science of Culture*. New York: Farrar, Strauss and Co., 1949.

Zumthor, Paul. *Essai de poétique médiévale*. Paris: Éditions du Seuil, 1972.

~ INDEX ~

Library of Congress Cataloging in Publication Data

Potter, Joy Hambuechen.
  Five Frames for the *Decameron*.

  Bibliography: p.
  Includes index.
  1. Boccaccio, Giovanni, 1313-1375.   Decamerone.
I. Title.
PQ4287.P67   853'.1   81-47942
ISBN 0-691-06503-9   AACR2